Explaining Federa

MW01074099

This book is a study that deals with the theoretical and empirical questions of federalism in the context of five case studies (Austria, Belgium, Canada, Germany and Switzerland). The central argument is that in the long run the political institutions of federalism adapt to achieve congruence with the underlying social structure. This change could be in the centralist direction reflecting ethno-linguistic homogeneity, or in decentralist terms corresponding to ethno-linguistic heterogeneity.

In terms of the relationship between institutions and society, federalism presents a unique opportunity for students of comparative politics. Federalism is both a societal and an institutional phenomenon, and thus presents an area where the two can be studied together. As an institutional phenomenon, federalism denotes the constitutional configuration of the political system. However, this formal division of political power between the center and substate units is just one side of the picture, as federalism is also a societal phenomenon. In this case one could have a federal society where societal differences like ethnicity, language and class tend to be territorially-based, or one could have a non-federal society where differences are nationwide and not territorially concentrated. It is the relationship between the institutional and the societal where the most thought-provoking theoretical questions can be found, and it is this logic of congruence that is employed here in order to explain the course of broad changes in the federal systems of the industrialized West.

Explaining Federalism will be of interest to students and scholars of federalism, comparative government, comparative institutional analysis and comparative public policy.

Jan Erk is Assistant Professor of Comparative Politics at the University of Leiden, the Netherlands.

Routledge series in federal studies
ISSN 1363–5670
Series Editor: Michael Burgess
Centre for Federal Studies, University of Kent, UK
Formerly edited by John Loughlin
Cardiff University, UK

This series brings together some of the foremost academics and theorists to examine the timely subject of regional and federal studies, which since the mid-1980s have become key questions in political analysis and practice.

Explaining Federalism

State, society and congruence in
Austria, Belgium, Canada, Germany and
Switzerland

Jan Erk

Routledge
Taylor & Francis Group

LONDON AND NEW YORK

Transferred to digital printing 2010

First published 2008
by Routledge
2 Park Square, Milton Park, Abingdon, Oxon OX14 4RN

Simultaneously published in the USA and Canada
by Routledge
270 Madison Ave, New York, NY 10016

Routledge is an imprint of the Taylor & Francis Group, an informa business

© 2008 Jan Erk

Typeset in Times by Wearset Ltd, Boldon, Tyne and Wear

British Library Cataloguing in Publication Data
A catalogue record for this book is available from the British Library

Library of Congress Cataloging in Publication Data
A catalog record for this book has been requested

ISBN10: 0-415-43205-7 (hbk)
ISBN10: 0-415-59955-5 (pbk)
ISBN10: 0-203-94049-0 (ebk)

ISBN13: 978-0-415-43205-4 (hbk)
ISBN13: 978-0-415-59955-9 (pbk)
ISBN13: 978-0-203-94049-5 (ebk)

To the memory of my father

Contents

Summary

Explaining Federalism is a study that deals with the theoretical and empirical questions of federalism in the context of five case studies (Austria, Belgium, Canada, Germany and Switzerland). The central argument is that in the long run the political institutions of federalism adapt to achieve congruence with the underlying the underlying social structure. This change could be in the centralist direction reflecting ethno-linguistic homogeneity, or in decentralist terms corresponding to ethno-linguistic heterogeneity. In this context, the book does two things:

1   Substantively, it fills a gap in the comparative federalism literature by analyzing the patterns of change and continuity in five federal systems of the industrial West. This is done by an in-depth empirical examination of the case studies through a single framework of analysis.
2   Theoretically, the manuscript contributes to a core debate in comparative politics. Here the aim is to show the shortcomings of new-institutionalist approaches in explaining change, and to highlight the usefulness of society-based approaches in studying change and continuity in comparative politics.

In terms of the relationship between institutions and society, federalism presents a unique opportunity for students of comparative politics. Federalism is both a societal and an institutional phenomenon, and thus presents an area where the two can be studied together. As an institutional phenomenon, federalism denotes the constitutional/institutional configuration of the political system. This formal division of political power between the center and substate units is one side of the picture. But federalism is also a societal phenomenon; one could have a federal society where societal differences like ethnicity, language, and class tend to be territorially based, or one could have a non-federal society where differences are nationwide and not territorially concentrated. It is the relationship between the institutional and the societal where the most thought-provoking theoretical questions can be found.

What is of interest in this manuscript is the long-run equilibrium between social structures and political institutions. In this context, the logic of congruence between society and institutions is employed in order to explain the course of broad changes in the federal systems of the industrialized West. Empirical evidence shows that political institutions change in order to reach a better fit with the society. Pressures in homogeneous societies are in the centralist direction; in heterogeneous societies they go the other way.

The case studies are a model of structured focused comparison, presented with a clear focus on the variables and causal chains of interest to the analysis. Evidence from these suggests that a society-based perspective presents a more reliable way to identify the political patterns in federal systems. In all the cases, institutions have changed towards congruence with the ethno-linguistic structure rather than the other way around. Not only do the empirical chapters display the role played by the underlying societal set-up in shaping the uncodified workings of federal systems; they also aim to explain why in many cases institutions proved to be malleable rather than sticky.

Preface

> [E]ach instance of a federalism ancient and modern is imbedded in a set of unique local institutions, which themselves must be appreciated and understood. To acquire the information about history, the sensitivity to culture, and the linguistic competence to examine all these societies is more than any isolated scholar can do.
>
> *William H. Riker*[1]

Good thing is that I was not isolated. Friends and colleagues in Austria, Belgium, Canada, Germany and Switzerland made sure that research and writing was not a completely solitary experience – although it certainly felt that way on a number of occasions. But Riker is right: archival research on original language sources was quite taxing, and I was only examining five such societies in which federalism was imbedded. At the same time, the fortunate by-product of field research was that I got to spend considerable time in the countries under focus. I would like to express my thanks to Murat Lütem and Idil Lütem in Bad Godesberg, Kaan Orbay and Neval Orbay in Vienna, Matthias Behnke in Geneva and Julien Descombes in Zurich for their hospitality and friendship. Colleagues in Austria, Belgium, Canada, Germany and Switzerland kindly gave me their time, answered my questions, directed me to material, and read parts of the manuscript. I thank Anna Gamper, Peter Bußjäger, Anton Pelinka and Wolfgang C. Müller in Austria; Matteo Gianni and Frédéric Varone in Switzerland; Guido von Raskaj, Niels Lange, Steffen Schneider and Christine Strähle in Germany; Geert Bouckaert, Wilfried Dewachter, Guido Dierickx, Philippe Van Parijs, André-Paul Frognier, Sophie Weerts and David Robichaud in Belgium; David R. Cameron, Steve White, Raffaele Iacovino, Jeffrey Osweiler, Brian Greene, Hudson Meadwell, Peter Moore, François Rocher, Jocelyn Maclure and Mark Brawley in Canada; Imke Harbers, Robbert Schuller, Roelof Smit and Maria Spirova here in the Netherlands. Two colleagues deserve special mention: Alain-G. Gagnon had an important impact on my thinking on federalism during my doctoral studies, and I was fortunate to work with another leading federalism scholar, Richard Simeon, during my post-doctoral research. I thank them both for their support and encouragement over the years. While I acknowledge their role in this book, I should also mention that I am solely responsible for all faults and inaccuracies that might have been overlooked.

Efficiency during the writing stage depends on certain intangible qualities of the work environment. In this respect, I should thank the petulant and elusive beauty of the city of Montréal, whose very problems only add to her indelible charm. Mother Nature has not given her a beautiful climate, but has surely endowed her with beautiful people. Her many twenty-four-hour cafés deserve much credit for the café allongé and nicotine induced creative breakthroughs. It would have probably been more appropriate if I had been writing post-modern poetry rather than a macro-social deductive inquiry into educational policy and mass media regulation in federal systems, but I guess none of the patrons realized. Despite her merciless winter, Montréal is undoubtedly a queen of a city and I owe her a lot for an atmosphere conducive for academic work.

During the writing of this book my father passed away. As a retired academic he was still carrying out research and publishing, albeit in the completely different field of cardiovascular surgery. I dedicate this book to his memory.

Jan Erk
Leiden, The Netherlands

1   Federalism and congruence

Introduction

This book aims to do two things, one substantive and one theoretical. The first objective is to contribute to the comparative federalism literature by analyzing the patterns of change and continuity in five federal systems of the industrial West. This will be done by an in-depth empirical examination of Austria, Belgium, Canada, Germany and Switzerland through a single framework of analysis. There is much to be learned about federalism by studying these five cases together. In addition to the study of federalism, the book seeks to contribute to the theoretical debate in comparative politics in general. Here the aim is to show the shortcomings of new institutionalist approaches in explaining change, and to highlight the usefulness of society-based approaches in studying change and continuity in comparative politics.

The study of federalism is a field that has not yet been at the core of the theoretical debates in comparative politics. In fact, it has been noted that federalism is often studied in country-specific terms with little systematic comparison.[1] The field tends to produce works of prescriptive nature instead of theory-driven analyses.[2] Yet, in terms of the relationship between institutions and society, federalism presents a unique opportunity for students of comparative politics. Federalism is both a societal and an institutional phenomenon, and thus presents an area where the two can be studied together. As an institutional phenomenon, federalism denotes the constitutional/institutional configuration of the political system. This formal division of political power between the center and substate units is one side of the picture. However, federalism is also a societal phenomenon; one could have a federal society where societal differences like ethnicity, language and class tend to be territorially-based, or one could have a non-federal society where differences are nationwide and not territorially concentrated. It is the relationship between the institutional and the societal where the most theoretically interesting questions lie. What is of interest in this study is the long-run equilibrium between social structures and political institutions. In this context, the logic of congruence between society and institutions is employed in order to explain the course of broad changes in federal systems in the industrialized West. The basic argument is that political institutions change in order to be congruent with the society. Such explicit theoretical objectives can help bring a field hitherto dominated by prescriptive concerns into the core of comparative politics.

As the empirical chapters on Austria, Belgium, Canada, Germany and Switzerland show, political institutions in these countries have gradually changed to reach a better fit with the ethno-linguistic social structure. Before its recent federalization, Belgium was a unitary state. However, a Belgian "nation" did not emerge to fit the unitary political institutions; these institutions changed to reflect the underlying ethno-linguistic divisions instead. Federal institutions also do not neatly correspond to the Swiss federal society. The federal constitution did not create twenty-six distinct societies for each canton, but the two large constituent communities in the form of Swiss Romand and Swiss German have continued to exist – together with the smaller Ticinesi and Rhaeto-Romance. In Canada, on the other hand, a federal structure based on ten provinces did not eliminate the Québec vs the rest of Canada social divide. In Canada and Switzerland there has been mid-range institutional change in the direction of congruence, but, more importantly, in both cases the federal system tends to bypass the federal constitution and works asymmetrically based on the constituent linguistic/cultural communities. That is to say, the constitutional symmetry between the French-speaking province of Québec and the other nine provinces of Canada is coupled with an asymmetry in the workings of Canadian federalism where Québec's behavior is markedly different from the other English-speaking provinces. Similarly, the constitutional symmetry among Swiss cantons coexists with Swiss-German and Swiss-Romand communities that transcend cantonal boundaries in the workings of federalism. The German case similarly indicates institutional change while the social structure remained constant. The Federal Republic of Germany started with substate competences and an accompanying degree of diversity in public policies in 1949, but it has since moved in the centralist direction. Austrian federalism has followed a parallel path towards nation-wide politics. Both cases exhibit the centralizing tendencies that accompany ethno-linguistic homogeneity. Altogether, the case studies suggest that a society-based perspective presents a more reliable way to identify the political patterns in federal systems. In all the cases, institutions have changed towards congruence with the ethno-linguistic structure rather than the other way around. Not only do the following chapters display the role played by the underlying societal set-up in shaping the uncodified workings of federal systems; they also aim to explain why in many cases institutions proved to be malleable rather than sticky.

State, society and federalism

The term "federalism" originates from the Latin word *foedus*, i.e. compact. Historically, the term represented a political compact between groups which had come together in an association. The sixteenth-century German Calvinist thinker Johannes Althusius is the most important intellectual forebear of federalism theory.[3] Althusius' thinking centered on the notion of shared sovereignty in a contractual union, *pactum foederis*, between the constituent political entities.[4] In the following century, a confederal compact based on such contractual ideas was formed between the provinces of the Low Countries. Elsewhere, three Alpine communities had already established such a union in the thirteenth century that eventually became the Swiss Confederation. Confederal arrangements, however, lacked a strong political center. It was the stronger federal union amongst the former British colonies in North America that gave the center direct political authority for the first time. A federal constitution combining the compact theory of federalism with the republican principle of democratic legitimacy had replaced the earlier confederal union between the thirteen American colonies in 1787.[5] In the following century, federalism was used as a tool towards German unification.[6] Around the same time, Austrians were experimenting with federal arrangements to keep their multinational empire together.[7] Despite these various uses to which federalism was put, it was generally considered as a transitory arrangement or a "second best" option in the path towards political existence.

Until the end of World War II, federalism was still seen as a lesser substitute to unitary state. In the late nineteenth century, British constitutional theorist A.V. Dicey wrote about the federalization of the British Empire as an inferior alternative to the unity of the Westminster model.[8] Following the Great Depression of 1933, the weakness of the United States government in face of the magnitude of macro-economic problems was attributed to the divided political order of federalism. In his provocatively entitled *The Obsolescence of Federalism*, British Labour politician and political historian Harold Laski argued that federalism produced weak governments, which were in turn incapable of dealing with the big questions of industrialization and mass democracy of the twentieth century.[9] According to Ronald Watts, prior to 1945 federalism was treated with benign contempt as an incomplete national government or a transitional model of political organization.[10] However, since World War II, federalism has come to be accepted as a potential way to manage diverse societies and as a way to combat remote, undemocratic and ineffective central governments. Correspondingly, a literature dealing with the theoretical and empirical questions of federalism has emerged.

Theories of federalism share the descriptive lowest common denominator of a political structure where authority is divided among two or more levels of government, but the common theoretical premises do not extend much beyond that. Until the 1950s the study of federalism was the study of federal constitutions. In fact, the very origins of comparative federalism lie in the field of comparative constitutional studies where a formal legal analysis is employed. The constitutional division of competences between the center and the substate units (provinces, states, cantons, Länder) remained the main focus of comparative federalism for long time. The most influential work within this tradition has been that of K.C. Wheare.[11] Wheare's legalistic analysis, which defined federalism as a form of governance where the orders of government are coordinate and independent, has often been quoted as the authoritative definition of a federal system. But there has been a parallel approach employing a society-based perspective. The most important voice of this persuasion has been a French thinker more widely known for his anarchist ideas, Pierre-Joseph Proudhon.

Pierre-Joseph Proudhon's *Du principe fédératif* is one of the earliest examples of sociological federalism.[12] Proudhon saw social and economic diversity as the reason for adopting federal political institutions, rather than seeing these institutions as the cause of diversity. Some of the intellectual descendants of Proudhon's idea of federalism can be found within the political economy approach to federalism.[13] According to this perspective, the socio-economic differences between regions influence the workings of a federal system. The leading advocate of the sociological approach to federalism is, though, William Livingston. According to Livingston, the focus of federalism studies had to be on societal factors rather than formal institutions. This idea was reflected in the notion of "federal society," i.e. a social structure with territorially based diversity. Livingston believed that such a federal society was the *raison d'être* for federalism. This approach was diametrically opposed to the dominant institutional/constitutional perspective in the study of federalism. Livingston argued that:[14]

> Institutional devices, both in form and function, are only the surface manifestations of the deeper federal quality of the society that lies beneath the surface. The essence of federalism lies not in the institutional or constitutional structure but in the society itself.

For Livingston, a federal society was one with territorially-based diversity; he was not very specific about what constituted diversity and, by extension, what it meant for a society to be federal or not. A number of students of federalism took up the notion of federal society and expanded on Livingston's insight. For example, Michael Stein elaborated on the definition of a federal society: "Where a society is constituted of territorially based communities which are clearly differentiated by language and ethnicity, then one can find a federal society."[15] Stein believed that factors such as religion, geography and economics reinforced the territorially based ethno-linguistic differences, but it was the ethno-linguistic patterns that were fundamental. Another student of federalism, Donald Smiley, preferred the term "federal nation" in his work: "A federal nation is one in which the most politically salient aspects of human differentiation, identification and conflict are related to specific territories."[16] The federal society argument was also taken up by Charles D. Tarlton in order to build a dichotomy between symmetrical and asymmetrical federalism: "following Livingston, an asymmetrical federal government is one in which political institutions correspond to the real social 'federalism' beneath them."[17] Symmetrical federalism, on the other hand, denoted a political order where the federal demarcations were drawn independently of the underlying social structure. This distinction runs parallel to one made by Aaron Wildavsky between "structural" and "social" federalism.[18] According to Wildavsky, social federalism is where economic, ethnic and religious diversities correspond to political boundaries. Structural federalism, on the other hand, refers to a federal institutional structure designed to decentralize political power regardless of the societal make-up. More recently, some scholars have made a similar distinction between "territorial" and "multinational" federal systems.[19] However, such approaches to federalism that take into account the social structure remain a minority in a field dominated by the institutionalist perspectives.

The study of federalism has long been a study of institutions, so the recent move in comparative politics towards new institutionalism has cemented intellectual continuity in federalism studies.[20] New institutionalist approaches, however, are somewhat different from the old tradition of institutionalist analysis in federalism. The focus of new institutionalism is predominantly comparative, and institutions are seen as an intermediate layer constraining and influencing politics. This is different from the earlier studies, which focused only on constitutions. New institutionalist works tend to take the federal structure as the independent variable and seek to explain its role in shaping society and politics. Richard Simeon describes this perspective in the following terms:[21]

> Institutions are not simply the outgrowth or products of the environment and they are not just dependent variables in the political system. They can be seen as independent forces, which have some effects of their own: once established they themselves come to shape and influence the environment.

Emphasis is now more on the institutional arrangements that shape political strategies and distribute political power. The new institutionalist logic suggests that political actors try to take advantage of the available channels for political activity, and actors are gradually socialized into the institutions as they form their preferences within these rule-bound settings.[22] Interests, therefore, come to be nested in prevailing institutional arrangements. As a result, institutions socialize political actors into the existing structure in such a way that prevailing institutional arrangements are reproduced over time. However, it is this very notion of continuity that appears problematic in the five cases under focus in this study.

As the following empirical chapters demonstrate, federal institutions have not ensured their continuity by providing rule-bound settings to political actors in Austria, Belgium, Canada, Germany and Switzerland. In fact, in many instances formal institutions were changed or bypassed. For example in the Belgian case, political institutions gradually changed in the direction towards a congruence with the constituent Francophone and Flemish cultural/linguistic communities. In Germany, similarly, there has been more change than continuity. An institutionalist logic would expect the federal division of responsibilities established in 1949 to lead to the development of substate interest group mobilization at the Länder level. However, the German federal system has not socialized the German nation into a federal society. In the end, German society has not changed; institutions have. What is common in both cases is the relative ease with which new institutions have been created while existing institutions were changed or bypassed. Due to its emphasis on continuity, new institutionalism has problems with explaining not only the direction of change, but also change itself. Various subfields of comparative politics have recently produced works that call into question the notion of institutional continuity.[23] New institutionalist scholars themselves have recently tackled what they call "the impoverished state of theorizing on issues of institutional change."[24] Limits to the institutionalist perspective are also acknowledged by some of the trailblazers of new institutionalism in federalism scholarship. According to Richard Simeon:[25]

> We have not done a very good job theorizing about change in the federal system.... Clearly institutional models alone are insufficient, since these changes have occurred ... within an essentially unchanged institutional framework.... But to fully explain change we are driven to revive our interest in societal forces and in political economy.

Newer works in comparative federalism have also come to acknowledge the limits new institutionalism has in explaining change. Instead of taking institutions as given and investigating their consequences, Erik Wibbels calls for approaching institutions as dependent variables to account for the ways in which the institutions of federalism evolve.[26] In view of that, Wibbels has drawn attention to the need to "understand how and why institutions emerge and evolve as they have across federations."[27] Jonas Pontusson echoes this observation in the context of new institutionalism: "the problem of explaining institutions – why they differ across countries and how they change over time – brings out the limits of institutionalist analysis most clearly."[28] According to Pontusson, "to understand the impetus for change, we need to analyze the process whereby 'extra-institutional' forces reshape the interests of powerful actors."[29] The ethno-linguistic social structure is the source of one such extra-institutional force.

The aim of this study is to give voice to the societal forces that influence the workings of federalism. This follows Riker's point that "in the study of federal governments, therefore, it is always appropriate to go behind the fiction to study the real forces in a federal system."[30] Here the focus is not on how institutions reproduce themselves over time, but on how societal factors bypass or in fact lead to institutional change. Accordingly, the workings of federalism in Austria, Belgium, Canada, Germany and Switzerland are explained through the ethno-linguistic social structure, and not through political institutions. Carl Friedrich had noted the benefits of structural perspectives in explaining the processes of federal change:[31]

> The study of social structure in relation to federalism has, therefore, helped us to understand better the dynamic nature of federal orders, to look upon a federal system as subject to continual change, rather than a static design fixed forever in an immutable distribution of factors.

It should be noted, however, that the social structure functions both as a unifying force and a cleavage.[32] For example, language divides French-speakers and

German-speakers in Switzerland, and French-speakers and Dutch-speakers in Belgium, but it also strengthens inner-group cohesion within linguistic communities otherwise divided over religion, class and region. The ethno-linguistic cleavage provides the social base for demarcating the borders of collective identity. The importance of ethno-linguistic factors, of course, depends on the decline of other significant social cleavages in terms of their political relevance. Decline in class voting is one such development;[33] another is the increasing secularization of European societies and the subsequent decline of religion as a politically salient social cleavage.[34] Parallel to the decline of other social cleavages, the broadening of mass politics and modernization have accentuated the unifying – and the dividing – force of language. As a result of a combination of these factors, language has emerged as the predominant social demarcator in most of the industrialized West since the end of World War II.[35]

In the last fifty years, language has grown into the main basis of collective identity in the five cases under study. While linguistic public space brings together Austrians, Germans and English-speaking Canadians otherwise divided over place, class or religion, it also divides Québécois from the English-speaking Canadians, Francophone Belgians from Flemings, Swiss Romands from Swiss Germans. According to French sociologist Dominique Schnapper, "language is an ethnic marker, but it is also the essential instrument through which democratic life is instituted and maintained."[36] Elsewhere Schnapper has argued that "a common language is essential in order to establish the exchanges which constitute a democratic order."[37] The role of language in providing public space for democracy has been noted by a number of other observers as well. For example, Margaret Moore argues that "in order to be a well-functioning national community, there has to be some form of common public life, a common framework of laws and a forum in which debates can take place."[38] A similar point is made by Brian Barry: "for democratic politics to work, the citizens must be able to communicate with one another, and must have access to the same forums of political debate."[39] According to Jeremy Webber, "language tends by its very nature to define the boundaries of political community. Language has this effect because, in addition to being a subject of public debate, it is the medium through which public debate occurs."[40] Webber believes that "there is thus an inevitable tendency towards autonomy in our linguistically defined political debates."[41] Consequently, linguistically demarcated public spaces become essential as forums of democratic deliberation. In other words, the linguistic community comes to perform the role of the default *demos*, i.e. the collectivity which functions as the primary base for democratic politics.[42]

The linguistic divisions in Belgium, Canada and Switzerland in fact demarcate the borders between separate *demoi*, i.e. communities which function as the default base for democratic politics. These three countries have federal societies along Livingston's formulation. In the presence of multiple *demoi* within one state, political institutions gradually change in order to be congruent with the social structure and come to reflect the underlying ethno-linguistic divisions. This process is most pronounced in cultural policy areas, like education and media, closely linked to use of language. Austria and Germany, on the other hand, have their respective nationwide *demoi* regardless of the formal federal demarcations. By employing Livingston's logic in the opposite direction, we can say that that these two countries have non-federal societies. Here, change has been in the opposite direction as political institutions have come to reflect the nationwide collectivities. Just as in Belgium, Canada and Switzerland, it is in similar cultural policy areas like education and media where the underlying ethno-linguistic homogeneity of Austria and Germany has found its first outlet. The idea of congruence between society and institutions has a broader intellectual heritage, of course.

In their influential 1963 book *The Civic Culture*, Gabriel Almond and Sidney Verba dealt with the question of congruence between political culture and political institutions: "Political cultures may or may not be congruent with the structures of the political system."[43] Their view was based on an understanding that viewed society separately from state institutions. However, the term congruence is probably more closely associated with Harry Eckstein. The first tentative step Eckstein took towards exploring the notion of congruence between state and society was in 1961.[44] In this working paper, Eckstein proposed a way to look at democracies through the lens of a congruence between state and society, or, more precisely, between the authority patterns in society and political structures. He believed that the relationship between the two carried the answers to what made certain democracies stable and others not. However, Eckstein acknowledged that his propositions did not yet have empirical validation.[45] It was in his work on Norway that he found evidence for his ideas through an examination of the relationship between authority patterns of the Norwegian society (i.e. in families, schools and economic organizations) and the authority patterns of the Norwegian government.[46] According to Eckstein, a congruence between these authority patterns ensured stability: "Democracies (and perhaps also other kinds of rule) tend to be stable if governmental and social authority patterns are highly congruent – if they involve considerable resemblances and thus have a certain fit."[47] For Eckstein the nature of the society was reflected in what he called the authority culture, which in turn made certain political systems more appropriate for certain social structures.[48] Eckstein continued exploring the notion of congruence and authority culture throughout his career, but he did not expand this into a general theory of congruence between society and state.[49]

Similar ideas propounding congruence between state and society can be found in other areas of the social sciences as well. Ernest Gellner's view on nationalism and political change is one such example: "Nationalism is primarily a political principle, which holds that the political and national unit should be congruent."[50] In many respects, there are strong parallels between structural-Marxist approaches and views on congruence and change. Different from Almond, Verba, Eckstein and Gellner, Marxist perspectives bring the socio-economic factors to the fore, but the emphasis is similarly on the social structure in order to explain political behavior. According to structural-Marxism, the source of politics lies in the socio-economic structure. This structure determines the workings of the political system and pressures political institutions to reflect the underlying socio-economic factors.[51] Structuralist works do not figure prominently in contemporary comparative politics, however. One such exception is Stefano Bartolini's study of the European left, which deals with the broad environmental constraints the macro-social structure imposes on political actors.[52] Another such study highlighting the role structures play in inducing and constraining the behavior of political actors is Gregory Luebbert's work on social classes and the origins of political regimes.[53] With regard to the emphasis it places on the ethno-linguistic structure, the present study employs a structural focus not unlike the angle used in the above works.

There is, of course, always a risk of social determinism inherent in such structure-based macro approaches. One way to prevent this is to focus attention on political actors and public policy concerns. As evidence from the case studies shows, the way the field of public policy functions tends to be the immediate reflection of the underlying social structure. In particular, the differences between federations with federal and non-federal societies are best observed in cultural policy areas where ethno-linguistic divisions strongly influence and delimit political choices. This should not imply that the institutional structure set up by the constitution is unimportant. When large-scale constitutional reconfiguration is unattainable, change is reflected through the workings of the system. This is often the case when there is imbalance in the respective sizes of linguistic/cultural communities. Various attempts to codify the national dualism of French and English Canada have historically stalled in the face of opposition from English Canada. Similarly, the overwhelming numerical majority of Swiss Germans makes large-scale institutional reform formalizing Romandie as a French-speaking constituent community of Switzerland unlikely. Formal institutional change, in both cases, has remained mid-range. As result, broader change has come through a growing discrepancy between *de jure* federal constitution and *de facto* federal practice. Without a large-scale formal revision of the constitution, the operation of the federal system has evolved to reflect the underlying social structure. In order to observe these patterns – without the assumption of an automatic process of change – one should focus on the choices made by political actors in the field of public policy.

In the absence of formal recognition, the federal society reveals itself through the workings of the system as the ethno-linguistic community becomes the primary collectivity; in other words the *demos*, which demarcates the frame of reference employed by political actors. Tactical decisions concerning public policy are of course constrained and influenced by the institutional set-up, but the broad choices made by political actors emanate from the social structure. This does not mean that the political choices are preset for the linguistic communities, since many political issues deeply divide these communities, but these issues are deliberated within these linguistically demarcated public spaces. In other words, language forms a distinct public space creating an "us" community in which political deliberations take place. When confronted with an ethno-linguistic structure that does not match the political one, the political structure gradually changes in the direction of congruence; not automatically, but through the influence of public policy concerns pursued by political actors. And when constitutional reform is blocked by the majority, the field of public policy becomes a substitute for large-scale institutional change. The assumption here is that choices available to political actors in the field of public policy are influenced and delimited by the demarcations of the societal composition. Decision-makers might disagree over the substance of the policies, but they share the choice of venue in the form of the ethno-linguistic "nation," i.e. the default *demos*. In the case of a discrepancy between the ethno-linguistic societal structure and the political structure, public policy concerns exert pressures towards congruence by demarcating the social collectivity for which policies are made. There is move towards congruence whenever these collective boundaries do not coincide with the jurisdictional boundaries of political institutions. Thus, if the "nation" is smaller than the unit defined by the political institutions, there will be devolutionary pressures on the unitary institutions. And in federations designed without a formal recognition of the federal society, public policy will bypass the constitution and function asymmetrically based on the constituent ethno-linguistic communities. Due to the existence of multiple *demoi*, one often finds political battles over "who gets to decide."

On the other hand, when the "nation" is bigger than the unit marked off by political institutions, the tendency will be towards centralization. In these ethno-linguistically homogeneous non-federal societies, contents of public policies and efficiency in delivering them are the issues of concern – whatever the institutional design. Public policies are debated in nationwide terms. Political actors compete to impose their version of public policies, and political struggles tend to center on the contents of these policies. Since the choices made by political actors are influenced and delimited by the demarcations of the *demos* regardless of the institutional division of power, in this case debates on public policies tend to follow national lines. Content thus trumps control. In sum, it can be said that in non-federal societies what is done is more important than who does it, as long as the job gets done.

Focus on public policies helps to bring social and institutional perspectives closer, in due course attaining a fuller apprehension of the political patterns at play. The two ideal models of federal state and unitary state are useful benchmarks to evaluate political institutions and constitutions, but a deeper understanding of the workings of the system can be attained by looking at the field of public policy. In general terms, examination of public policies would likely show that the workings of a unitary state with a federal society might be less unitary than what the institutional set-up conveys. And similarly, in federations with non-federal societies, the workings of the system might be more unified than what the *de jure* federal structure suggests. One is likely to find standardization and nationalization of policies within substate competence even while the constitution remains federal. The pressures towards congruence – both the centralist and the decentralist variants – are most pronounced in cultural policy areas of education and media, where ethno-linguistic factors find their first expression.[54]

The central line of reasoning employed here is not based on the assumption of automatic process of congruence. The starting point is the societal structure, but the link between structure and change is reflected in the choices agents make about public policy. Change is gradual towards a better fit with the frames of reference employed by the political actors. It is clear that this perspective takes the social structure not as something to be explained, but as a given. The ethno-linguistic social structure is employed in order to explain change. The preceding long process of ethno-linguistic identity formation is not a part of the inquiry. This is different from many studies on nationalism that approach national identity as something to be explained – the dependent variable, in other words. And when they seek to explain change, students of nationalism are often inclined to use agency-based rational action models.[55] This study has a different take on the notion of agency; the emphasis is on how the social structure influences and delimits political choices. It is certain that in many instances ethno-linguistic divisions provide political elites with raw material to mobilize and use to their own ends, but this does not mean that elites have full control over these divisions. Put differently, political leaders did not create the ethno-linguistic social structure. They might have benefited from the divisions on many occasions, but at the end of the day the ethno-linguistic fault-lines are too deep to be mere products of elite manipulation.[56] It all comes back to the difference between society-based and institutionalist approaches in the study of federalism. The two differ in terms of their approach to identity. Societal approaches tend to see identities themselves as the independent variable to which federal institutions respond, while institutionalist approaches hold identity to be a product of federal institutions and the entrepreneurship of central and local politicians.

In terms of the primacy it accords to the social structure in explaining change, the theoretical foundations of this study are clearly society-based. The intellectual lineage of this macro-social perspective can be found in the works of Pierre-Joseph Proudhon, William Livingston and Harry Eckstein.[57] This is a scholarly tradition which holds the uncodified social structures indispensable to the analyses of how political systems function. Claus Offe calls this approach "the sociology of political institutions;"[58] others have described it as the "sociology of politics."[59] Works of this persuasion share a similar emphasis on the role social structures play in inducing and constraining politics. In other words, this is a tradition which puts the society before the state.

Federalism in Austria, Belgium, Canada, Germany and Switzerland

The empirical chapters on the cases record the processes towards congruence in detail. Evidence shows that in all five, political institutions have been rather pliable when social and political structures do not coincide. It is worth reiterating, however, that the processes of change tend to come through the workings of public policy, not through a grand design towards congruence.

Germany and Austria are two cases with ethno-linguistically homogenous non-federal societies. The theoretical argument devised in the preceding section suggests that, in both cases, the contents of public policies would be the main public concern. The jurisdictional division of responsibilities would thus be of secondary importance since issues are couched in nationwide terms. In this context, one should expect the harmonization and standardization of education and media policy – which are within the jurisdiction of the substate units, i.e. the Länder – and a general tendency for public policies to be debated in "national" terms. In both cases, empirical evidence corroborates theory. Chapter 5, on Germany, shows that, despite disagreements between the political left and right over the contents of policies in education and media, political actors in the Federal Republic of Germany shared an all-German frame of reference. As a result, all political actors approached these policies in nationwide terms. Empirical examination demonstrates that Länder governments – including the parties in power and the Länder bureaucracy, opposition parties, interest groups and professional associations – have all been active in translating societal homogeneity into federal change. Regardless of differences over the contents of the policies, issues were tackled at the national level. Political battles over education and media were fought in an all-German arena, despite strict constitutional clauses imposing exclusive substate jurisdiction in these policy areas. A complete overhaul in the direction of a unitary state is impossible under the German constitution, since the federal character of the state is non-amendable. Change, therefore, came through the operation of the federal system. The picture on the Austrian side is much the same. Despite exclusive substate Länder jurisdiction in education and media, there have been centralizing tendencies fostered by nationwide cultural homogeneity. The Austrian Länder were in fact active participants in the "nationalization" of education and broadcasting. There were deep disagreements and intense rivalry between the two main parties in Austria, the Social Democrats and the Christian Democrats, but in spite of the partisan differences over the contents of policies, all political actors involved set the issues in nationwide terms.

In contrast with these two cases, Belgium, Canada and Switzerland are ethnolinguistically heterogeneous federal societies. There are certain differences between these three, however. While Belgium is closer to a balance between the linguistic communities, Canada and Switzerland have dominant linguistic majorities – English-speakers in Canada and German-speakers in Switzerland constitute around 75 percent of their respective populations. What unites these three cases is the existence of linguistically demarcated public spaces. According to the theoretical argument formulated in this chapter, the operation of education and media policy should display the inner workings of the federal system based on these divisions. That is, pressures on public policies to correspond to the constituent linguistic/cultural communities should be expected. Within this context, "who gets to decide," i.e. the Federal Government of Canada or the Québec Government, should be more important than what is to be done. Evidence from these three cases confirms the theory.

Chapter 3, on Belgium, traces a relatively linear process of change from a unitary state to a federal one. In the decades following the end of World War II, political actors started to take their respective linguistic communities as their frame of reference and competed within the boundaries of these communities despite national competence over education and media assigned by the constitution. Consequently, these two policy areas gradually devolved towards the Francophone and Flemish constituent communities of Belgium until a satisfactory level of congruence was attained. The most recent constitutional changes in 1993 have formalized Belgium's federal society. Canadian and Swiss cases are not as straightforward, however.

Canada and Switzerland differ from Belgium not only in terms of having a dominant linguistic majority, but also in terms of already having the formal structures of a federal system. In both cases, change is not from a unitary state to a federal one recognizing the ethno-linguistic divide. Here, change is from a federal constitution that did not formally recognize the multinational aspect of the country to a federal system that has come to function in congruence with its constituent communities. While the relative balance between the two linguistic communities allowed Belgium to pursue the goal of federalization in spite of the differences regarding the terms of this process, Québec's demands for change have often stalled in the face of opposition from the rest of Canada. In Switzerland, similarly, large-scale constitutional change towards a multinational federation has little chance of likelihood. The result is mid-range institutional change and, more importantly, a *de facto* practice which diverges from the *de jure*. In Canada, education and media policy have been important outlets for identity politics – and hence they are the immediate reflections of the underlying ethno-linguistic duality of the Canadian social structure. What neither constitutional reform packages nor sovereignty referenda have managed to bring about has largely been attained by the workings of public policy. The cooperation between the nine provinces of English-speaking Canada is much closer than that which a reading of the constitution would suggest, while Québec prefers to do things on its own. There are certain similarities between Switzerland and Canada. The Swiss public space is also divided into linguistic halves which function independently of the structure set up by federal demarcations. Evidence shows that Swiss federalism has come to reflect the underlying ethno-linguistic divide between the French Swiss and German Swiss, despite a formal federal system based on twenty-six cantons (the Italian-speaking canton of Ticino is too small to be a major partner). In particular, the French-speaking cantons of Romandie have established common education and media policies that follow the ethno-linguistic divide.

In sum, all five cases show evidence of institutions changing to conform to the societal structure rather than the other way around. In all five there has been a fair degree of disagreement across the political spectrum concerning the contents of public policies, but these political battles have been fought in arenas which correspond to the underlying ethno-linguistic composition. Detailed examination of the case studies will follow a brief discussion of the methods used in the empirical investigation.

Method of comparison

The core of the empirical inquiry was carried out in archives. Preliminary research on secondary sources had suggested a number of key formative moments. Field research tried to capture these turning points of institutional change through the analysis of archival material, but original-language secondary literature was also used to help identify issues that deserved focus. The archival research was based on primary sources in German, French and Dutch.[60] Parliamentary minutes, public opinion polls, court decisions, publications of special bodies and advisory committees, treaties, agreements, ministerial reports, political party policy documents, and publications of numerous semi-public and public bodies were examined. This pattern of empirical inquiry was duplicated for each case study.

Austria, Belgium, Canada, Germany and Switzerland are all advanced democracies of the industrialized West. Obviously these are not identical cases, but they are reasonably close to enable comparison. It is not the conclusion that the five are comparable, but rather the starting point for investigation. Since the objective of the study is to explain federal change, the case studies are examined within the confines of a common framework of analysis. In doing so, some of the *sui generis* characteristics of the cases are relegated to the background. This of course brings to the fore the tension between generalizability and idiosyncrasy in the social sciences. All comparative works face a difficult choice between exactness in description and comprehensiveness in explanation. Despite the demarcation of the range of choices by these two opposite ends, most students of comparative politics tend to follow a path somewhere in between. It is often the particular combination of the two approaches that determines where one is situated within the field. This study tries to retain a balance between the two paths; it seeks to build an explanation that has parsimonious clarity without sacrificing in-depth exactness.

Historical/comparative case studies provide a particularly fertile ground for analyses that seek to balance exactness in description and comprehensiveness in explanation.[61] Such studies allow for a combination of historical accuracy and generalizability through the method of focused comparison.[62] This is the approach employed in this study as well. At the core lies a macro-level deductive argument applied to particular events where the analysis seeks to combine a general structural theory with historical contingency and human agency. The focus is on the five cases of Austria, Belgium, Canada, Germany and Switzerland, but the inquiry is based on the premise of broader applicability to other cases. The aim of the study is to provide a "thematized story" of congruence in federal systems by combining theory and history. Donald McCloskey describes this middle ground in the following way: "A thematized story, or a dynamized model, stands between the pure (and mere) metaphor and the pure (and mere) story."[63] This approach is justified by its aim to provide an explanation while capturing empirical complexity at the same time. More recently, some leading rational choice theorists have used an approach similar to thematized story.[64] In what they call "analytic narratives," these authors present in-depth case studies informed by deductive theorizing. Accordingly, analytic narratives retain "sensitivity to the particularities and richness of stories while actually offering the microfoundations that permit illumination of general theory."[65] Both thematized stories and analytic narratives seek a balance between exactness in description and comprehensiveness in explanation; in other words, they seek to combine explanation in principle and explanation in detail.[66] This is also the path followed by this study. The inquiry started with an explanation in principle, followed by explanation in detail to see if the principle held true in the face of facts. This is an approach similar to the analytic narrative elaborated by rational choice theorists, but differs in one important respect: while rational choice theorists use a micro-level deductive theory to approach their cases, this study uses a macro-level deductive theory. The empirical investigation was carried out through the parameters set by the theory of congruence. However, the initial theoretical formulation was occasionally revised during the empirical research in the face of empirical findings. Such successive interaction between theory and data produces a tighter-knit study – a point noted by Margaret Levi in the context of analytic narratives: "The process of inquiry begins with a deductive model, but the inductive investigation transforms and produces a fuller elaboration of the deductive model."[67]

Analytic narratives and thematized stories are useful tools to combine scientific objectives with respect to history. This is a way to attain a parsimonious explanation that makes sense of the complexity, but also remains firmly couched within the case studies. Nevertheless, there is an inherent tension between rigor in historical precision and the quest for scientific generalizability. History should not turn everything into a *sui generis* configurative story. At the same time, one does not want the theory to rewrite history in order to fit it in with the research model. Theorizing introduces an order to the case and variables to build an explanation, but, as Donald Green and Ian Shapiro caution us: "formalization … cannot be an end in itself; however analytically tight and parsimonious a theory might be, its scientific value depends on how well it explains the relevant data."[68] Focus on parsimony and formalization should not equal collection of convenient data and a research model which omits or lumps with little understanding of what the variables signify. In other words, parsimony is useful insofar as it helps to illuminate reality. For a reliable and valid explanation, one needs full immersion in the context to understand what the variables represent. Since comparative politics consolidated itself as a discipline during the behavioral revolution in reaction to the earlier historical/institutional study of comparative government, it has always contrasted itself with configurative historical single case studies and has thus inflated the importance of large-*n* case studies in building the scientific foundations of a social science discipline. However, explanatory power and generalizability are not necessarily in conflict with descriptive accuracy and small-*n* case studies. A wider description of cases does not mean that one is sacrificing explanatory zeal at the expense of historical story-telling. On the contrary, this is carried out in order to dig deeper and reach for the closest approximation to social reality while the premise of generalizability is retained. Besides, Austria, Belgium, Canada, Germany and Switzerland represent the major examples of federalism in the industrialized West anyway. The lessons gained from the study of these five federal systems should have broader applicability to the cases where similar questions of state and society are under investigation. The editors of a recent volume on the benefits of small-*n* comparative studies defend their methodology in the following terms:[69]

> The social sciences today are torn apart by a tension between two desires: to richly describe the world, showing its complexity and variability, and to robustly model the world, showing its relationships and regularities. We argue in this volume that engaging in comparisons of a few, well-understood cases reduces this tension.

William Riker has made a similar point by highlighting the role focused studies play in combining precision and generalizability. Riker suggests that investigating well-defined small events rather than undefined grand questions presents a more promising way for scientific progress.[70] This is the reason behind limiting the empirical investigation in this study to the policy areas of education and media. Miriam Golden shares Riker's view on the benefits of concentrating on well-defined small puzzles:[71]

> A narrow focus to attain a proper solution is a better research strategy than a broad focus that fails to generate conclusive results.... By narrowing the focus of the phenomena under study, we reduce the trade-off between analytic rigor and empirical accuracy.

In the end, it all comes down balance between exactness in description and comprehensiveness in explanation – or, better put, between analytic rigor and descriptive accuracy.

2   Austria

Introduction

Since its inception in 1920, Austria's federal system has moved in a centralist direction. The standard explanation credits the Austrian constitution as the reason for this pattern of change.[1] According to this view, the Austrian provinces (*Länder*) were constitutionally in a weaker position vis-à-vis the federal government (*Bund*). In the following decades, the Bund took advantage of its initial powers and expanded into policy areas under Länder jurisdiction. As a result, the Länder have been relegated to the position of administrative subunits in a decentralized state, rather than retaining their position as the constituent members of a federal union. Austrian scholars tend to use the term "centralistic federation" (*zentralistischer Bundesstaat*) to describe this system.[2] Empirical evidence, however, suggests that a perspective based on the social structure is more helpful in explaining the broad pressures towards centralization.[3]

The 1920 Constitution had provided certain jurisdictional bridgeheads for the Länder, so their failure to utilize this cannot be explained by the institutional structure alone. In fact, the federal constitution included exclusive competences for the Austrian Länder. The so-called *Generalklausel* of Article 15 gave the Länder competence in all areas not explicitly mentioned in the constitution. Most Länder competences are determined through this residual clause – i.e. anything that is not specified as federal competence is Länder competence by default. Armed with this clause of residual jurisdiction, the Austrian Länder should have been able to protect their prerogatives and add many more over the years as new policy areas emerged. This has not been the case, however. The Länder have weakened, and this process took place without large-scale political opposition. This chapter seeks to demonstrate that the answers to the workings of the Austrian federation lie not in its formal constitution but in its social structure. It is argued that territorially-based social diversity is a *sine qua non* for a federal frame of mind in the public consciousness. Without the territorially-based distinctiveness necessary to sustain such a federal outlook and a principled commitment to the division of constitutional competences, Austria's federal system has moved in a centralist direction.

According to its constitution Austria is a federation, but in practice the country works as a unitary state. Politicians, bureaucrats, interest groups, professional associations, trade unions and, most importantly, voters see politics in nationwide terms and act accordingly. In other words, Austria is a federation with a "non-federal" society; the *demos* is a nationwide one. The federal constitution establishes nine Länder, but there is no corresponding societal distinctiveness along the federal demarcations. The absence of territorially based ethno-linguistic heterogeneity generates broad centralizing pressures on Austria's federal system. The workings of the federal system are therefore much more unified than is the case in federations with federal societies like Canada, Belgium and Switzerland. This chapter shows that Austria's federal system has moved in a centralist direction due to the ethno-linguistically homogeneous societal structure where divisions are nationwide rather territorial.

Federalism in Austria

World War I ended with Austria's loss of most of the non-German territories of the Habsburg Empire. As the French Minister Georges Clemenceau remarked in 1918: "*L'Autriche c'est ce qui reste.*"[4] Consequently, a unitary state under the name of *Deutschösterreich*, soon to be changed to *Republik Österreich*, was set up in the German-speaking parts of the Habsburg Empire. But this was a time of uncertainty; conservative groups still had attachment to the monarchy, socialists wanted to unite with Germany, and there was a very real threat of revolutionary Bolshevism. In addition, there were growing separatist inclinations in parts of the country. The central government in Vienna failed to establish unchallenged authority over the regional governments based in the crown lands of the Austrian monarchy in Vorarlberg, Tyrol, Salzburg, Styria, Upper Austria, Lower Austria and Carinthia.[5] In the post-war political vacuum, most of these Länder had gone back to the provincial charters introduced by the imperial *Landesordnungen* of 1861. Regional sentiments were especially strong in the western Länder, where the strength of Catholic conservative views fuelled anti-Vienna sentiments toward the socialist-dominated capital.[6]

In May 1919, Länder-based Christian Socials came up with a federal blueprint opposing the idea of central state advocated by socialists in Vienna. Socialists then put forward a modified version of their constitutional proposal. The Länder representatives came together in Salzburg on 15–17 February 1920, and later in Linz on 20–23 April 1920, to discuss the proposals. Following the meeting in Linz, a constitutional committee was set up in Vienna with members of the provisional government seeking to find a middle ground between the opposing ideas.[7] After extensive negotiations, a federal compromise was reached as the crown lands of the Habsburg Empire were reinvented as the Länder of the Austrian federation,[8] and the federal constitution (*Bundesverfassung*) was accepted on 1 October 1920.[9] The constitution established a directly elected National Assembly (*Nationalrat*)[10] and a weaker Federal Council (*Bundesrat*) composed of Länder representatives.[11]

Post-World War I Austria, however, became the battleground between the

Socialist and Christian-Social camps trying to win control of the new regime. These two groups came to be known as the encampments (*Lager*),[12] and the conflict between them eventually escalated into a civil war in 1934. The Christian-Social Lager emerged victorious, and an authoritarian clerical regime was established under the leadership of Chancellor Engelbert Dollfuss in 1934. That political experiment ended with the 1938 *Anschluss*, when Austria became a part of the Third Reich.

At the end of World War II, the Austrian Länder were recreated within their 1938 borders. Under the leadership of Karl Renner, a coalition was formed between the Social Democrats (SPÖ),[13] Christian Socials or Austrian People's Party (ÖVP),[14] and Communists (KPÖ) on 27 April 1945. The Allied forces allowed the reinstitution of the 1920 Austrian Constitution with the extensive amendments that had been introduced in 1925 and 1929. Austria's political future was, therefore, settled much earlier than Germany's, due to a compromise between the Western Allies and the Soviets. The new Austrian state became a neutral country between the West and the East. Between the years 1947 and 1966, the country was run by a permanent coalition of ÖVP and SPÖ. Due to this political arrangement, Austria is often seen as an example of a consociational democracy between the Conservative Catholic "black" and left-wing "red" Lager.[15] The red–black division became the defining political cleavage of the new Austrian state as the public sphere was divided between the two groups according to the system of proportionality (*Proporz*). All bureaucracies and public corporations, from their governing boards to the rank and file, were divided between the two Lager. In the meantime, the occupation status ended on 15 May 1955 and Austria regained full sovereignty. In 1966, the ÖVP was able to form the government on its own; later the SPÖ became the governing party from 1971 to 1983. Thereafter, the government moved back and forth between these two parties, often with the much smaller Austrian Freedom Party (FPÖ) as a junior coalition partner. The system of proportionality between the SPÖ and the ÖVP, however, remained intact during this period.

The federal structure also took on the characteristics of the red–black political cleavage, especially within the Länder. For most of this time the majority of the Länder implemented the proportionality system of *Regierungsproporz*, which divided the provincial cabinets between the parties represented in the provincial parliaments. In broad terms, however, Länder politics do not receive much public visibility; Länder politicians are not as well known as national ones, media rarely focus on Länder political debates, and *Landtag* elections are generally seen as test elections for federal politics.[16] Due to the unitary social structure, all regional issues are interpreted according to a nationwide perspective. Political parties, trades unions, interest groups and professional associations are all organized along national lines. According to Fried Esterbauer, "in Austria, the political subsystems of parties, associations, media, and public opinion are predominantly composed of anti-federalist forces, more so than it is the case in other federal states."[17]

The asymmetry between Vienna and the countryside has some federal implications, however. As the former capital of the Habsburg Empire and with a population of almost two million, Vienna dominates the political, cultural and social life of this country of eight million inhabitants.[18] Furthermore, Vienna has historically been the stronghold of the red Lager, while most of the countryside votes Conservative. Six of the remaining eight Länder have had continuous ÖVP governments since 1945. Even though there is an anti-Vienna sentiment within these Conservative Länder, the political issues are more about the relative strength of national parties in certain regions rather than a territorially divided Austrian society.[19]

Over the years, the Bundesrat, which was designed to represent Länder interests, has become a part of nationwide party politics as well.[20] The voting patterns of the Bundesrat members correspond to party affiliation rather than provincial interests. Especially in the case of different majorities between the two Houses of Parliament, party competition defines Bundesrat–Nationalrat relations. This might appear to corroborate Riker's point about the importance of political parties in federal systems,[21] but the nationwide party structure in Austria is more of a reflection of the country's unitary social structure rather than the cause. Gottfried Heindl refers to this phenomenon as the "unity of duality" (*Einheit der Zweiteilung*).[22] The two main political parties represent the defining ideological cleavage of Austrian politics going back to the nineteenth century; furthermore, all other societal associations are based on national terms as well, leading Anton Pelinka to remark: "A comparison of the existing political picture with the constitution necessarily leads to realization that a discrepancy and a tense relationship exists between the constitution and political reality."[23]

The unitary social structure exerts a strong centralizing pressure on the workings of the federal system even while the constitution formally remains federal. The centralization process was particularly strong in the decades following the end of World War II. According to Theo Öhlinger, during this process "the federal structure of the constitution was formally maintained, but increasingly it was hollowed-out in favor of a global steering mechanism ..."[24] This observation seems to be shared by many students of Austrian federalism. An example of this perspective is the study by Christa Altenstetter, who described the process of centralization in the following terms:[25]

> Although the Länder had very different historical experiences and their populations' identity with their Land were quite distinct, an overview shows a far-reaching substantial homogeneity of the population, parties, and interest groups. This strong social and political homogeneity is reflected in the organization of the federal order from 1920 which has constituted the procedural framework for the federal process in Austria.

Along similar lines, Friedrich Koja points out to societal homogeneity as factor working in favor of centralization: "Since 1945, the homogeneity of the Austrian population, the imposition of party and special interests above Länder interests, but most importantly the trend towards large-scale unitary governance have undermined federalism."[26] Devoid of any inherent social opposition to centralization, all actors have supported the centralist drive. Political parties are clearly the primary players in this game.[27] They are followed by interest groups and the bureaucracy. Even Länder governments have played a part as they have actively sought nationwide policies that have reduced their role to administrators of national policies. Granted, through the ad hoc body of the provincial governors' conference (*Landeshauptmännerkonferenz*), Länder leaders periodically influence federal politics, but their collective action in the national arena is hardly an example of a federal society at play. The nationwide approach to Austrian politics is endorsed by Austria's voters as well. The Austrian Constitutional Court (*Verfassungsgerichtshof*) responsible for settling the competence questions between the Bund and the Länder tends to employ a centralist reading of the federal system.[28] The Court has also introduced the principle of the duty of federal consideration (*bundesstaatliche Rücksichtnahmepflicht*), which prescribes concerted action and reciprocity, and thus effectively limits Länder autonomy.[29]

It is interesting to note that, in the Austrian context, the notion of "cooperative federalism" is generally seen to be a principle which restores some of the original prerogatives of the Länder. This informal system of cooperation and collective effort by the Länder and the federal government has allowed the Länder to re-enter some of the policy areas in which they had lost a voice. In other federal systems cooperative federalism is often interpreted as a measure facilitating centralization, but in Austria it is a way to bring the Länder into decision-making. Such centralist views of federalism would likely provoke major constitutional crises in federations with federal societies, like Canada and Belgium, but Austria has no equivalent of a Québec or a Flanders to oppose an idea of federalism which expects and prescribes uniform action nationwide. In Austria, the Court's approach is merely a reflection of the prevailing views on federalism in political circles.

The main political parties also adhere to a unitary interpretation of federalism. In their political programs, parties often refer to the cooperation between the Bund, Länder and municipalities (*Gemeinden*) as the three levels of government. In Austria, federalism seems to denote the collective effort of all three levels of government. In federal societies like Canada, Belgium or Switzerland it would have been quite problematic to include the municipalities in a federal order. In these societies, federalism is inseparable from the notion of self-rule in constituent units, and municipalities are thus under provincial jurisdiction. An example of the centralist outlook prevailing in Austria is the SPÖ program, which states that "federalism should not be allowed to stop at the Länder."[30] The ÖVP, on the other hand, adds the professional associations (*berufliche Körperschaften*) to its notion of federalism. Similarly, the emphasis is on solidarity and cooperation between all these entities.[31] In contrast with the notion of self-rule of constituent units found in federations with federal societies, in Austria federalism seems to be interpreted as a top-down system of multi-level public administration and the collective action of the actors within this system. According to a recent report of the Institute for Federalism: "a major barrier to real reform [of federalism in Austria] lies in the absence of a federal frame of mind among key political actors and mass media."[32] The term "federalism" in contemporary Austrian politics has come to denote administrative decentralization rather than a union between self-governing entities.

It has to be noted, however, that, starting with the mid-1970s, the Länder have come together on a few occasions to assemble lists of Länder demands (*Länderforderungen*) from the federal government. These initiatives are often led by the two western Länder, Tyrol and Vorarlberg. The Länderforderungen call for more voice in drafting policies and, of course, more financial transfers from the federal government to carry out these policies. In other words, these are attempts to reclaim some of the provincial competences assumed by the federal government over the decades. As a result, some modest reversal has taken place in certain policy areas, but an overall review of the federal system is rarely on the agenda, especially in its 1920 form. An exception was the "Pro-Vorarlberg" initiative in 1979.[33] That year, the Land parliament of Vorarlberg adopted a resolution calling for an increase of the powers of the Länder in the Austrian federal system:[34]

> The Land ought to have competence in those areas that it can deal with alone in order to take into consideration the needs of the population and the relations between the Länder, to protect cultural diversity, and to make public administration less costly. The application of this principle calls for the strengthening of the competences of the Länder and their participation in decision making, in particular in the following areas:.... The school system (participation in writing syllabi and textbooks), continuing education, broadcasting (more consideration for Länder concerns, stronger regionalisation), protection of historical monuments.

As a Land with a claim for a modest degree of cultural distinctiveness (Vorarlbergers see themselves as Alpine *Alemanni* like their Swiss neighbors), it is notable that education and broadcasting are core parts of the Pro-Vorarlberg resolution. However, this initiative by tiny Vorarlberg failed to change the Austrian federal system. The motion was indeed supported by 69 percent of Vorarlbergers, but it did not materialize into a nationwide movement for federal reform.[35] It is worth noting that the two policy areas of education and media are of foremost importance to constituent communities in federations with federal societies. Because education and media are the areas where societal distinctiveness is supposed to be most prevalent, they can be seen as critical policy areas where one is expected to get the strongest demands for self-rule. The following two sections on education and media show that such demands did not exist in Austria. In fact, all political actors involved sought nationwide solutions to issues within the cultural sphere. There were important differences between the ÖVP and the SPÖ in terms of the contents of the national policies they favored, but they entertained the same nationwide frame of reference. This national disposition was shared by civil society associations, unions and, most importantly, the Länder themselves. It should therefore not be surprising that, failing to strike a responsive chord from its society which would preserve and strengthen federalism, the Austrian federation has moved in the centralist direction.

Education

During the constitutional discussions in 1920, the Social Democrats and Christian Socials failed to reach a common position on education; consequently, this policy area was left out of the constitutional framework of the new Austrian republic. One key point of contention was jurisdiction over education. The Social Democrats favored strong Bund control over education, while the Christian Socials preferred Länder jurisdiction. The second point of disagreement was the role of religion in education. A number of divisive issues emerged, such as the role of the Catholic Church in education, the question of religious instruction in public schools, and state subsidies to private church schools. Socialists were in favor of secular public education controlled by the state, while Christian Socials were skeptical of the *étatiste* policies of the socialists and wanted to keep the Church in education, favoring Länder control over the cultural sphere. Consequently, the constitution avoided the legal question of competence over education in 1920; culture in broad terms, however, was deemed to be under Länder sovereignty (*Kulturhoheit*).[36]

Education was left to be governed by a collection of imperial decrees (*Reichsgesetze*) dating back from the Habsburg Empire. These did not add up to a comprehensive education system, so education policy was to be managed by additional ad hoc agreements (*paktierte Gesetzgebung*) between the Bund and the individual Länder outside the constitutional framework. This system remained in effect until 1934, when the new authoritarian clerical regime signed a concordat with the Vatican and gave the Church extensive control over education. In 1938, Austrian education became a part of the Third Reich's Ministry of Education.

At the end of World War II, the Allies restored the Land-based education system. In compliance with Allied directives, the school boards of the Austrian Länder (*Länderschulräte*)[37] began to eliminate Nazi influence from the curriculum and the ranks of the teaching staff. In 1947, the Allies established the Quadripartite Committee on Educational Affairs to harmonize education in their zones of occupation. A Federal Ministry for Instruction (*Bundesministerium für Unterricht*) was set up to coordinate these efforts. The involvement of the Bund, however, lacked a clear constitutional base. The Federal Chancellor's Constitutional Affairs Office (*Verfassungsdienst des Bundeskanzleramtes*), together with provincial governors (*Landeshauptmänner*) and heads of provincial bureaucracies (*Landesamtdirektoren*), sought ways to bring a legal base to a national education policy.[38] Religion re-emerged as the most divisive issue between the SPÖ and the ÖVP. Issues like subsidies to private Catholic schools, religious instruction in public schools, and the renewal of the concordat with the Vatican were the roadblocks on the path to a settlement. So education, once again, was kept out of the constitution. However, in 1960 a compromise between the Church and the SPÖ (*Konkordatskompromiß*) opened possibilities for an agreement between the Social Democrats and the Christian Socials.

A parliamentary negotiation committee between the two parties (*Verhand-lungsausschuss*) began meeting in December 1960 to settle the question of education policy. The committee came up with a School Law program (*Schulgesetzprogramm*) in 1962, which was subsequently passed by the Nation-alrat on 18 July 1962 as a constitutional amendment. The new law settled the competence questions and added a special clause for future amendment of the Education Bill. Accordingly, any change in the field of education has to pass a special requirement of two-thirds of Nationalrat votes. This was included in order to protect the original compromise from future unilateral activism by one side.[39]

However, the constitutional amendment bringing education under Bund com-petence is in conflict with the spirit of Article 15 of the constitution which estab-lishes the residual clause (*Generalklausel*) of Länder competence for policy areas not explicitly put under Bund jurisdiction. According to the principle of residual jurisdiction, any competence not explicitly mentioned in the constitu-tion lies with the Länder by default. Furthermore, in general terms culture is considered to be Länder jurisdiction.[40] However, no questions of Länder compe-tence were raised during the discussions at both Houses of Parliament. During the vote for the draft law at the Nationalrat in July 1962, all parties expressed strong support for a nationwide policy. According to an ÖVP member:[41]

> Very difficult competence issues had to be resolved between the Bund and the Länder, especially the question of whether the Länder should keep their far-reaching competences in the school system, or, considering certain necessities, whether the Bund should be given greater powers in school administration.

This point was echoed by the SPÖ:

> Surely – and here I am referring to the division of competences – our responsibility towards future generations urgently demands from us a school system that is as unitary as possible in order to provide these genera-tions with the tools to function in a modern economy.[42]

The Federal Minister of Education at the time, Heinrich Drimmel, summed up the developments in the following way:

> with this law, we will end the provisionary and transitory Austria of states, which is a notion that has for long deteriorated and even disappeared due to the weakness of belief in distinct provincial identities and existence. We will finally have a unity in the cultural political field.[43]

During the debate at the Bundesrat, the law received similar support from Länder representatives. According to the SPÖ representative for Upper Austria, Franz Fruhstorfer:

> These series of school laws open up the path towards amending the laws on university organization. This is especially fortunate for the federal Länder, because through the establishment of new universities they will be able to assume a stronger part in the spiritual life of our fatherland.[44]

Fruhstorfer concluded his speech by stating that "extreme federalism brings division and disarray because it overlooks the fact that we actually live in the same house."[45]

As a critical policy area where identity politics are assumed to be most dominant, the field of education has become a primary outlet for the centralizing tendencies that accompany the unitary social structure of the Austrian federation. As a result, the Austrian Bund has moved into a policy area constitutionally under Länder jurisdiction and has created a national education policy. This move was carried out with Länder cooperation and public support. In fact, the move toward a nationwide education policy was implemented with the active participation of the provincial governors' conference, which was instrumental in facilitating this process. According to the new Austrian education policy, each Land passed identical legislation based on national standards. Reinhard Rack labels this legislative process "rank-xerox federalism".[46] Felix Ermacora is somewhat harsher in his evaluation: "[the 1962 constitutional amendment] meant the complete destruction of Länder sovereignty in the field of school policy which certainly constituted one of the strongest setbacks for Austrian federalism."[47] In a study on Austrian federal cultural policy, Peter Pernthaler seems to agree with Rack and Ermacora, and adds that such standardization led to the erosion of any distinctiveness that might have existed among the Länder:[48]

> The intensive centralization, concentration, and administration of the entire educational curriculum for all Austrian schools and universities by the Bund has had a wide impact in terms of an effective weakening of federalism in the consciousness and political formation of teachers and pupils thereby further contributing to the collective togetherness of the nation (*Gesamtbevölkerung*).

It has to be stressed that the process of centralization took place with the broad support of all relevant social groups, political parties and orders of government. According to Peter Bußjäger, Länder politicians have displayed no desire to reverse the trend toward centralization.[49] The Bund has gone as far as to set up Land offices (*Landesschulbehörden*) to oversee the execution of Länder education policies. Even the ÖVP program, from a party traditionally more sympathetic to questions of Länder competence, stresses the national element in the education system, mentioning the need for close cooperation between the Bund, Länder and municipalities.[50] This follows from the societal consensus of seeing education as a national concern. A recent Austrian study on education is a good example of this prevailing view, which considers educational federalism to be an unnecessary differentiation in an important policy area and equates it with inefficiency: "How can the Länder work together in their autonomous competence areas in a way as to carry out the common tasks and preserve the compatibility of education systems in Austria without unreasonable additional costs?"[51]

The interpretation of education as a nationwide concern is closely associated with the unitary social structure in Austria. In federations with federal societies, regional diversity in education policies is not seen as unnecessary but as a natural state of affairs. In Austria, political actors seem to discern no justification for retaining education federalism and the differentiation in policies associated with it. As the experiences of federations with federal societies suggest, territorially-based societal distinctiveness seems to be vital in instilling a principled attachment to cultural self-rule.

Media

Media form the second critical policy area where strong pressures for subnational competence are expected to exist in federations where federalism has strong societal roots. Along with education, media provide an important outlet for claims of societal distinctiveness. In federations with federal societies, media and education are the two most sensitive areas where substate units jealously protect their prerogatives and seek further competences. In the Austrian case, however, there have been pressures in the opposite direction. Voters, politicians, interest groups and Länder governments themselves have sought nationwide solutions to questions of broadcasting and the press. Particularly in the field of broadcasting, the framework of reference has resolutely been a pan-Austrian one as the constitutional notion of Länder cultural sovereignty has been bypassed by interpreting broadcasting as a telecommunications matter rather than a cultural issue.[52]

At the end of World War II, the Allies immediately set up broadcasting corporations in their zones of occupation. Their broadcasts were coordinated by the Federal Ministry of Traffic (*Bundesministerium für Verkehr*). The Federal Ministry for Instruction (*Bundesministerium für Unterricht*) also had responsibility for some aspects of broadcasting. In 1949, the provisional Telecommunications Law (*Fernmeldegesetz*) left the Bund in charge of telecommunications for an indefinite period. This law was based on the policy competences the Bund had acquired in 1924 over the telegraph system. The Telecommunications Law of 1949 passed the National Assembly with a minor amendment.[53] The same proposal endowing the Bund with exclusive jurisdiction over radio transmissions was approved without a formal debate in the Federal Council,[54] and the federal government consequently assumed the right to dispense radio broadcasting licenses (*Konzessionverleihung*).

In 1952, as the Allies started to hand the administration of their broadcasting stations over to the Austrians, some Länder governments tried to assume control over the broadcasting facilities left by the Allies.[55] However, Länder activism was short-lived and without much success. The issue quickly moved to the federal level and pitted the Ministry of Instruction against the Ministry of Traffic. The competition between these two ministries did not produce a winner, but ensured that the issue remained a federal one.[56] In 1953, the first nationwide broadcasts started under the framework of *Radio Österreich*, but there was still no specific legal act establishing a national broadcasting corporation. Broadcasting was subject to the guidelines applicable to public administration in general. The composition of Radio Österreich was based on the prevailing practice of proportionality. In addition to the bipartite division of staff and programming, Radio Österreich was supervised by two public administrators, one from the ÖVP and one from the SPÖ. The Land of Vorarlberg, however, challenged this system and claimed that, according to the constitution, the Länder had the right of sovereignty over broadcasts (*Sendehoheit*). In the meantime, the two public administrators of Radio Österreich made their views on broadcasting and federalism public:[57]

> I don't stand for a "centralistic" but a "common" Austrian broadcasting. That is to say, there should be neither federal broadcasting nor Länder broadcasting. Besides, the public administration [of Radio Österreich] has for long fulfilled its responsibility. The next step can only be a broadcasting law.

The second public administrator was less apologetic: "A certain centralization is the only way to manage broadcasting economically. Austrian broadcasting is already more federal than before 1938."[58] In the end, the Constitutional Court decided that the Bund had competence over broadcasting – both in technological and programming aspects:[59]

> The Länder have the possibility to set up and run their own broadcasting facilities, because this is not an act of public law but private law, which is not subject to the distribution of competences outlined in the constitution. Yet the Länder are required, as all other legal subjects, to follow the legal provisions, which in this case give the Bund the responsibility in the field of telecommunications licensing.

The Constitutional Court's 1954 decision to interpret broadcasting as a part of telecommunications and hence Bund responsibility, rather than culture which would fall under Länder jurisdiction, paved the way for further centralization. Vorarlberg and Tyrol protested against the Vienna-based centralism, but the issue failed to draw the interest of the broader public.[60] On 11 December 1957, the Austrian Broadcasting Company (*Österreichische Rundfunk*) was set up and also divided up along SPÖ and ÖVP proportionality lines. The exclusion of all other social groups led to protests that culminated in a public petition for a referendum (*Volksbegehren*), signed by 833,389 voters, in 1964.[61] The issue of coalition partisanship control of the broadcasting company was more important to the public than the Bund–Land division of competences over broadcasting. The public petition came with calls for solutions affirming national unity above partisan loyalties.[62] The ÖVP managed to play the public disillusionment with the system of proportionality well, and the 1966 elections produced an ÖVP majority government.

The new government in due course put a draft broadcasting law (*Rundfunkgesetz*) before the Nationalrat on 8 July 1966. During its discussion in the parliament the draft law received considerable criticism from SPÖ and FPÖ members, but most of the criticism was over partisan issues; federalism was not on the agenda of the opposition. For example, the FPÖ was broadly critical of the proportionality practice but supported the bill. An FPÖ member of the Nationalrat put it in the following terms: "The reform should definitely guarantee that the Austrian Broadcasting Corporation is changed from a tool of the black–red coalition to a cultural institution of the entire nation."[63] But the same FPÖ member concluded his talk on a supportive note: "The new broadcasting law is a beginning. It would hopefully fulfill the expectations which accompanied its formulation. For nation and state, radio and television should serve our fatherland as cultural instruments."[64]

A general theme in Nationalrat discussions was criticism of Vienna's political, social and cultural domination in the country. In a federation with a federal society, the first topic would have been federal encroachment into subnational jurisdiction – but not in Austria's case. The discussions at the Federal Council were even less heated. There were a few occasions of partisan bickering, but federal involvement was not part of the disagreements, and the law was passed.[65] As a result, broadcasting was put under the control of a new entity called the Austrian Broadcasting Corporation, ORF (*Österreichischer Rundfunk Gesellschaft bmH*). The ORF was constituted along corporatist lines, as trades unions, associations, and the Catholic Church, as well as Bund and Länder representatives, acquired representation on its board and in its ranks.

The final step toward centralization came in 1974 with the government proposal to place media formally under federal jurisdiction. There was some opposition to the government plan and the proposed constitutional amendment, but these matters were largely partisan concerns over the contents of the bill rather than a principled opposition to the change in the Bund–Länder balance. On the 10 July 1917, the bill came to the Nationalrat. Here, the only dissenting voice on the amendment's impact on federalism came from Professor Felix Ermacora (ÖVP), a Professor of Constitutional Law, who pointed out the violation of the spirit of federalism:[66]

> Ladies and gentlemen, federalism is probably for me, and also for my friends in the ÖVP group, the necessity to provide a corresponding structure to the differentiation in the federal Länder along demographic, geographic,

economic and social conditions; and thereby, to provide the federal Länder with a consciousness of their Land and their people.

However, Ermacora failed to convince his colleagues. The bill placing media under Bund competence easily passed the Nationalrat and arrived at the Bundesrat the following week. Here, another Professor of Constitutional Law was the lone voice of opposition to placing broadcasting under federal jurisdiction. At that session on 17 July 1974, Professor Herbert Schambeck (ÖVP) argued against the bill as all others voted in favor of the changes: "Ladies and gentlemen; another problematic question concerns federalism. We can say that here federalism has not increased but decreased."[67] It is interesting to note that, as the Upper House of the Austrian Parliament, the Bundesrat is supposed to protect the prerogatives of the Austrian Länder; yet members of the three parties represented here voted for the proposed constitutional change making broadcasting an exclusive federal jurisdiction. In this context, the view expressed by Lower Austria's representative is closer to the prevailing mindset: "Austria as a federal state lives through the unity of the state as a whole and through the strength of its member provinces, that is to say the core principle of the state order is federalism."[68] As a result, the ORF formally became the national broadcaster under the jurisdiction of the federal government. Until 1998, the ORF had a monopoly over broadcasting in Austria. Since then, private broadcasters have entered the Austrian market, but the legal basis of broadcasting remains nationwide.[69]

Conclusion

The preceding analysis shows that the workings of the Austrian federal system are more unitary than is suggested by the federal constitution. In fact, the Austrian federation seems to work more as a unitary system because all political issues are set in a pan-Austrian frame of reference. This is because the federation lacks territorially-based societal heterogeneity to sustain a principled commitment to federalism. Societal homogeneity induces a centralist political outlook at all levels of government which undermines the notion of self-rule in constituent units essential for federalism. Empirical evidence strongly suggests that the Austrian federation's centralist disposition stems from its social structure, not its formal constitution.

This conclusion was reached as a result of an in-depth analysis of the two policy areas of education and broadcasting. Education and broadcasting were chosen as critical policy areas because identity politics are assumed to be especially dominant in the cultural sphere. Any form of societal distinctiveness is expected to reflect itself in subnational demands for further competences in the cultural sphere, or at least the use and protection of the already existing constitutional prerogatives. Similarly, nationwide cultural homogeneity is expected to make its presence felt by fostering centralizing tendencies in these policy areas. The Austrian Länder were active participants in the nationalization of education and broadcasting. There were deep disagreements and intense rivalry between the two main parties, the SPÖ and the ÖVP. Yet, despite partisan differences over the contents of policies, all the political actors involved set the issues in nationwide terms. These findings suggest that society-based perspectives, rather than the more commonly used institutionalist approaches, provide a richer understanding of federalism in Austria.

3   Belgium

Introduction

Federal change in Austria was in the centralist direction; in Belgium it has followed a decentralist path. For many years, the two main linguistic/cultural communities of Flemings and Francophones inhabited the unitary constitutional shell of Belgium. However, over the past forty years the unitary Belgian state has federalized its institutions through successive state reforms, eventually leading to a constitutional revision formalizing its federal character in 1993. The process of federalization has permeated all spheres of political activity, but the particular focus of this chapter is on the institutional changes within education and mass media. Nationwide systems in these two policy areas were gradually replaced by Flemish and Francophone halves.[1] The aim of this chapter is to trace this process of federalization.

The federalization process is described by the term "communitarization" (*communautarisation/communautarisering*) in Belgium. This is due to the role the constituent linguistic/cultural communities played in decentralization or, more precisely, in the move towards a congruence between state and society. Empirical evidence shows that Belgian political institutions gradually changed in order to be congruent with the frames of reference employed by the political actors. Political actors approached issues of public policy within the confines of their respective language groups which came to function as the *demos*, i.e. the community which functions as the default base for democratic deliberation. Until congruence, the so-called *question communautaire* was the defining political cleavage for predicting political behavior in terms of the constraints and choices it provides to political actors.

Federalism in Belgium

Belgium is composed of two main linguistic groups. Flanders is the northern Dutch-speaking half of the country, constituting 60 percent of the population; Wallonia is the southern French-speaking half, where 30 percent of the population lives. The remaining 10 percent of the population lives in Brussels, a French-speaking city geographically situated in Flanders.

The Belgian state was formed in 1830 by a Francophone elite. The expectation at the time was that Belgium would gradually become a French-speaking state.[2] However, various Flemish dialects of Dutch persisted in the northern half of the country. In the late nineteenth century, tensions began to emerge over the exclusion of the Dutch from public life. The growing Flemish movement began to demand the recognition of the cultural distinctiveness of Flanders. Flemish nationalism continued to gain strength during the interwar period and managed to win certain concessions from the Belgian state; most importantly, Dutch was made an official language in 1935. In the meantime, the southern part of the country begat a defensive reaction to the Flemish movement in the form of Walloon nationalism. Walloon nationalism did not share Flemish nationalism's linguistic/cultural agenda; their demands have been mostly in the economic sphere.[3] In response to Flemish demands for political redistribution, though, Wallonia found Francophone Brussels to be an ally. As a French-speaking enclave within Flanders, residents of Brussels have a separate Bruxellois identity, albeit less consolidated as a "national" identity than that of Walloons and Flemings. Historically, Brussels had a Dutch-speaking majority, but, starting in the mid-nineteenth century, French gradually became the dominant language in the city.[4]

During the late 1950s, Flemish nationalism and the Walloon reaction it sparked off brought the Belgian state to a standstill. Only a wholesale reform of the Belgian political system appeared to be a way out from the impasse. The first reforms towards recognizing cultural duality of the Belgian state were carried out in 1962–63, but these were immediately followed by negotiations for a new set of reforms. On 18 February 1970, Prime Minister Gaston Eyskens announced that the Belgian unitary state had come to an end: "The unitary state with its guiding laws and its structures and functions is overtaken by events. The communities and regions should take their place in the reformed structures of the state, better adapted to the specific situations of the country."[5] The 1970 reforms were followed by new reforms in 1980 and 1988, and the latest constitutional revision was carried out in 1993. As a result, the new Article 1 of the constitution declares Belgium a federal state, thereby legally recognizing a process that has been in play since the 1960s.

The Belgian federation that emerged from the 1993 state reform is not a neat symmetrical federation with clearly defined responsibilities for its orders of government. Its institutional complexity reflects the societal complexity that underlies it. As a result of the successive state reforms, the Belgian constitution now recognizes three language groups as "Communities". The French and Flemish Communities together with the tiny German-speaking Community constitute the non-territorial units of the Belgian federation. The French Community of Belgium is composed of Walloons and Brussels' Francophones. In territorial terms, the federal arrangement is based on three "Regions": Dutch-speaking Flanders, Francophone Wallonia – with its small community of German-speakers along the German border, and the cosmopolitan but mainly Francophone Brussels-Capital Region. In practice, the Flemish Community and the

Region of Flanders have merged to become one entity, while Brussels and Wallonia not only together constitute the French Community of Belgium but also pool the competences they have as Regions. However, the focus of the empirical investigation in this chapter is less on the details of the contemporary federal system and more on the processes of change that paved the way for the constitutional settlement of 1993.

As the following sections show, the practice of federalism preceded the official federalization of the country. That is to say, many policy areas came to function in terms that reflected the linguistic/cultural duality of Belgium while the constitutional shell remained unitary. Public space was divided in two along linguistic fault-lines, and the workings of public policy reflected the divisions. As Kris Deschouwer put it, "[in Belgium] there is no central public forum for political debates. There are two unilingual debates."[6] Gradually, numerous policy areas were devolved to the constituent communities of Belgium. During this process, many issues which divide societies and engender political partisanship were subsumed under the *question communautaire*. For example, Flemish Christian Democrats (CVP, now renamed CD&V), Flemish Liberals (VLD, formerly PVV), Flemish Socialists (SP, now renamed SP.A) and Flemish Nationalists[7] all teamed up in their demands for further self-rule. While Flemings of various political colors were joining forces, Francophones fought a mostly defensive retreat. Brussels and Wallonia were forced into a partnership in the face of the Flemish onslaught for political redistribution, and many of the institutions of Francophone Belgium reflect the continuation of this difficult duality. Now that there is an adequate degree of congruence between political institutions and the societal structure, Flemings have increasingly turned their attention towards the contents of their policies and have accordingly carried out reforms which aim to increase efficiency and effectiveness, while Bruxellois and Walloons still ponder the future of their political community.

Education

In the last forty years, nationwide standardized education in Belgium has been replaced by two separate educational systems. The devolution of education to the Flemish and Francophone constituent communities has also been accompanied by increasing differences between the two educational systems.[8] Historically, education was a deeply divisive issue in Belgium, pitting Catholics against the anticlerical alliance of the Liberals and Socialists. The religious/philosophical conflict over education was finally solved with the school peace of 1958. The status of both religious schools and secular schools was settled as two sides agreed to receive the same amount of subsidies from the state.[9] The settlement of the religious conflict in education brought the language issue to the forefront, however, and the educational system subsequently became the battleground for Belgium's ethno-linguistic communities.

The process towards differentiation in education had begun before the official federalization of the country. From 1961 onwards there were two Ministers of

Education within the same ministry: a French-speaker and a Dutch-speaker. The first state reform demarcated the linguistic boundary and changed the constitution in order to recognize two unilingual regions and bilingual Brussels. Prime Minister Théo Lefèvre of the Christian Democrat–Socialist coalition which introduced the 1962–63 reforms explained the need to communitarize Belgian education in the following terms:[10]

> It seems that in the creation of cultural councils, equipped with real competences, we have the best means of encouraging the developments of two communities with respect to their own character. Within the same spirit acknowledged, in the same structure of government, there is the need for a profound transformation of the departments of public education and cultural affairs according to the existence of two cultures within the country.

The 30 July 1963 Law on Education divided primary and secondary education into Francophone and Dutch language halves, but higher education was left untouched. Education was to be organized in the language of the Region, i.e. French in Wallonia and Dutch in Flanders. Brussels was a special case where education would be in French or Dutch depending on the mother tongue. The 1962–63 reforms also abolished the bilingual schools in Brussels which offered courses in both languages. All schools had to become unilingual and, depending on the mother tongue, Bruxellois students were divided into two groups. The outcome was a gradual consolidation of the inter-communal partitioning, *cloisennement*.

All the major state reforms carried out in 1970, 1980, 1988, 1993 and 2001 had an impact on the educational system. In addition to these constitutional reforms, there was constant institutional change and fine-tuning through legislation. With the law of 25 September 1969, national education and cultural affairs were split into two. Consequently, the Ministry of National Education and Culture was divided along linguistic lines, but education still did not become fully a Community competence. In 1971 the Ministry of Education was officially divided into two separate ministries, each responsible for one section of the population, but there would still be a national education policy until 1980. Flemish Nationalists had failed to realize their goal of the full communitarization of education. The frustration of the Volksunie leader Hugo Schlitz displays the importance Flemings attach to educational self-rule:[11]

> A community that does not have the right to show that on education and/or subordinate administration it has more or less expressed consent is not autonomous in its domain. It becomes a cashier, a box-office counter, an office of the central state.

Education remained a national competence after the 1980 state reform, but the Ministry of Education continued to function in two linguistic sections, with two Ministers – one Francophone and one Dutch-speaking. The Francophone

Socialists (PS), the strongest party in Wallonia, were initially lukewarm to the idea of communitarization in education, fearing that once communitarized they would be unable to fund the extensive public educational system in the Walloon Region. However, French-speakers, both Walloons and Bruxellois, gradually came to terms with the Flemish-driven communitarization of education and recognized the essentially political character of educational self-rule. As a *Front démocratique des Francophones – Rassemblement wallon* (FDF-RW) Member of Parliament announced to his colleagues at the first meeting of the newly renamed Council of the French Community in 1980: "In fact, the educational project is always by nature a political choice, a choice which is intimately connected, in this case, with the future of our French Community."[12] It was clear that this recognition was a defensive one largely carried out in response to the movement towards Flemish cultural self-rule. The words of the Minister of the new Council of the French Community display the defensive game played by the French Community in the reforms: "Our problem is protecting our dignity as Francophones; that is, being capable to correctly assume our autonomies with our own means."[13]

In a report published in 27 April 1983, the Flemish executive outlined its position concerning the changes in educational policy.[14] In order to establish the communitarization of education, the Flemish executive demanded that Article 59 of the constitution, which gave the federal government competence over education, be repealed.[15] It furthermore demanded that all the institutional, structural, financial and administrative measures necessary for the communitarization of education be introduced.[16] In an agreement signed in 1984, all four political parties (CVP, SP, PVV, VU) represented in the Flemish government pooled their resources and declared their support for the communitarization of education.[17] During the debate on the communitarization of education, a Flemish Christian-Democrat Member of Parliament tried to explain the reasons behind the Flemish demands educational self-rule:[18]

> Why is the communitarization of education now so important? ... The history of the Flemish movement above all has been a history of fight for cultural autonomy. The various steps in the Dutchification [*vernederlands-ing*] of education were the steps on the road to cultural autonomy for the Flemish nation/people. What is more evident than a community administering its education?

For a long time, Francophone Christian Democrats (PSC) resisted the communitarization of education because they feared that such communitarization would adversely affect Catholic education in Socialist-dominated Wallonia. However, receiving guarantees about the free Catholic schools in Wallonia from the other major parties in 1987, PSC relented to the process of communitarization. The 1988 reforms expanded the power of the Communities over education, except for a few issues which were left at the federal level. The beginning and end of the study year, minimum requirements for diplomas, and pensions for teachers were issues that would continue to be administered at the federal level.

Communitarization of education was introduced on 15 July 1988 through a special majority vote in the two Houses of Parliament which changed three articles of the constitution. Article 59b of the constitution placed education exclusively within the jurisdiction of the Communities. This amendment was a part of the broader state reform of 1988. As a consequence, the *ministre de l'Education national du rôle Français* became the *ministre de l'Enseignement de la Communauté française*. However, disagreement between Socialists and Christian Democrats prevented a uniform approach to education within the French Community. This division was exacerbated by the divisions between the Socialist-dominated Walloon Region and the rest of the French Community in the Brussels-Capital Region. After complex and difficult negotiations, the new Ministry of Education of the French Community was divided between one Socialist and one Christian-Democrat Minister. The outcome was two Ministries: the *ministre de l'Education et de la Recherche scientifique* and the *ministre de l'Enseignement et de la Formation*.

Following the 1988 state reform and the communitarization of education, financial problems emerged within the French Community. This led to an initiative between the executives of the French Community and the Walloon Region to create a joint entity called the "*Etablissement*" to administer education.[19] This initiative was based on a clause introduced by the state reform which allowed the Communities and Regions to set up joint services and institutions for their common tasks. However, this effort did not succeed in solving the problems. Difficulties continued to affect the ability of the French Community to administer educational policy. In 1990 there was another round of negotiations between the Francophone substate entities, and the Walloon Region and the Brussels-Capital Region agreed to help the French Community in financing education. Notably, the theme of the second "The Future of Wallonia" (*Wallonie au future*) congress in 1991 was the "Challenge of Education" (*Le défi de l'éducation*), and the preliminary statement of the congress was "building up a country is building up its education" (*Bâtir un pays, c'est construire son education*).

The 1993 constitutional reform removed the remaining federal competences over education. The new system did not even establish a national framework for consultation. The French Community, however, delegated the implementation of its constitutional competence over education to the Walloon Region and the Commission of the French Community of the Brussels-Capital Region. At the moment, the future of the educational system in Francophone Belgium is still unclear. Questions still revolve around deciding who will be the competent authority for education. There appears to be a general malaise within French-speaking Belgium concerning educational policy. Not only are the French Community and Walloon Region facing difficulties in financing education; there also seems to be widespread public disappointment with the communitarization of education and the subsequent confusion over competences and the declining quality of education.[20] Despite the new funds the 2001 Lambermont Accord has allocated to education in the French Community, financial and administrative problems seem to continue for Brussels and Wallonia.

In contrast with the experience of French-speaking Belgium, competence questions seem to be settled on the Flemish side. The focus is increasingly on the content of educational policy, and presently there appears to be an extensive reorganization of the Flemish educational system. The Flemish government continuously reiterates the importance it attaches to education. In a recent publication by the Ministry of the Flemish Community entitled "A Government for the Flemings," educational policy is presented as the most important responsibility of the Flemish Government: "Education remains an essential pillar of the Flemish Government. It surely remains our first concern towards each other."[21]

As Flemings and Francophones acquired control over their educational systems, the content of their educational policies gradually changed in line with their political priorities. Communities developed and changed their educational policies without any coordination with one another. Between 1980 and 1988, the educational policy between the two Communities started to differ considerably. While the French Community remains divided over many aspects of educational policy, the Flemish government has followed a reorganization of the educational system which ran parallel to the communitarization process. There have been institutional reforms as well as standardization of curricula and programs for all schools in Flanders. The Flemish Community, in particular the Flemish Ministry of Education, has delegated its authority to a number of autonomous public institutions.[22] According to Jan De Groof, this asymmetry between the Flemish and French Communities is natural and should remain as it is:[23]

> The split between the "legal" country and the "real" country, together with the progressive distancing between the two educational communities, would give the appearance of artificiality to national legislation on the matter. Divided and thus differentiated responsibility, best epitomized by the field of education, cannot be corrected by unitarist interventions after a complete transfer [of competences].

During the communitarization process of education from 1962 until 1993, all major political parties in Flanders (CVP, PVV, SP and VU) joined forces as a common front seeking educational self-rule. Once the question of control was finally settled in 1993, the content of educational policy began to divide the political scene in Flanders. The Flemish Socialists are a good example of this change. After having lost a considerable portion of their traditional blue-collar support to the far-right xenophobic *Vlaams Blok* (recently renamed *Vlaams Belang*[24]), Flemish Socialists have recently renamed themselves "Social Progressive and Alternative" (SP.A) and re-embraced the secular/humanist cause in education. The liberal VLD (formerly PVV) is also distancing itself from Christian-Democrat education objectives. Following the attainment of congruence and the settlement of the politics of identity, we have started to see the emergence of politics of interest as Flemish parties compete over the contents of educational policy.

On the Francophone side, the religious/philosophical divisions over education traditionally pitted the Francophone Christian Democrats (PSC, now renamed CdH) and the Francophone Socialists (PS) against one another. For different reasons, both parties initially opposed the communitarization process. The PSC feared that communitarization would give the Socialists control over Wallonia and put the independent Catholic schools at risk. The PS, on the other hand, feared the financial costs of running an extensive public education system in Wallonia. However, in the face of a united Flemish front seeking self-rule in education, they joined forces within the Francophone Wallonia–Brussels camp together with the Francophone Liberals (PRL), Brussels Francophones (FDF) and Walloon Nationalists (RW). Recently, though, the political scene has changed, as the Francophone Christian Democrats are now marginalized, and the PRL and FDF have joined forces together with the citizens' movement MCC in the form of a stronger new Liberal Party (MR). The content of education is now emerging as an issue in Francophone Belgium, while control issues remain.

Media

The communitarization of mass media predates the official federalization of the Belgian state. In print media this has taken the form of *de jure* recognition of the linguistic division which already existed. For radio and television broadcasting, the process towards communitarization has been more explicit. The Belgian national public broadcasting corporation, which enjoyed monopoly over radio and television broadcasts, was first split along linguistic lines, and as the Communities acquired jurisdiction over mass media, Belgian broadcasting bifurcated into two autonomous sections. Self-rule in mass media resulted in an asymmetrical picture, as Flanders privatized most of the broadcasting while the French Community retained the Francophone half of the public broadcasting corporation. This has come as result of a steady process of communitarization in media accompanying the successive state reforms in the last forty years.

In terms of print media, radio broadcasting and television broadcasting, the country is clearly divided into two. Viewers/listeners/readers seldom cross linguistic lines. In parallel, newspapers and broadcasters do not target audiences across the linguistic divide. In other words, in terms both of consumers and producers of media, the country is split into linguistic halves. Television viewership is a good indication of the underlying divided societal structure. Belgian viewers appear to be strongly divided along linguistic lines, and there is very little cross-Community viewing; 75 percent of Flemings watch Flemish channels, 10 percent watch Dutch channels and 15 percent watch non-Dutch language channels. Only 3 percent of this non-Dutch group watches Belgian French channels.[25] The same thing appears to exist on the Francophone side as well.[26] As Dewachter puts it:[27]

> The organization of the media in Belgium – with which one creates a bridge between economics and culture – is clearly divided into two separate networks.... There are Dutch-language newspapers, radio, television, weekly

papers and there are French-language ones. They hardly penetrate one another's language region.

This division is reflected in the frames of reference employed by political actors as well. That is to say, the behavior of political actors was determined by their membership in their respective linguistic communities as long as the institutional structure of mass media was incongruent with the social structure. All Flemish political parties across the political spectrum joined ranks in their quest for self-rule; Francophones, on the other hand, were forced into a defensive alliance against Flemish demands. Nonetheless, the communitarization of the Belgian mass media has been a much less controversial affair than that of education. In education, the stumbling-block in the path of a smooth and early settlement was the linguistic status of Brussels. In the field of media, such a distinct point of contention does not exist between Flemings and Francophones. Different approaches to public and private broadcasting, however, augment the linguistic divisions.

French- and Dutch-language print media were historically always separate, but the legal competence of the cultural Communities over mass media is a product of the last forty years. Subsequent state reforms brought media under the legal and technical competence of the French and Flemish Communities, but the beginnings of institutional changes in Belgian mass media lie in an earlier time period. The origins of the communitarization process in media go back to the recommendations of the Harmel Report of 1959, which constituted the basis of the first state reform of 1962–63. Long before the federalization of the country, the report suggested community control over broadcasting in an endeavor to ease the tensions afflicting the relations between the two linguistic groups: "For radio broadcasting and television a Walloon council of management and a Flemish council of management should be created."[28]

In many ways, the legal communitarization of mass media competences is a belated response to social disunion. Press always remained separate, and for many years the Belgian public broadcasting corporation used "deconcentration" as a substitute for communitarization. That is to say, the public body was divided into two linguistically separate parallel sections without officially devolving media competence to the substate entities. This process of deconcentration, *dédoublement* in French, helped contain the linguistic tensions until the constitutional changes arrived. Starting with the 1980 state reform, competences over media were gradually devolved to the Communities.[29]

Belgian print press strictly follows the language division. In addition to readership, there is also a strict separation between Flemish and Francophone print media in terms of ownership. While cross-ownership is widespread within linguistic groups, there is no cross-ownership across the linguistic divide. There seems to be a great deal of press concentration within the Communities, as three leading press groups in each linguistic group control most of the daily newspapers. Due to the clear divisions between Flemish and Francophone newspapers and readership, the *de jure* recognition of the linguistic divisions in print media has been a colorless technical development without the tensions which characterized the communitarization of public broadcasting. This is of course aided by the fact that print media are entirely based on private ownership, which means that many of the divisive issues of public funding and subsidization are safely bypassed. In public broadcasting, however, the difficulties the French Community has in financing public broadcasting and the neo-liberal policies of the Flemish government complicated the communitarization process.

The origins of Belgian public broadcasting go back to the SBR (*Société Belge Radio-Electrique*) created in 1922. With the law of 18 June 1930, the state monopolized broadcasting under the newly established Belgian public broadcasting service INR/NIR (*Institut National de Radiodiffusion/Nationaal Instituut voor Radio-Omroep*). Along the prevailing consociational practice, INR/NIR divided its broadcast into three; *Radio-Catholique*, *Radio-Libérale* and *Radio-Socialiste*. After the war, INR/NIR gradually replaced the consociational practice of programming with one based on linguistic lines as broadcasting was divided into French- and Dutch-language sections. Along with this development, the name of the national public broadcasting institution also changed. It became *RTB/BRT* (*Radio-Diffusion-Télévision Belge/Belgische Radio en Televisie*) with the law of 18 May 1960. This marked the beginning of a decades-long reform process: "The Harmel Law (of 18 May 1960), born as a result of the long negotiations on the reform of the status of INR, opened – and this was the first time in the Belgian context – perspectives on cultural autonomy."[30] RTB/BRT was accordingly divided into three autonomous units; a Francophone section, a Dutch-language section, and a third section dealing with common issues. As the state reform of 1970 devolved most of the mass-media policy to the cultural Communities, the common-affairs section was gradually split along linguistic lines into two sections as well. Based on the constitutional amendments of 1970, the public broadcasting corporation was divided into two administrative boards in 1971, which would follow different policies from then onwards.

In 1977, the division of the Belgian public broadcasting corporation was completed and the common-services section was fully abolished. With the end of the common services, even the musicians of the RTB/BRT symphony orchestra were divided between the two broadcasting institutions according to their language registry.[31] With the 1977 reform, RTB became RTBF (*Radio-Télévision Belge de la Communauté culturelle française*), and BRT became BRTN (*Belgische Radio en Televisie, Nederlandse Uitzendingen*). The institutional ties between RTBF and BRTN were completely dissolved as the two corporations became fully autonomous.

In the years to follow, BRTN gradually decreased its nationwide reach and effectively became the public broadcasting corporation of Flanders only. In 1995 it changed its name to *De Nederlandse Radio- en Televisie-uitzendingen in België, Omroep van de Vlaamse Gemeenschap*.[32] The absence of a nationwide programming policy was finally legally incorporated into the BRTN charter. The 25 January 1995 Decree of the Flemish Community and Region on Radio and Television regulates broadcasting in Flanders. According to Article 4 of this treaty, BRTN is responsible for public broadcasting in the Flemish Community: "The programs should contribute to the further development of the diversity of Flemish culture and of a democratic and tolerant society."[33] Most recently, on 1 January 1998 BRTN officially became the public broadcasting corporation of Flanders by adopting the name VRT (*Vlaamse Radio en Televisie Omroep*), thereby dropping any reference to Belgium proper. The name change has been accompanied by an extensive administrative reform of the institution as VRT has done away with the institutional relics of the consociational system.

While major reforms are implemented on the Flemish side, RTBF is still known as the "Belgian radio-television of the French Community," and it follows the original principles of Belgian public broadcasting. Despite its resistance to institutional reform, RTBF has gradually lessened its Belgium-wide character and accepted its role in bipolar Belgium. Article 8 of the decree of 14 July 1998 makes this recognition explicit by stating that RTBF is responsible "for ensuring the cultural development, in particular by installing the values and the promotion of the cultural activities of the French community, its heritage in Wallonia, in Brussels and abroad, as well as the appropriate advancement of regional specificities."[34]

During the communitarization of public broadcasting, financial questions pitted the Flemish Community against the French Community because there was a common public broadcasting corporation whose functions and finances had to be divided between the two linguistic groups. Naturally, this brought with it a fair deal of disagreement over the proper means of the institutional splitting and the future of public subsidies, since Flanders is richer than its Francophone counterpart. Private broadcasting, on the other hand, came after self-rule in media; therefore, it was not a point of discord between the two sides during the communitarization process. The Flemish side allowed the introduction of private broadcasts of licensed stations in 1987, but this did not become a community issue because Flemish decisions were exclusively aimed at the Dutch-language media.

Once a sufficient degree of congruence was achieved between the institutions for mass media and the social structure, the different political priorities of the two linguistic communities started to become visible. Once the "control" issue was largely settled – at least for the Flemings – the "content" issue increasingly became a primary concern. In this context, changes in mass-media policy after the communitarization of the field follow the same pattern seen in education – i.e. concerns about the contents of public policy and efficiency in delivering them dominating the Flemish public agenda, inertia and confusion on the Francophone side. As a consequence of the divisions between Brussels and Wallonia, public policies are not approached with the same considerations of efficiency that seem to be prevailing on the Flemish side. In Flanders, extensive reforms have been carried out and new institutions have been established, while such activism is absent on the Francophone side. There is still some degree of incongruence between the political institutions of Francophone Belgium and its social structure based on a complex mix of Walloons and Bruxellois.

Consequently, questions about control still make their presence felt and prevent a complete restructuring of the media system along the lines of the Flemish example. Nevertheless, questions of control have also led the Francophone political parties to join forces against the Flemish onslaught for political redistribution. Walloon historian Philippe Destatte puts it in the following terms: "Institutional choices should go hand in hand with choices about the media: it is necessary to build spaces of communication which correspond to political structures."[35]

As a result of the communitarization process in media, the two linguistic sections of Belgium look less and less alike. This asymmetry is reflected in the different paths the public broadcasting corporations took, and also in the approaches towards private broadcasting. Another difference is the method for media regulation. The French Community prefers to regulate directly through the government apparatus, while the Flemish government has set up a number of autonomous public institutions (*openbare instellingen*) with quasi-governmental character – a pattern similar to the developments in education.[36]

During the process towards congruence, Flemish political parties were united in seeking self-rule in the policy area of media; focus is now increasingly on the contents of policies. On the Francophone side, despite the common stance against Flemish demands, questions of political competence remain. This flows from the fact that for Francophones there is still more institutional engineering in the waiting, while congruence between the society and political institutions is almost complete on the Flemish side. And as far as a nationwide mass-media system is concerned, Dewachter sums up the picture in the following terms: "It is clear that, in the field of media a Belgian society no longer exists."[37]

Conclusion

Following the school peace settlement of 1958, linguistic divisions assumed the center stage of politics in Belgium. From then onwards, the process has been towards a congruence between the educational system of the country and its ethno-linguistic social structure. Without the complexity of Brussels, congruence would have been achieved much more easily. In other words, had the country been neatly divided into two unilingual sections, the issue of educational self-rule would have been settled as early as 1962, when the first linguistic laws were put into effect. The process towards congruence in the field of media, on the other hand, has been much smoother.

Empirical examination of parliamentary minutes, proposals, inter-party accords, government publications and public inquiry reports suggests an inexorable tendency towards communitarization which gradually led to the division of all aspects of education and media into two linguistic sections. Print media were already divided long before the legal recognition of the two linguistic Communities. The *dédoublement* of the RTB/BRT, on the other hand, has been gradual and relatively problem-free, compared with the divisive issues in educational policy. The only issue that led to a major political debate in the field of mass media was that of private television channels and commercial advertisements on the television channels of the Belgian public broadcasting companies. Parliamentary minutes display almost no major debates when the issues under discussion are related to media and communitarization. These issues are dealt with in a technocratic manner with little substantive discussion. Between the two sides, it appears that there was an overall agreement concerning the direction of institutional changes, i.e. towards increased Community control over the mass media. It was largely regarding the technical and financial aspects of this process that the negotiations took place.

What the empirical research demonstrates is the power of the ethno-linguistic structure in providing the direction of change. The specific terms and details of the consecutive deals would have been difficult to predict, but the goals of the political actors were preordained by their ethno-linguistic background. During the process towards congruence, social class, political affiliation and ideology do not appear as reliable indicators of political behavior. The institutions of the unitary state also appear to have failed in molding the society into a "unitary" one. That is to say, the institutional set-up of national education and national media has proved to be malleable rather than sticky.

One factor other than the ethno-linguistic structure was relevant in the field of educational policy. The division between anticlericals and Catholics, despite its declining intensity over the years, continued to make its presence felt in the changes to the country's educational system. However, the decreasing importance of religion as a politically salient cleavage and the increased marginalization of anticlericals in Flanders and Catholics in Francophone Belgium have prevented religion from undercutting the primacy of the ethno-linguistic social structure. Religion has very much been internalized into this structure in the form of devout Flanders and anticlerical Wallonia.[38]

It has to be said, however, that the process of congruence has not been an entirely smooth one. There have been many disagreements, but these tended to be over the details rather than the broader notion of demands for cultural self-rule. What is clear from the empirical research is the commitment of both sides to the communitarization process, even if they differ over the specific terms of the solutions.

4 Canada

Introduction

As a federal system, Canada is quite different from the Austria and Belgium discussed in the previous chapters. Federal change in Canada is not a simple linear process along the centralizing–decentralizing axis. Canada's federal society does not match the institutional demarcations of the federation. Change is therefore towards a congruence between society and institutions, and this is reflected in decentralist pressures concerning French Canada. The province of Québec, where the overwhelming majority of Canada's French-speakers live, jealously guards its constitutional prerogatives, prefers to do things on its own, and continuously seeks further autonomy. Change in English-speaking Canada, on the other hand, is in the centralist direction. The nine English-speaking provinces of Canada frequently come together with the federal government in order to put together nationwide solutions to what they see as national issues. As a result of this asymmetry, the Canadian federal system tends to bypass the federal constitution and works in a way to reflect the constituent linguistic/cultural communities.[1]

The following sections demonstrate the role ethno-linguistic factors play in the operation of Canadian federalism. The way public policies function tends to be the immediate reflection of the underlying social structure. Empirical evidence shows that public policy concerns exert pressures on the political institutions to change towards congruence with the ethno-linguistic composition of the country – even if such pressures do not always translate into large-scale institutional change. In this context, the constituent linguistic/cultural communities of Canada function as default *demoi* bypassing the formal structures of the federation. This process is particularly visible in education and media where identity politics find their first outlet. As a result, in the absence of formal recognition, the duality of the Canadian society tends to reveal itself through the workings of the system.

Canadian federalism

After decades of conflict that ended with France's defeat in North America, the colony of New France was formally given to Britain in 1763. Most officers and nobles returned to France, but the majority of the French-speaking inhabitants of this colony remained. French Canadians mostly withdrew to the countryside around the St Lawrence valley and sought to maintain their way of life with a minimum of interference from their new masters. In turn, the British recognized their laws, customs, language and religion. A degree of self-rule was formalized with the Québec Act of 1774.

American Independence and the consequent immigration of the United Empire Loyalists together with new settlers from the British Isles fundamentally altered the future of the St Lawrence valley and the remaining British colonies in North America. Lower Canada (present-day Québec) was no longer a French-only province, while Upper Canada (present-day Ontario) became overwhelmingly English-speaking. The provinces of Upper and Lower Canada were given representation in the first legislative assembly through the Constitutional Act of 1791. During the 1820s, the so-called *patriote* movement started to demand further autonomy for French Canada. The movement ended with a rebellion in 1837, which was put down by the British. A Royal Commission under Lord Durham arrived in Canada to investigate the causes of the uprising and seek solutions to the troubles in the colony, where Lord Durham found Canadian dualism to be the cause of the problems: "I have found two nations warring in the bosom of a single state. I have found a struggle not of principles but of races."[2] He recommended reuniting the province of Canada under a single system of responsible government. With the strong influx of immigrants from the British Isles, Lord Durham believed that the French element would soon become a minority. This would speed up the process of assimilation, thereby eliminating cultural duality, which he believed caused unrest. The Act of Union of 1839 did fuse the two parts of Canada into one, but failed in the assimilation. The political system continued to work in two halves with Canada West and Canada East. Each section was given equal seats; there were two prime ministers, twinned ministerial portfolios, and parallel departmental establishments.

The United Province of Canada, however, did not work very well. Frequent political deadlocks immobilized decision-making. This was also a time when the United States remained a military threat. Together with the other British colonies of North America, Canadian provinces feared the dominance of the powerful and expansionist neighbor to the south. In the meantime, Britain had begun to dismantle the system of colonial preferences that had given Canadian imports a competitive edge in Britain. The small separate colonies were deep in debt and unable to borrow the funds needed for their economic development, and the solution seemed to be the creation of a new market reaching from sea to sea. However, it was clear that, due to the French-Canadian faction, a unitary system would not work. As the first Canadian Prime Minister, John A. Macdonald, put it:

I have always contended that if we could agree to have one government and one parliament, legislating for the whole of these peoples, it would be the best, the cheapest, the most vigorous, and the strongest system of government we could adopt.[3]

The alternative was a federal system. First, the province of Canada was restored to its two parts as Ontario and Québec; then, together with Nova Scotia and New Brunswick, the four created the Canadian federation under the British North American Act of 1867. Protected by provincial autonomy and religious, linguistic and social barriers, French-speaking Québécois found a way to maintain their way of life and group identity. French minorities outside Québec, however, had no such provincial protection. In the following years, the Canadian federation expanded to include new provinces. These were also years of growing French–English tensions as English-speaking majorities annulled linguistic equality clauses in Manitoba and the Northwest Territories (later to become Alberta and Saschatchewan). In 1913, Ontario abolished its French schools. The federal government's failure to protect the rights of French-speakers outside Québec led many French-Canadians to see the Québec provincial government as their primary object of loyalty. In the meantime, English-speaking Canadians took part in the creation of an ocean-to-ocean Canadian nation. The result is a federal system that works asymmetrically based on the two linguistic/cultural communities of Canada; in other words, a federation with an incongruence between political institutions and social structure. Despite their formal equality under the constitution, Québec and the remaining nine provinces of English Canada display different patterns of behavior in the practice of federalism.

The distance between written constitution and actual practice in the Canadian federal system is recognized by students of Canadian federalism.[4] Most observers tend to point out that the centralism inherent in the British North America Act (BNA Act) failed to work in the face of practical realities like linguistic divisions and geographical size. Another area where what appears on paper is not always what takes place in practice is the field of public policy. In his study on the welfare state and Canadian federalism, Keith Banting notes that institutional and constitutional patterns are not very helpful in understanding how the field of public policy works.[5] Banting's focus is mostly on social policies, but his observation could be extended to other policy areas as well. In particular, there appears to be a visible difference in the way the nine English-speaking provinces and Québec approach public policies. Will Kymlicka describes the attitudes towards federalism and public policies in English Canada the following way:[6]

> Survey data has repeatedly shown that most English-speaking Canadians have no principled commitment to respecting the existing constitutional division of powers. On the contrary, their expectations and attributions of responsibility are naturally directed to the federal government even in areas of provincial jurisdiction (the most commonly cited area for federal action is education), and they would support federal intervention in almost any area of policy so long as it provided good governance.

Kymlicka's point is supported by the final report of the *Citizens' Forum on Canada's Future* delivered in 1991. In the provinces of English Canada, respondents declared that they were in favor of a stronger federal government.[7] Only in Québec did the majority of respondents express support for more provincial powers. Andrew Petter's research on federal spending power corroborates this asymmetrical picture. Petter notes how little controversy increasing federal involvement has created outside Québec.[8] Similarly, in an article summarizing the results of their recent polling survey, Fred Cutler and Matthew Mendelsohn conclude that "Canadians outside Québec have little attachment to particular divisions of powers in the *BNA Act*.... They have little respect for the classical federal principle and little interest in attempting to implement 'watertight jurisdictions.'"[9] Cutler and Mendelsohn expanded on this point in an op-ed piece they wrote for the newspaper *The Globe and Mail*:[10]

> Overall, our survey results show that Canadians have no deep commitment to the principle of federalism, have little knowledge of the existing division of powers, and care little about which order of government exercises which power. In important policy areas they care about results, and they see cooperation between governments as best able to achieve this.

In Québec, on the other hand, issues of jurisdictional control still dominate the politics of the province and its relationship with the rest of the country. The contents of public policies mean less since battles are fought along issues of control. To quote Kymlicka once again:[11]

> Having the ability to collectively debate and determine policies on issues that matter to them is not just a *symbol* of Québécois nationhood, it is the *substance* or *practice* of nationhood. Having developed a strong sense of national identity, Quebecers want to act together as a political community – to undertake common deliberations, make collective decisions and cooperate in political goals. They want to make these decisions with each other, not because their goals are different from other Canadians, or from Americans or Belgians, but because they have come to see themselves as members of the same society, and, hence as having responsibilities to each other for the ongoing well-being of that society. That is just what it means to think oneself as forming a nation.

However, constitutional reform in the direction of recognizing the duality of the Canadian political system has constantly failed in the face of political intransigence. According to Kenneth McRoberts, official bilingualism and the Charter of Rights and Freedoms promoted by Pierre Trudeau's Liberal governments are partly responsible for the strong opposition from English Canada.[12] The aim of such policies had been to build a bilingual and multicultural Canadian nation from coast to coast, replacing the duality of Québec vs the Rest of Canada. The result has been a public aversion within English Canada to practices of dualism, which have come to be seen as the special treatment of Québec and élitist. Such views have been largely responsible for the demise of the Meech Lake Accord that sought to codify some aspects of dualism. In response, Québecers attempted to take the initiative and declare sovereignty, but the 1995 referendum – like its 1980 predecessor – failed to deliver majority support. In the face of institutional non-recognition, dualism has continued to influence the workings of the system in the field of public policy. The division of the public space into two linguistic sections has been particularly visible in the two policy areas where identity politics loom large, i.e. education and media.

Media

Radio broadcasting in Canada started off in a legal vacuum, as it was not clear under which level of government this new policy area fell. In 1929, a Royal Commission was set up to examine radio broadcasting. The prevailing tendency within the Aird Commission – named after its chairman – was in the direction of a national broadcasting policy; however, during the deliberations of the commission, Québec passed its own bill on radio broadcasts, which was followed by additional legislation two years later in 1931. As the question of political control of airwaves began to emerge, the federal government referred the question to the Supreme Court of Canada, asking if Ottawa had jurisdiction to regulate and control radio communication. The BNA Act was not clear on which level of government had constitutional prerogatives in this field. The Supreme Court referred the matter to the Judicial Committee of the Privy Council in London, which was the final court of appeal in Canadian law until 1949. The Judicial Committee of the Privy Council ruled in favor of Ottawa, based on the residual competences of the federal government to legislate for "peace, order and good government" in areas not explicitly listed in the BNA Act.

Based on this ruling, the federal government established the Canadian Radio Broadcasting Commission in 1932. After a brief experiment with national broadcasts with French-language segments, the CRBC started dividing its broadcasts into French and English. Marc Raboy points out that "as early as 1934, Canadian Public Broadcasting served two audiences, two markets, and two publics with one policy, one mandate and one institution."[13] The CRBC was replaced by the Canadian Broadcasting Corporation in 1936, but the separation of services continued through the French-language Radio Canada and the English-language CBC. In response to the openly partisan position of Radio Canada during the conscription crisis, Québec political parties gave support to Premier Maurice Duplessis' 1945 proposal to create Radio Québec. The bill (*Loi autorisant la creation d'un service de radiodiffusion provinciale*) easily passed the Québec Legislative Assembly, but it was never put into effect because of Ottawa's declaration that it would refuse to grant provincial licenses. Duplessis considered Ottawa's refusal to be a violation of Québec's constitutional prerogatives: "Québec holds the centralization of broadcasting into the hands of the federal bureaucracy to be contrary to the fundamental principles ratified by the Canadian constitution and the fathers of the confederation."[14]

The post-war political climate in Canada witnessed increasing federal

powers. The recommendations of the Royal Commission on National Development in Arts, Letters and Science (The Massey Commission 1949–51) high-
lighted the role of media in building national unity. The work of the Massey
Commission was followed by the Royal Commission on Broadcasting (The
Fowler Commission 1955–57), which made more specific recommendations for
a national media policy. But as Austin Weir pointed out in his study on national
broadcasting in Canada at the time, "there were, in effect, two countries."[15] In
the meantime, the Quiet Revolution was underway in Québec and was consum-
ing the political interests of that province. Formally a federal crown corporation,
Radio Canada was a leading force in disseminating the modernist reform project
of Québec's Quiet Revolution. Despite the internal changes, Québec's position
vis-à-vis the rest of the country remained constant as it regarded itself as different from the other provinces of English Canada. In this context, Premier Jean
Lesage opposed the process of harmonization of provincial legislation. He
explained Québec's position as follows:[16]

> We understand that the federal government is seeking uniformity in admin-
> istration together with uniformity in the services provided to the population
> across the country. I would respond that such a concern with administrative
> uniformity does not justify centralization and unilateral decisions....
> Québec does not adhere to this type of uniformity because we believe that
> our national community has the right to blossom as it sees fit.... It is rea-
> sonable to expect that the administrative decisions of the government of
> Québec will not be necessarily identical to those of other provincial govern-
> ments.

In 1966 Daniel Johnson's Union Nationale government came to power, but
the reforms started by Jean Lesage's Liberals continued. Johnson also continued
Lesage's position on seeking more powers for Québec over media policy:[17]

> Another area to which the government of Québec attaches great importance
> concerns the instruments of education and culture, particularly radio and
> television.... Québec can no longer tolerate being absent from an area
> where its vital interests are clearly evident, especially if one takes into
> account the future of mass communication in audio-visual media.

In 1968, the Québec government decided to put into action Duplessis' original
1945 bill on Radio Québec. The following year, Jean-Jacques Bertrand's
government established a Ministry of Communications (*Ministère des communications*) and a Québec Broadcasting Bureau (*l'Office de radio-télédiffusion du
Québec*). Robert Bourassa's Liberal government, which came to power in 1970,
continued the position of successive Québec governments and made "cultural
sovereignty" a key demand in its dealings with Ottawa. In his so-called "green
book" on the development of cultural policy, the Minister of Cultural Affairs,
Jean-Paul L'Allier, spelled out Québec's claims for autonomy in all aspects of

cultural policy – including the media.[18] The Parti Québécois government that came to power in 1976 continued this position. In April 1977, the new Minister of Communications, Louis O'Neill, wrote an open letter to his federal counterpart, Jeanne Sauvé, asking the federal government to exit the policy area of broadcasting.[19]

In the meantime, the Canadian Radio-television and Telecommunications Commission had set up a Committee of Inquiry into the National Broadcasting Service (The Boyle Committee). The final report of the Boyle Committee, published in July 1977, pointed out the bifurcation of media in Canada, calling it "cultural apartheid:" "There is a mutual lack of interest between the networks of each linguistic group accentuated by the marked differences between the English-language and French-language journalists in terms of their points of view, attitudes and work methods."[20] In an editorial in *Le Devoir* entitled "The Two Solitudes of CBC-Radio Canada," Claude Ryan – who would later become the leader of the Québec Liberal party – commented on the findings of the report: "the dualism of the networks that was present from the start has survived all the changes. This cannot be explained as a random outcome or persistence, but as a concern for being faithful to reality."[21]

The failed 1980 referendum and the repatriation of the constitution without the approval of Québec's National Assembly continued to poison Québec City–Ottawa relations in the early 1980s. The persistence of the problems led the new Conservative government, under Brian Mulroney, to seek various mechanisms to officially recognize Québec's distinctiveness. The first sign was an agreement between Ottawa's Communications Minister, Marcel Masse, and his Québec counterpart, Jean-François Bertrand, concerning the future of Francophone television. Accordingly, both sides agreed to "recognize the distinctiveness of the French-language television network in Canada, which would mean the existence of two different television broadcasting policies in the country."[22]

In 1985, The Task Force on Broadcasting Policy, co-chaired by Gerald Caplan and Florian Sauvageau, began to study the question of media policy in 1985. Their final report was released the following year: "French radio and television broadcasting in Canada, in terms of productions, stations and audience, is almost entirely from Québec. Canadian content here essentially means Québécois content."[23] Consequently, the report recommended that "the two sectors, serving distinct societies, should be allowed to take different approaches to meeting the objectives assigned to public broadcasting."[24] This was a belated recognition of what was already taking place in practice. As the 1986 report of the Royal Commission on the Economic Union and Development Prospects for Canada (Macdonald Commission) concluded: "Quebec does have a de facto special status in Canada. The question is how much de jure special status Quebec should have."[25]

At present, Canadian media remain divided into two linguistic sections. Public broadcasting is under exclusive federal jurisdiction, but a steady process of congruence has led to the bifurcation of Canadian broadcasting. This is not only with respect to the public administration of broadcasting. According to

Mary Jane Miller, Canadian television is broadly divided into two systems of national symbols.[26] The issue of French–English divisions in Canadian broadcasting is well documented by other observers as well.[27] The same pattern characterizes the print media. Rowland Lorimer notes that the country is divided into two distinct markets in publishing with very little flow of material in between,[28] while Arthur Siegel sees major differences between the two linguistic sections of the country in terms of newspaper styles, coverage and interest.[29] The discrepancy between the uncodified workings and the unworkable codes in Canadian politics is thus particularly visible in this policy area. Mark Raboy sums up the picture in the following terms: "Basically, inevitably, the institutions and practices of Canadian communications have reflected the inconsistencies of Canada rather than the national unity designs of their architects."[30]

These patterns indicate a clear difference between Québec and the nine provinces of English Canada. While Québec wants, exercises and sometimes gets more self-rule over media policy, the rest of the country is content with entrusting the federal government with this competence.[31] Official bilingualism prescribes a coast-to-coast policy based on individual rights, but in practice what we have here is a picture of Québec vs English Canada. Thus, there is a clear asymmetry: one province – which should be like the others according to the constitution – is the counterpart of the federal government in this policy area.[32]

Education

While French–English dualism characterizes both print and broadcasting media, education remains a provincial jurisdiction. However, the distance between the letter of the law and actual practice is visible in this policy area as well. The nine provinces of English Canada frequently collaborate to standardize their policies, often with federal involvement; Québec, on the other hand, is very sensitive about federal encroachment and remains an outlier.

Such duality can be traced back to the Québec Act of 1774, which recognized the role of the Catholic Church in education. The United Province of Canada continued such *de facto* dualism, which acquired limited *de jure* recognition in 1867 as the two parts of the province of Canada regained self-government.[33] In the years following the end of World War II, the country witnessed a massive increase in the scope and reach of public policies. Education was amongst the first policy areas that were subject to this expansion. Based on the recommendations of the Massey Report in 1951, the federal government introduced a program of direct subsidies to post-secondary education. Québec, however, opted out from most of Ottawa's conditional grant programs. The Union Nationale government of Maurice Duplessis was particularly opposed to letting the federal government into the field of education through direct federal grants to universities. In 1954, Québec also withdrew from the Dominion–Provincial Student Aid Programme. In addition to these opt-outs in educational policy, Québec decided to tackle the expansion of Ottawa in matter of principle as well. The response was the creation of the Royal Commission of Inquiry into

Constitutional Problems (Tremblay Commission). In 1955, the Commission's dossier on education was published:[34]

> Since confederation, the sentiments of Quebecers, and French-Canadians in general, have not changed: exclusive provincial jurisdiction over education is one of the most important federal compromises. It should be jealously guarded and it should remain as comprehensive as possible.

In 1958 Duplessis' successor, Paul Sauvé, reached a deal with John Diefenbaker's federal government where Québec remained outside Ottawa's conditional grant program in education but received compensation. This was beginning of the pattern of Québec opt-outs from federal–provincial shared-cost programs with financial compensation.

In 1960, Jean Lesage's Liberals came to power and the modernization process of the Quiet Revolution began to transform the internal political structure of Québec. The opposition to Ottawa's role in educational policy, however, continued without interruption. Jean Lesage appointed a neo-nationalist, former Rector of Laval University, Monsignor Alphonse-Marie Parent, to head the provincial Royal Commission on Educational Reform. Based on the recommendations of the Parent Commission, the Québec state re-entered the field of education, which had been within the prerogative of the Church since 1875. The new Québec Department of Education was established in 1964, with Paul Gérin-Lajoie as the Education Minister. Québec Liberals continued the policies of opt-outs that Duplessis had established.[35] Michael Behiels explains the reasons behind Québec's position as follows:[36]

> Underlying the neo-nationalist rejection of federal grants to universities and support for cultural and linguistic development in general was the firm conviction that a national minority could not relegate, even in the smallest measure, responsibility for its future to federal institutions controlled by another majority culture.

Conditional federal grants and shared-cost programs that were welcomed by the nine provinces of English Canada were opposed by all shades of political opinion in Québec. As the leader of Union Nationale, Daniel Johnson, put it in 1963:[37]

> What is possible, however, is to allow Quebec to retain, in virtue of its responsibility for a given cultural group, those rights, powers, and constitutional freedoms of which the other provinces no longer feel the need, since they prefer to entrust to the central government the responsibility for the culture they share.

This idea found support in English-speaking Canada as well. As the New Democrat Party leader at the time, Tommy Douglas, remarked in 1968: "Thus, it may mean that in any area such as education and housing, where Quebec feels that a strong federal power may erode provincial rights, it may be necessary to have two programs – one for English-speaking Canada and one for Quebec".[38]

During the first half of the 1970s, the Québec Liberal party was in power under the leadership of Robert Bourassa. Bourassa continued Québec's traditional policy of jealously protecting exclusive provincial jurisdiction over education. He reaffirmed the policy of seeking cultural sovereignty (*souveraineté culturelle*) for Québec. However, those who were in favor of a Canada-wide approach to education found an unlikely ally from outside. In 1976, the Organization for Economic Cooperation and Development (OECD), as part of its series on the education systems of its members, published its report on Canada. The report called for a national education policy and a federal–provincial bureau of education.[39] Not surprisingly, Québec's Minister of Education at the time, Jean-Marie Beauchemin, voiced his objections to the recommendations of the report: "Why did [the OECD examiners] not base their report on the undeniable reality of two national identities? Did they not feel the pulse of the political will of Québec, or not see the necessity of developing two majority cultures?"[40]

This year, 1976, was also the year the Parti Québécois got elected to power in Québec. The new Premier, René Lévesque, was in favor of a large-scale rearrangement of the federal system. Lévesque advocated a system of sovereignty-association between Québec and the rest of Canada in a binational framework. The Federal Government responded with the creation of a Task Force on Canadian Unity. Named after its co-chairmen, John Robarts and Jean-Luc Pepin, the Pepin–Robarts Commission drafted a report that advocated the formal recognition of dualism in the Canadian federation. However, Trudeau's federal government resisted such a redrawing of the federal map, and in fact decided to take the offensive – especially in the field of education. The comments made by the federal Secretary of State, John Roberts, in 1978 display the increasing tensions between Québec and the rest of the country:[41]

> The constitution does not exclude the setting of national goals in education. It does not absolve the federal government of responsibility for educational processes inevitably carried out by instruments within federal jurisdiction. Above all, the constitution does not rule out the federal–provincial cooperation in the evolution of educational policy for Canada.

In response to the federal offensive, Lévesque decided to call a referendum on sovereignty and economic association. The vote was to give the government the mandate to negotiate a sovereignty-association with the federal government. The Québec Liberal Party did not go as far as seeking a large-scale transformation of the system into a binational confederation, but supported the move towards increased self-rule. The constitutional committee of the party declared in 1980 that "in these two areas [i.e. education and culture], we propose to maintain Québec's historical position – an affirmation of the primary role of the provinces and an attitude of opposition to federal initiatives."[42]

Ottawa's position, however, was quite different. In 1981, at a national symposium entitled *Education in Canada: Federal–Provincial Relations in Education*, the federal Secretary of State and Minister of Communications, Francis Fox, made the following point: "Education in Canada is a subject that must be of basic concern to all Canadians. For that reason the federal government must be both present and involved."[43] Provinces of English Canada did not see this as an unacceptable encroachment into an area of exclusive provincial jurisdiction, and were open to Ottawa's participation. At the same symposium, the Minister of Education of British Columbia, Brian Smith, declared that "the provinces have a duty to cooperate and work towards some common educational goals and the federal government has a role in post-secondary education to articulate those goals and provide vital funding."[44]

In the late 1980s, the new Progressive-Conservative government in Ottawa, under the leadership of Brian Mulroney, tried to institutionalize Québec's distinctiveness through a round of negotiations that culminated in the Meech Lake Accord of 1987. However, Meech Lake faced strong opposition from English Canada; its diluted successor, the Charlottetown Accord of 1992, faced opposition from both Québec and the rest of the country. Once again, it was the workings of the system that filled the void between an unworkable constitution and the underlying ethno-linguistic duality. Education continued to be a policy area where the differences between Québec and the rest of the country were most pronounced.

In the 1990s, the divisive question of the federal role in workforce training took on the long-standing pattern of asymmetry between Québec and the rest of the country. The Québec government saw workforce training as part of education and hence as under provincial jurisdiction. The federal government, however, was picking up the tab for workforce-training programs in other provinces. This is yet another reflection of the existence of two linguistic public spaces in Canada. Public opinion in English Canada tends to favor a more harmonized approach to education policy. The excerpt below, from a 1993 *Globe and Mail* editorial entitled "For a Federal Role in Education," is a good example of the prevailing approach to educational federalism outside Québec.[45]

> Yet there is much Ottawa could do without overstepping its jurisdiction and without asking the provinces' permission. Can do and should do.... Why have a federation, anyway? Because while some things are best left to local governments, some things can only be done at a national level.

This perspective was endorsed by the news magazine *Maclean's*, the same year, in its special issue on Canadian education: "Clearly, what is lacking is a national set of goals and standards that all provinces endorse – and strive to achieve."[46] This seems to follow Will Kymlicka's observation that "while most Québécois want an even more decentralized division of powers, most English-speaking Canadians favor retaining a strong central government."[47]

Recently, the tensions have re-emerged between Québec City and Ottawa over the federal government's Millennium Scholarship initiative. While all nine provinces of English Canada welcomed these new funds to education, Québec saw this as federal intrusion into its prerogatives. Another recent example is the Social Union Framework Agreement between the federal government and the nine provinces of English Canada, signed on 4 February 1999. Amongst other things, this agreement aims to increase mobility within Canadian post-secondary education by eliminating the residency-based policies of the provinces. Alain Noël notes that many provinces shared the pan-Canadian vision of the federal government in terms of a preference for national solutions.[48] This reduced their bargaining leverage in negotiations with the federal government. In addition, according to Noël, "English-Canadian public opinion on these questions is either indifferent or favors the federal government."[49] As a result, the country has come to function in two parts, where one side has reached a fair degree of standardization in education policy while the other jealously protects its prerogatives.

Conclusion

The written constitution of the Canadian federation is of limited use in explaining how the federal system works. In fact, some students of Canadian federalism believe that "federalism in Canada is less a state than a process."[50] A fuller apprehension of the political processes at play requires the use of a society-based approach. In particular, it is in the policy areas of education and mass media where one finds the greatest degree of disparity between the letter of the law and the true workings of the system. These two areas of public policy are particularly important outlets for identity politics – and hence they are the immediate reflections of the underlying ethno-linguistic duality of the Canadian social structure.

Starting with the BNA Act of 1867, Québec has demanded, in one way or another, the codification of its distinct status into the constitution. Changes in Québec led to changes in who was doing the demanding. What started as a conservative Christian-Democrat demand symbolized by the Tremblay Report of the 1950s evolved into a progressive Social-Democrat position of the PQ and the soft nationalism of the PLQ. What remains constant, however, is a deep-seated conviction that the Québec *demos* is separate from the Canadian one, and that the constitution should acknowledge this. However, neither constitutional reform packages nor sovereignty referenda have managed to bring this about. While there has been no codification of the distinctiveness into law, the system has come to function in an asymmetrical way in its day-to-day running. The cooperation between the nine provinces of English-Canada is much closer than a reading of the constitution would suggest, while Québec prefers to do things on its own. Thus it appears that the uncodified workings of the federal system reflect the underlying ethno-linguistic social structure more closely than the letter of the law. Since the linguistic communities determine the public spaces in which political deliberations take place, public policies tend to be the first reflection of the dualism of the Canadian social structure. The field of public policy, in this respect, indicates how the federal system really works.

The different approaches to federal involvement and nationwide public policies between Québec and the other provinces was noted by Richard Simeon some time ago in his influential study of federal–provincial relations in the 1960s. Simeon noted how in Québec: "policies will be examined from the point of view of Québec first; Québec, not Canada is the reference point."[51] For the rest of Canadians, the reference point was the nation as a whole, and there tended to be strong public support for national policies.[52] Will Kymlicka's observation suggests that these differences might suggest a bigger phenomenon than just the choice of the public policy provider: "One way to describe the problem is to say that there is a disjunction between the legal form of multination federalism and its underlying political foundations."[53] And in the absence of codification, duality tends to reveal itself through the workings of the system.

5 Germany

Introduction

At the end of World War II, the Allies encouraged the West German provinces (*Länder*) under their occupation to adopt a federal system. Political decentralization was seen as a safeguard against an expansionist strong Germany and as a way to denazify and re-educate German people by preventing the concentration of political power and bringing politics closer to the citizen. However, the decentralized institutions designed for the Federal Republic of Germany in 1949 were organized according to a political logic that ran against the grain of its unitary ethno-linguistic structure. In the following fifty years, the political system moved towards a congruence with the underlying social structure as political actors mobilized in all-German terms rather than following the federal demarcations. The unitary characteristics of this non-federal society brought about demands for uniform nationwide policies. The federal character of the German state, however, constitutes a non-amendable clause of the constitution. As a consequence, centralizing tendencies manifested themselves through the workings of the system rather than a large-scale state reform. In particular, collective action of the German Länder together with Länder–federal government (*Bund*) cooperation paved the way for nationwide public policies. Policy areas within the exclusive jurisdiction of the Länder were first harmonized and then standardized, eventually leading to *de facto* national policies. A student of German federalism has suggested the label of a "unitary federal state" for these patterns in which the Federal Republic of Germany came to function.[1]

This chapter deals with the two policy areas of education and media in detail, both under exclusive Länder jurisdiction. Empirical evidence shows that the decentralized federal structure failed to socialize political actors into a system of provincial education and media. The ethno-linguistically homogeneity of the non-federal German society played an important role in merging Länder concerns into national ones. Different from the experiences of other federations with federal societies, like Belgium, Canada and Switzerland, the substate units of the German federation frequently joined forces to form Germany-wide policies in areas where they have exclusive jurisdiction. This pattern is not confined to the behavior of the Länder. All political actors shared a national frame of reference, despite disagreements over the contents of policy. In other words, the default base of politics, i.e. the *demos*, is a nationwide one. According to Heidrun Abromeit:[2]

> From the beginning, the central problem of German federalism has been the lack of congruence between form and content. Federal institutions operate with unitary actors, characterized by predominantly unitary ideas and interests that only by chance coincide with regional interests.

As result, Germany has come to function as "a decentralized state and centralized society."[3] The following observation made by Hermann Brill shortly after the creation of the Federal Republic of Germany epitomizes the core of the federal question in Germany: "The essence of the question is the issue of power deconcentration, that is to say, the demarcation of the territory ... against the unitary tendencies of the societal life in Germany."[4]

Federalism in Germany

Federalism in Germany has a long history going back to the Holy Roman Empire of the German Nation and the nineteenth century German unification process, but this chapter's focus is limited to federalism in the Federal Republic of Germany.

The federal structure of 1949 was designed under Western Allied supervision. The Allies had already set up administrative institutions in their zones of occupation. This was followed by the demarcation of the occupation zones into Länder, most of them artificial creations for administrative expediency. The Allies were predisposed towards restructuring German politics through a federal system designed to disperse political power. Under Allied guidance, Länder Minister-Presidents of the Western zones of occupation met throughout 1948 in order to put together a constitution for West Germany. Länder representatives were ready to draft a working arrangement for the Western zones of occupation, but they were reluctant to agree on a constitution for all of Germany, fearing that this would permanently seal the East from the West. After a series of meetings between the Länder representatives, the constitution, called the Basic Law (*Grundgesetz*), was accepted on 8 May 1948. Upon its ratification by Land Parliaments on 23 May 1949, the new Federal Republic of Germany, with its capital in Bonn came into being.

The Basic Law establishing the Bonn Republic instituted a decentralized federal structure based on a strict separation of powers. The levels of government were to have exclusive jurisdiction over the policy areas given to them and function autonomously through their own financial means. For a few policy areas, the constitution introduced a system of joint Bund–Länder responsibility. With the exception of these areas with concurrent powers, the system comprised two separate levels of government, with the Länder enjoying residual powers of jurisdiction. This federal structure, however, was not to remain as intended by the Allies. The Federal Republic gradually assumed unitary characteristics in the subsequent fifty years as the two separate levels of government merged in many areas. However, the changes towards congruence between political institutions and social structure did not come about as result of a major state reform; changes came as minor steps towards nationwide public policies instead. This pattern is especially evident in areas where the Länder constitutionally enjoy exclusive competences. A federal system based on exclusive competences was slowly replaced by an interlocking system of functional federalism based on cooperation between levels of government and ad hoc committees.[5]

Similar to the Austrian case discussed in Chapter 2, the Federal Republic of Germany also has a non-federal society. In general, the borders of German Länder do not correspond to traditional or historical demarcations; they owe their existence to Allied imposition of administrative decentralization on the territories under their control. Some of them are amalgamations of previous principalities and states, while some are just arbitrarily drawn. A couple of Länder claim a certain amount of historical continuity, but this is more a result of Allied planning rather than political will. In addition to their rather arbitrary demarcation, the Länder were created at a time of massive population mobility. The loss of the territories in Eastern Europe and Soviet occupation in Eastern Germany led to an influx of refugees amounting to one-fifth of the population in Western Germany. As well as the twelve million refugees from the East who arrived in the closing days of World War II, an additional 3.5 million arrived before German reunification. This continuous influx and mobility helped dilute any cultural distinctiveness that might have existed at the Land level. Consequently, the Länder came to function more as administrative units rather than representations of territorially-based social distinctiveness. This is reflected in the prominence national issues enjoy in Land elections.[6]

From the early days, the ethno-linguistic homogeneity of West Germany found reflection in broad societal pressures towards centralization. In a public opinion poll conducted in 1952, 29 percent of respondents declared that it was a "very good" idea to dissolve Länder and have one government in Bonn, 23 percent thought this a "good" proposal, 29 percent were indifferent or without an opinion, and 19 percent were against the proposal to dissolve the Länder.[7] In the following year, the percentage of those who strongly supported the dissolution had increased to 36 percent, while 24 percent thought it was a good idea and those who opposed had decreased to 17 percent.[8]

Demands for a more centralized political system were shared across the political spectrum, but since federalism was the foundation of the new political system according to Article 79(iii) of the Basic Law, it could not be changed by constitutional amendment. Modification, however, was possible through implementation. As the following sections on education and media demonstrate, in both policy areas nationwide policies were seen as natural solutions to all-German problems, and they were subsequently put in place. In the absence of territorially-based societal distinctiveness, diversity in the provision of public policies was seen as unnecessary and inefficient. Consequently there was an overall pressure to standardize, harmonize or, better put, to "nationalize" public policies. All political actors approached culture as a nationwide concept and not an exclusive Länder competence. Länder governments – including the parties in power and the Länder bureaucracy, opposition parties, interest groups and professional associations – were all active in translating societal homogeneity into federal change. This process of congruence does not necessarily mean that the political actors involved always agreed with the contents of policies, but that Germany was their frame of reference rather than their respective Land. Empirical evidence shows that political affiliation played no role in the choice of a nationwide approach to public policy. Regardless of political affiliation and level of government, all German decision-makers tended to view educational policy and mass media as nationwide concerns.

In a number of decisions, the Federal Constitutional Court (*Bundesverfassungsgericht*) lent legal support to the centralizing tendencies and introduced the principle of "federal friendly behavior" (*bundesfreundliches Verhalten*) which prescribes cooperation between levels of government.[9] In connection, the principle of "federal comity" (*Bundestreue*) was also introduced. This is an informal principle limiting Land autonomy through its emphasis on concerted action. In subsequent decisions, the court continued to expand on these, although having to concede that they were unwritten extra-constitutional principles.[10] The emphasis on concerted action should be seen as part of the notion of cooperative federalism bringing the two levels of government together in a shared system of governance. Cooperative federalism does not include a constitutional reallocation of competences, but is instead based on a network of coordination, cooperation, joint responsibilities and federal financing.[11] Such collective action of course constrains the likelihood of autonomous substate activity.[12] The courts thus took part in a nationwide drive towards circumventing the federal division of responsibilities. Philip Blair notes that although federal friendly behavior and federal comity were not integral to the 1949 federal structure, they have since come to be seen as constitutional conventions guiding the federal structure of the Bonn Republic set up by the Basic Law.[13] Centralizing tendencies in the Federal Republic are often explained by using these principles, but a more correct interpretation would be to see them as reflections of already existing pressures towards congruence.

Länder financial dependency on the Bund is another often used explanation for the centralizing tendencies in German federalism. However, the Basic Law created a federal system which provided the levels of government with their own finances. The system of financial equalization (*Finanzausgleich*) between the Bund and Länder was introduced later, in 1955.[14] The Länder thus came to rely on the federal government for financial resources through their own volition, and not the constitution. The following sections show that the answers to the centralist workings of German federalism lie in its unitary social structure. As a result of a combination of social pressures toward uniformity, and constitutional caps to centralization, collective Länder public policy has almost become a substitute to a unitary state. According to Ludger Helms:[15]

It is important to point out that unitarization in the Federal Republic of Germany has not come exclusively through the centralization of legislative competences by the federal government. To a great extent this is the result of the extensive self-coordination activity carried out by the Länder.

Wolfgang Rudzio believes Länder collective action to be closely related to nationwide societal homogeneity: "In a homogenous country like the Federal Republic popular pressures in favor of unity have already often secured advantageous solutions through such self-coordination before the need of a competence shift to the Bund."[16]

Media

Media policy is a part of the cultural sovereignty (*Kulturhoheit*) of the Länder as set up by Article 30 of the Basic Law.[17] This was part of Allied plans to reform and reshape Germany. Against the background of the Nazi propaganda machine, federalism was seen as a way to guarantee the freedom of press. Allied plans for media decentralization went against the wishes of the post-war German politicians, but German leaders were in no position to resist the occupation authorities. During the meetings of the Parliamentary Council discussing the new constitution for West Germany in 1949, the representative of the Land Württemberg-Baden, Theodor Heuss, who was later to become the first President of the Federal Republic, was very explicit about what was wanted and what was possible under Allied supervision:[18]

> I would rather not consider these affairs of broadcasting installations and public corporations here, because that would anticipate legislation which is currently a mixture of issues and one which we obviously want to place in the hands of the Bund. We do not want three or four different kinds of radio law.

Attempts to overcome the decentralized media structure imposed by the Allies got underway immediately after the ratification of the Basic Law. Changes, however, had to operate around the constitutional clause of cultural sovereignty. There were many disagreements concerning various aspects of a potential nationwide media policy, but these disagreements were submerged within a collective effort to bypass the institutional barriers.

The first reflection of a nationwide public opinion was in the field of print media. As the Länder acquired responsibility for the regulation of mass media in 1949, each Land passed its own press law. However, across the political spectrum there was a shared belief in the need for a national standard in press laws. In 1960, the Standing Conference of Länder Interior Ministers established a joint Länder Commission to produce a draft Land press law which was to be the model for all the Länder. The outcome was the 1963 draft press law which would function as a model for all the Länder. This allowed for the establishment and maintenance of a harmonized legal system for the press in the Federal Republic of Germany. As John Sanford has put it: "On the whole ... the press laws of the ten Länder and West Berlin are very similar, and in some cases virtually identical, and this elevenfold duplication rarely causes any serious problems."[19] It is interesting to note that even the strong Länder with enough resources to take independent action embraced the emergence of a national press law. Baden-Württemberg was the first Land that adopted the model draft law.[20] The significance of this bill is described by the Land government in the following terms: "With the Land press law, Baden-Württemberg could therefore also provide an essential contribution to the legal uniformity in the federal territory."[21]

Broadcasting is another component of media policy that falls under exclusive Land jurisdiction. The Länder thus have the right of legal supervision (*Rechtsaufsicht*) in the field of broadcasting. That is to say, the Länder legislate and oversee media law. Länder governments, however, have worked towards a nationwide media policy by standardizing their broadcasting regulations and delegating broadcasting to nationwide entities, and in 1950 the six Länder-based broadcasting corporations came together in the form of the Association of Public Broadcasting Corporations in West Germany (*Arbeitsgemeinschaft der öffentlich-rechtlichen Rundfunkanstalten in der Bundesrepublik Deutschland ARD*). According to its statute, the ARD's aim is "to look after the collective interests of the public broadcasting corporations in carrying out their sovereign rights in the field of broadcasting."[22] In 1956 the remaining three broadcasting corporations, together with Sender Freies Berlin, became ARD members.[23] In 1959, the ARD acquired its own budget. A leading student of German media law, Günther Hermann, believes that integration was justified by the public benefits which would ensue from ARD's ability to carry out tasks more efficiently than individual Land-based broadcasting corporations:[24]

> Also for the broadcasting sphere united behavior is obviously useful so that no further justification is needed when, for example, the joint behavior of all broadcasting corporations in and through ARD (especially central institutions) is more efficient than the different separate activities of the individual broadcasting corporations.

Hermann's views demonstrate the prevailing German perspective on the question of media policy. The concern is mostly about issues of content and efficiency in public policy. As the chapters on Belgium, Canada and Switzerland indicate, in federal systems with federal societies, similar questions are first interpreted through the lens of control – i.e. who gets to decide.

While the Länder were successfully pooling their resources within the context of ARD and setting up a nationwide broadcasting entity, the federal government was also taking initiatives in the field of broadcasting. In 1959, the CDU/CSU government presented a draft law to set up a second television channel (*Deutschland Fernsehen GmbH*). As a part of the same bill, two national broadcasting corporations aimed at foreign audiences, *Deutsche Welle* and *Deutschlandfunk*, were also created on 5 December 1960.[25] However, the Länder Minister-Presidents' Conference challenged the constitutionality of the federal government's proposal before the High Administrative Court (*Bundesverwaltungsgericht*). In response, the court delivered one of the most important rulings in the field of mass media. In its ruling delivered on 28 February 1961, the Court upheld the Länder competence in broadcasting: "It is the Länder, and not the Bund, which have competence in the field of the organization and programming of broadcasting."[26] The court also affirmed broadcasting as a "cultural" phenomenon within Land competence.[27] It is interesting to note that the ruling of the High Administrative Court also included a section which criticized the federal government for not cooperating with the Länder. The issue here seems to be the independent action of the federal government, not the level of governance. The court ruled that the federal government offended the principle of federal friendly behavior.[28] As a consequence, Deutschland Fernsehen GmbH was abolished, but Deutschlandfunk and Deutsche Welle remained due to their international mandates.

Following the court's decision, the Länder Minister-Presidents came together to draw up a treaty for another nationwide public broadcasting corporation. In June 1961, the public broadcasting corporation of the second national television channel, ZDF (*Zweites Deutsches Fernsehen*), was established. In due course, the Federal Constitutional Court upheld the right of the Länder to form a common broadcasting corporation through an interstate treaty. In line with the Constitutional Court's decisions, in 1966 the Federal Administrative Court had to invent a legal grounding for national broadcasting:

> There is no rule in the Basic Law which states that a Land can exert its state authority only in its own territory, and by extension, [there is no rule which states] that only the federal government has competence for the whole of federal territory.[29]

A reading of the decision shows that the court accepted not only the legality but also the necessity of establishing such a nationwide corporation:[30]

> In addition, it should be noted that in spite of Article 30, there were new, unanticipated state tasks which could not be ignored and which could only be regulated in common or by a central authority for the entire country, even though the Bund has no legal authority, and – given the short time span – could not be made responsible. This calls for an interpretation and implementation of the Basic Law which would enable the Länder to agree to uniform regulations as well as to establish central authorities for the fulfillment of such tasks.

This was a period when questions of cultural federalism and the need for a nationwide broadcasting policy were widely debated. Many interpreted the decentralized structure in media as an impediment to a national cultural policy. Klaus Furchner epitomizes the sentiment felt at the time: "Many difficulties in the German broadcasting system arise from the fact that nation-wide tasks have not always been solved in accordance to their importance. This can certainly be traced back to this organizational chaos."[31] In an article entitled "Federalism and the Reorganization of Broadcasting," after acknowledging the constitutional impossibility of amending the federal foundations of the West German state as set up in Article 79(iii), Friedrich von der Heydte called for efforts to seek common solutions to the questions of broadcasting:[32]

> It is one of the largest mistakes of the federal structure of our Basic Law that it only recognizes a separation of competences and a division of tasks between the Bund and the Länder, but it does not acknowledge the common tasks that have to be carried out jointly by the Bund and the Länder.

In order to solve this problem, Heydte suggested a somewhat unusual interpretation of federalism: "Federalism can also mean the renunciation of competences for the sake of the common good. It can mean the transfer of sovereign rights – supposed and real sovereign rights – to the *Foedus*, to the Bund."[33] The widespread desire to surpass cultural federalism is described by John Sandford in the following terms: "Politicians and the press are increasingly prone to point out that the present organisation of broadcasting, with its lavish ninefold multiplication of resources, is a luxury that is hard to justify."[34] Interestingly, these views were endorsed by the Länder as well. The 1969 report of the Research Commission on Broadcasting Policy in the South West (i.e. Baden-Württemberg) came out in support of a broader nationwide broadcasting policy:[35]

> The fact that the Länder have the authority for coordinating and harmonizing their tasks is no longer a question which should be seriously discussed. ... The federal principle provides the Länder with the possibility of handling their constitutionally assigned sphere of tasks differently, but this right of divergence in the implementation of competences does not correspond to a requirement to engage in acts of disunity.

In a report published in 1971, the Minister-President of another powerful Land, North Rhine-Westphalia, called for a "rationalization" of the federal system into a five Länder model, particularly in the field of broadcasting:[36]

> It is surely not at all certain that we can cope with the future tasks with the federal system of institutions we have today. This holds true for the Länder as regards their constitutional tasks they have to carry out for their citizens in cultural, economic, social, administrative and other areas. And it is valid for the broadcasting corporations and their special function of providing communication services to their populations by broadcasting.

In the 1980s, private broadcasting emerged as a divisive issue between the SPD and the Christian Union parties. The interesting point concerning this conflict between the left and the right is that the choice of venue was once again the national level. In 1984, SPD members at the Bundestag brought the issue of satellite-based private broadcasts in the Land of Lower Saxony before the Federal Constitutional Court. The SPD claimed that satellite broadcasting was a national issue which should not be decided by Land governments. While the SPD was seeking legal means to annul private broadcasting, business was lobbying for a federal policy regulating private satellite broadcasts. Meanwhile, the Länder Minister-Presidents' Conference met in 1984 with the aim of reaching a common position on the issue, but failed to reach a compromise.

In its decision on Lower Saxony Media Law delivered in 1986, the Constitutional Court ruled that a dual system through public and private broadcasting was possible under the Basic Law. The Court also suggested recourse to the principle of federal friendly behavior for reaching a coherent nationwide policy. As a part of its decision, the Federal Constitutional Court called for common action and asked the Länder to harmonize their regulations. The Court's decision subsequently opened up the possibility of an interstate treaty (*Staatsvertrag zur Neuordnung des Rundfunkwesens*) brokered by the federal government in April 1987. The new system effectively standardizes the media policies of the German Länder. In order to license and regulate private broadcasters, the Länder began to establish Land-based institutions for media regulation (*Landesmedienanstalten*) separate from the existing public broadcasting corporations. The establishment of these regulatory agencies was carried out with a high degree of standardization and federal involvement. Länder regulatory agencies for private broadcasting also formed a nationwide association (*Direktorkonferenz der Landesmedienanstalten*) to harmonize their regulations.

The 1987 State Treaty became the norm for united Germany two years later. Article 26 of the Unification Treaty of 31 August 1990 called for the establishment of new public broadcasting corporations in the five new East German Länder. The new Länder were also asked to establish the necessary private broadcasting regulations based on the dual West German system. Despite Article 30 of the Basic Law on Länder cultural sovereignty, the East German Länder were asked to conform to the standard West German media policy. Accordingly, a new treaty titled the United Germany Broadcasting Treaty (*Staatsvertrag über den Rundfunk im vereinten Deutschland*) was signed on 31 August 1991. The contradiction in granting cultural sovereignty to the new Länder and imposing a uniform media policy at the same time was an issue that failed to ignite political interest. The readiness to ignore the constitutional division of responsibilities is perhaps best exemplified by the following minutes attached to the 1997 interstate treaty on media:[37]

> The Federal Government and the Länder have come to an understanding on July 1 1996 to create in the framework of their constitutional jurisdictions, a uniform legal framework in the form of a Federal Law and an inter-Land

State Treaty. It was agreed that the necessary regulations should not be allowed to fail to materialize due to different interpretations of constitutional authority.

Education

Together with media, in 1949 education was put under exclusive provincial jurisdiction through the constitutional premise of Länder cultural sovereignty (*Kulturhoheit*).[38] However, education policy followed a nationwide direction, quite alike the process that took place in media policy. An all-German education policy was seen as a natural response to national concerns. Just as in media policy, one of the main driving forces in this process was the collective action of the Länder.

An important entity in the nationalization of education is the Standing Conference of Ministers of Culture (*Ständige Konferenz der Kultusminister* or *Kultusministerkonferenz* KMK) established between the Länder in 1949. The KMK charter states the purpose of the institution as follows:[39]

> The Standing Conference of the Ministers of Culture of the Federal Republic of Germany (Culture Ministers Conference) deals with issues of cultural policy with supra-regional significance with the aim of building common opinion and will, and the representation of common concerns.

From the outset, the aim seemed to be to find a way around the federal division of responsibilities. In 1949, the Minister for Education for Hesse, Edwin Stein, evaluated the KMK's performance in the following terms: "Despite the distinctiveness of the Länder, the culture ministers will contribute to the purpose of protecting and promoting the unity of the German spiritual life."[40] In 1988, at a special meeting of the KMK to commemorate its fortieth anniversary, Stein repeated similar views: "KMK had understood the need to co-ordinate the minimum uniformity of educational systems with the federal constitutional structure, and to maintain Germany's intellectual unity."[41] Bernard Vogel, who was the Minister of Culture for Rhineland-Palatinate between 1967 and 1976, and later the Minister-President of the same Land, believes that "the Standing Conference brought a minimum level of comparability of education systems in Germany to an extent that no other federal state has attained."[42] Vogel also states that during the early years of the Bonn Republic, there was widespread support across the political spectrum not only for the creation of the Standing Conference of the KMK but also for the establishment of a Federal Ministry for Culture.[43] The Bavarian Minister for Instruction and Culture between 1970 and 1986, Hans Maier, explains this centralist mindset in the following terms:[44]

> Especially in the fragmentation and division of the state after the Second World War, if one did not yet live in a common state and a common constitution for all Germans could not be found, one kept a firm hold on what

appeared to guarantee national unity, on the uniting power of history, language, literature, music.

Maier continues by stating that:[45]

> In Germany one expected from cultural federalism, paradoxically, not only the preservation of the federal distinctiveness of the Länder as in other federations, but especially, almost in the same breath, the establishment of cultural unity and political homogeneity in the entire state.

The first formal agreement of the Standing Conference of KMK, the Düsseldorf Agreement, was signed in 1955. The aim was to standardize educational assessment, the timing and duration of the study year, curricula, and the recognition of qualifications. In a report released in 1955 after the ratification of the agreement, the President of the KMK, Willy Dehnkamp, remarked: "Better cooperation between the Bund and Länder is in the interest of the German youth, German science and research, German culture and the German nation."[46] One important objective of the agreement was to remove the educational barriers to inter-German mobility.[47] With the Düsseldorf Agreement the KMK managed to establish a degree of harmonization in the education system, leading two students of German education policy to remark that "self-coordination amongst the Länder prevented cultural federalism from leading to a complete dispersion of school legislation."[48] The public, however, wanted more than harmonization.

Observers credit general public displeasure with educational divisions as one of the main reasons behind the efforts of the Minister-Presidents to seek further standardization.[49] A public opinion poll from 1953 shows that 60 percent of the respondents saw the "school question" as the most important political issue at the time.[50] A poll from the following year shows 69 percent support for a uniform teaching scheme for the whole of West Germany, as opposed 15 percent who wanted a differentiated system to remain.[51] Public demand for educational uniformity is a theme prevalent in the literature on German educational policy, and the issue appears to have dominated public life in the early decades of the Federal Republic.[52] The saying "father moves, son flunks" from those days symbolizes the relationship which was seen to exist between educational federalism and geographic mobility.[53]

In 1953, the Länder Ministers of Culture and the Federal Ministry of the Interior (*Bundesinnenministerium*) established a Special Committee on Education (*Deutscher Ausschuß für das Erziehungs und Bildungwesen*) to make recommendations for educational reform. In its advisory report, the Committee suggested an overhaul of the entire system, stating that:[54]

> [The Committee] is convinced that the intellectual unity of our nation – which should be strengthened and held above all ideological and social differences – demands a unified education that is common for all school types. This could not be achieved by only a binding outer structure through the

organization of a single educational establishment and one aptitude standard. Many additional pressing needs in education have to be met in order to establish the consciousness of this internal connection.

The report continued by stating that: "The educational structure must contribute to the intellectual unity of the nation in the basic experience, exercise and insights; and it must strongly support the establishment of a broad and common ground for the consciousness of this unity."[55]

The following years witnessed a number of initiatives aimed at devising various nationwide responses to the questions of education and culture. In 1957, the Council for the Sciences (*Wissenschaftsrat*) was created by a state administrative treaty between the Bund and the Länder. In 1959, the two levels of government signed the Königsten state agreement on scientific and educational research, effectively bringing the Bund into the exclusive Länder jurisdiction. The result was the establishment of the Ministry for Scientific Research at the federal level in 1962, followed by agreements in 1964 and 1968 expanding the role of the Bund in higher education. In the meantime, the 1964 Hamburg Agreement of the KMK continued the standardization process started by the Düsseldorf Agreement. The German Educational Council (*Deutscher Bildungsrat*) established in 1965 is another entity set up in the context of the nationalization of education. A public opinion survey (1965–67) shows widespread acceptance of the necessity for national reforms in education – 64 percent of respondents declared unqualified support for the educational reforms proposed by the Council for Sciences.[56]

An important event within the context of German educational policy was Georg Picht's 1964 article "The German Educational Catastrophe," which brought the issue of cultural federalism to the center of public debate. Picht's piece became one of the most influential arguments of the time, and was widely quoted in policy circles. In this article, Picht pointed to the problem of the so-called "school chaos" and the need for central planning, and he was very direct about the solution: "We need a federal Ministry of Culture and a central administration of culture. Therefore, we need an amendment to the Basic Law."[57] Picht also argued that, since the problem was immediate, the Länder should make every effort to seek solutions until a constitutional amendment was made. It is interesting to note that instead of defending their exclusive constitutional prerogatives over education, the Länder responded to Picht's article by trying to show that they were in fact cooperating with one another and with the Bund in establishing a national education policy.[58]

In 1969, the CDU/CSU/SPD grand coalition of Kiesinger and Brandt passed a constitutional amendment that made higher education and research joint Bund–Länder responsibility. The Free Democratic Party (FDP) initially opposed these changes, not because the constitutionally-entrenched competences of the Länder were violated, but because the reforms were not going far enough. The FDP opposition attacked the joint responsibility proposal as a "small solution" (*kleine Lösung*) to the issue of education:[59]

Our criticism is directed at the fact that the Bund is not given sufficient competences for an urgently needed reform in the educational system which would allow our youth to have a secure future in international competition and, thereby, remove a trouble from our state.

Later that year, the CDU/CSU/SPD coalition established the Federal Ministry of Education. To be precise, the existing Federal Ministry of Scientific Research was transformed into the Federal Ministry of Education and Science. Thus the Bund created a ministry in a policy area where it originally did not have constitutional jurisdiction. The first Federal Minister of Education and Science, Hans Leussink, believed the federal involvement in education to be the "flexibility" of federalism:[60]

The Federal Government is of the opinion that through joint educational planning, the debate on constitutional competences in the educational system will lose considerable significance if the Bund and the Länder can agree on an educational reform which guarantees the individual right to learning and teaching and which ensures society a productive and efficient educational system; the flexibility of federalism will reveal itself, in the end, as a force for the good.

Notably, the above introduction to the 1970 Education Report of the Ministry of Education and Science is subtitled "Educational Policy as an All-State Task." The new Ministry was not only the culmination of the process towards centralization; it also actively pursued further integration. In the following passage from the report, the authors appear to be either unaware of, or unperturbed by, the contradiction in their statement:[61]

The Federal Government has no desire, with its extended financial participation, to reduce the competences of the Länder in the shaping and influencing of education. Instead, the aim is to improve co-ordination and agreement on the establishment of priorities, irrespective of Länder boundaries.

The process of turning education into an "all-state task" continued with the Bund–Länder Commission on Educational Reform and Advancement of Research (*Bund-Länder-Kommission für Bildungsplanung und Forschung-förderung* BLK), set up in 1970. Arthur Gunlicks describes the position of the Commission as follows:[62]

Generally, there seemed to be a consensus ... all parties seemed to agree on a need to co-ordinate *Land* policies. In addition, the federal government seemed to believe that it had a responsibility to create greater uniformity of opportunities and living conditions across the nation.

The speech the State Secretary for the Federal Ministry of Education and Research of the new SPD–FDP coalition government, Hildegard Hamm-Brücher

(FDP), made to the Bundestag in June 1970 displays the confidence decision-makers had in BLK's chances of bringing about a federal educational policy:[63]

> If there is really a short-term escape from the dilemma of cultural federalism, here is the way! The creation of the Bund–Länder Commission (BLK) is an event of great political significance, and hopefully, it is the beginning of a new era in the development of the educational policy of our country.

Drafting a unified university education system through the BLK was aided by the 1972 decision of the Federal Constitutional Court on the need for a nationwide approach to student placement: "It is the joint responsibility of the Bund and the Länder to ensure the allocation of all available seats for university study through a supra-regional placement under the application of a uniform selection criteria."[64] A public opinion poll from the same year shows 50 percent support for a constitutional amendment that would give the federal government full authority over education, while 34 percent of the respondents declared they were in favor of Bund–Länder cooperation.[65] The process that got underway culminated in the Universities and Higher Education Law (*Hochschulrahmengesetz*) of 1976.[66] The outstanding question, however, remained the constitutional clause which still placed education under the exclusive jurisdiction of the Länder. An article entitled "Planning of Higher Education and the Basic Law" from that period provides an example of how explicit the discussion on bypassing the Basic Law had become: "How far could centralization, unitarization and coordination really be further pursued without violating Article 79(iii) of the Basic Law which establishes an absolute guarantee for the federal state?"[67] But the German frustration with the institutional parameters of the federal system bequeathed by the Allies is probably best exemplified by Helga Schuhardt's (FDP) calls for more federal involvement: "The discrepancy between factual necessity and constitutional possibility in the reorganization of education is simply unbearable."[68]

Within the context of this debate, the federal government released its report on the structural problems of education in December of 1978. In this so-called "deficiencies report" (*Mängelbericht*), the Bund recommended a constitutional revision in the field of educational policy. After laying out the effects of educational federalism, the report claimed that the absence of a uniform nationwide educational system left Germans at a disadvantage:[69]

> Those first in line to be affected from [educational policy] decisions – pupils, trainees, students, parents and teachers – rightfully expect that in a federal state, as a prerequisite for the freedom of movement, mobility and equality of opportunity in the educational and occupational system, a minimum degree of necessary uniformity in the educational system should also be guaranteed.

An article from 1980 shows the prevailing mindset at the time which associates educational diversity with inefficiency: "The persistent issue is to what extent differences in educational systems and resulting hindrances to mobility should be accepted for the sake of the advantage of federal pluralism."[70]

The process of German unification is another indication that, when deemed necessary by all parties involved, the federal division of responsibilities in education can easily be bypassed. The process of standardizing East German education with that of the West preceded the official reunification. The five East German Länder became members of the KMK and BLK before formal unification.[71] During July 1990, the Council of the Sciences evaluated the higher education and research organizations of East Germany and made suggestions as the new Länder joined. Following the recommendations, the educational structures of the East German Länder were changed in order to correspond to the standardized national educational system in the West. It is interesting to note that this was done while the East German Länder were also being granted the principle of cultural sovereignty – that is, the right of legal supremacy over their educational systems under Article 30 of the Basic Law.

The nationwide approach to education is shared by all the political parties as well. There are important differences between the three main parties in terms of the contents of education policy, yet they all share a nationwide perspective. The 1993 CDU report on education from 1993 states the party position in the following terms:[72]

> Federalism and the cultural sovereignty of the Länder are indispensable for the competition of different approaches and ways. But the Länder also have a responsibility, not only for uniformity in the operation of education, but also to ensure uniformity in the results in the different operations of education.... These results are the steps and marking stones on the path towards uniformity.

The SPD differs from Christian Union parties concerning the contents of education policy, and specifically objects to the three-tier traditional educational system which divides students into separate streams of secondary education based on their grades, but at the same time the SPD believes in a nationwide approach to education as a tool for social emancipation.[73] The political party most committed to a nationwide uniform educational system is the FDP. As early as 1950, the FDP declared its views on educational federalism: "To prepare the unity of the educational system for the future state territory, the individual Länder should adjust their available organizational structures with one another for a uniform federal regulation."[74] Forty years later, the views of the FDP had hardly changed:[75]

> FDP will conserve the principle of Länder competence to the extent that this does not endanger the inter-German compatibility of education operations. To this end, the federal government must be provided with necessary framework competences. The mobility of the teachers and students within the European integration process should not be allowed to run aground at the borders of the Länder.

Support for nationwide policies is not confined to the political parties, but spans the whole of Germany. Empirical investigation covering the debates on education in the Federal Republic of Germany found that no political actor challenged the perceived need for a nationwide approach to education policy in Germany. There were differences over content, but the federal government, political parties, teachers' unions, parent associations, industry, trades unions, and Länder governments and bureaucracy all shared an all-German frame of reference. Calls for further reforms and standardization continue.[76]

Conclusion

The preceding sections dealing with the changes in education and media demonstrate the prevailing centralist mindset shared across the political spectrum. In particular, there appears to be an overall consensus which associates federal diversity with inefficiency. The nationwide approach, on the other hand, appears to be the imperative of common sense to many German decision-makers. As an insider to the policy process puts it: "The cooperation between the Länder is a daily matter of course in the Federal Republic of Germany. And furthermore, cooperative federalism is a command of the constitution – and of common sense!"[77] Of course, this attitude to federalism should be seen within the context of an all-German *demos*. According to Gerhard Lehmbruch, the reason for such views is simply because "the public prefers the homogenization and uniformity of policies throughout the federal system.... And the manifest raison d'être of this interlocking relationship is the production of homogeneous policies."[78] This point is echoed by Steffen Schneider, who argues that "a homogenous society ... does not tolerate diversity in public policy."[79]

Analysis of the last fifty years of the Federal Republic shows that the institutional structure set up by the Allies failed to reproduce itself over time. Provincial jurisdiction did not led to provincial politics, since all political actors fought their battles at the national stage. The Länder, the federal government, political parties, and interest groups all found means to circumvent the constitution. When deemed necessary, a constitutional clause believed to create unnecessary and inefficient diversity was easily bypassed. Despite partisan differences concerning the contents of policies, the venue was always an all-German one.

6 Switzerland

Introduction

Switzerland is one of the oldest federations in the world. It is often seen as a success story in terms of management of ethno-linguistic diversity. This small federation, where four languages and two religions coexist with deep regional economic disparities, seems to have found the way to manage diversity successfully. The following sections, however, show the inconsistency that lies at the core of Swiss federalism. Swiss federalism rests on a state/society incongruence where the federal constitution creating twenty-six cantons coexists with a social structure composed of two main linguistic/cultural communities. In addition to these two large groups of French-speaking Swiss Romand and German Swiss, there are two smaller linguistic groups in the form of Italian-speakers and Rhaeto-Romansche speakers. To add to the complexity, the cantonal borders do not neatly correspond to either linguistic or religious fault-lines.

Starting with the second half of the twentieth century, language has increasingly come to function as the main basis of identity in Switzerland. The result has been a federal system under pressure to reflect the mismatch between the Swiss federal society and the Swiss federal constitution. The focus of this chapter is on these discrepancies between the formal institutions and the workings of Swiss federalism.[1] In particular, due to the important role they play in identity politics, the two policy areas of education and media are analyzed in depth. The aim is to reveal the processes of change that contribute to the growing distance between *de jure* constitution and de facto practice.

Federalism in Switzerland

The origins of the Swiss federation go back to the thirteenth century. The three alpine communities of Uri, Schwyz and Unterwalden managed to establish independence from the Holy Roman Empire in 1273. These three communities signed an oath of cooperation (*Eidgenossenschaft*) on the meadow of Rütli by Lake Lucerne in 1291, and this symbolic oath became the name of the confederation they established. Their union gradually expanded to include thirteen cantons where two religions and four languages came to coexist. In addition to the religious and linguistic heterogeneity, the expanded confederation also included urban and richer new members like Zurich and Basel, in contrast to its original alpine founders. The confederation was a patchwork of prince-bishoprics, city-states, republics, oligarchies, alpine democracies, affiliated lands and colonies, all united under the oath of cooperation. The confederation managed to stay out of the Thirty Years War between Protestants and Catholics despite its divided population, and hence continued to prosper.

In 1798, Napoleon's armies occupied Switzerland and established the "one and indivisible" Helvetian Republic, named after the first Celtic inhabitants of the country, the Helvetii, and the Roman province of Helvetia. The creation of a modern centralized state with national citizenship was supported by large segments of the Swiss population, but met with hostility from the ruling class and the conservative Catholic cantons. In order to solve the problems, Napoleon restored some of the original powers of the cantons with the 1803 Act of Mediation. Following Napoleon's defeat, the Swiss confederation was re-established in 1815. French republican ideas remained influential, however, as the restored confederation soon faced strong state-building pressures from its richer Protestant cantons. The driving force was the so-called "radicals," i.e. anticlerical liberals mostly from Protestant cantons. There were deep divisions between the conservative rural Catholics, who resisted a strong national executive, and these radicals from the industrializing cantons who pushed for a stronger union. In 1847, the radical cantons went to war to prevent the conservative *Sonderbund* from seceding. The industrialized Protestant cantons emerged victorious from the brief civil war which lasted only twenty days, with a loss of 120 lives. The outcome was the federal constitution of 1848, which stripped the cantons of sovereign state rights and turned them into members of a federation but stopped short of a unitary state. In 1872, the constitution underwent further revisions increasing the powers of the federal government.

Following the constitutional settlement, the former adversaries, i.e. anticlerical radicals and conservative Catholics, periodically joined forces against the burgeoning socialist labor movement. However, religion remained the predominant social cleavage during most of this time, dividing the country almost evenly into Protestants and Catholics. Starting with the end of World War II, though, religion gradually lost its predominance as the main social divide, while language emerged as an important marker of collective identity.[2] Around 75 percent of Swiss are German-speakers – or, more precisely, speakers of various Swiss German dialects grouped together under the name of *Schwyzertütsch*. French-speakers constitute 20 percent of the population inhabiting the six western cantons. They tend to refer themselves as *Suisse Romand*, while German Swiss generally use the term *Welschschweiz* to refer to the Francophone Swiss and *Welschland* for the French-speaking western parts of Switzerland. Italian-speakers make up only 4 percent of the population, and are concentrated in the southern canton of Ticino (*Tessin* in German and French). Finally, a tiny group of Rhaeto-Romansche speakers live in the isolated alpine canton of Grisons, forming less than 1 percent of the Swiss population. Even in the canton Grisons, they constitute only 17 percent of the population. This old Latin language is further subdivided into four distinct dialects; *Surselva, Sutselva, Surmeira* and *Ladin*. To add to the complicated picture, the tiny Romansche-speaking community is divided into Protestant and Catholic sections.

The formal federal structure, however, is not based on linguistic constituent communities but on cantons. With a population of only seven million,[3] Switzerland has twenty-three cantons (three of which are further divided into half-cantons) ranging from Appenzell-Inner-Rhoden with 14,800 inhabitants to Zurich with 1,170,000.[4] In addition, there are more than 3,000 communes which enjoy a wide range of powers. In many ways Switzerland has remained a pre-modern political entity, often referred to as "special case Switzerland" (*Sonderfall Schweiz*). According to Herbert Lüthy:[5]

> Switzerland is not a nation-state, not a unitary state, not a state based on homogenous unity. In its present structure of unbroken continuity of communal autonomy preserved from the medieval ages, it is in great measure the antithesis of the modern state established in Europe since the 19th century. In its origin and its historical self-consciousness, Switzerland is nothing other than an alliance of medieval particularisms against the historical tendency towards unification of territorial, dynastic, administrative or national states in central structures, and this historical consciousness forms the Swiss political civilization.

Steinberg shares the same view: "Switzerland represents a model of Europe that might have evolved if the French Revolution had not succeeded in transforming the European state."[6] In German Switzerland, the tradition of isolationist conservative alpine democracy going back to medieval times remains strong. The term often used to describe this phenomenon is *Kantönligeist*. Until recently, most small Catholic cantons of central Switzerland had the annual open air vote called the *Landsgemeinde*. These are no longer practiced in most cantons, but a tradition of direct politics remains intact in Switzerland. The Swiss not only vote in communal, cantonal and federal elections; they also vote for frequent government amendments to the constitution and numerous referendum initiatives brought by voters, interest groups or political parties, as well as cantonal referenda.[7]

The 1848 Constitution established a directly elected Federal Assembly with two houses; a National Council (*Nationalrat – Conseil national*) composed of 200 members, and an Estates Council (*Ständerat – Conseil des États*) composed of forty-six members representing the cantons, also directly elected. Their joint session in the form of the Federal Assembly (*Bundesversammlung – Assemblée fédérale*) elects seven members to the national executive, the Federal Council (*Bundesrat – Conseil fédéral*), for four years. The positions of President and Vice-President rotate between the members of the executive. According to an agreement reached in 1959, the composition of the Federal Council is based on the formula of 2:2:2:1 – that is, two members come from the Radical Democrats

(FDP), two from the Social Democrats (SPS), two from the Christian Democrats (CVP) and one from the People's Party (SVP).

The Swiss federal system does not have a constitutional court in the traditional sense like other federations. Political decisions have priority over the interpretation powers of the Federal Tribunal (*Bundesgericht*). The court has therefore stayed clear of constitutional questions and has focused on administrative questions instead.[8] This is partly due to the role direct democracy plays in the Switzerland. Along with federalism, direct democracy is a central characteristic of the Swiss political system. Numerous referenda have led to more than 150 constitutional amendments since 1848 – including the creation of the new canton of Jura in 1979.[9] The most comprehensive constitutional revision since 1872, however, is a very recent one. On 19 April 1999, the majority of Swiss voters and Swiss cantons voted in favor of a proposal aiming to reform the federal constitution. The new constitution came into force the following year. Article 7(1) of the former constitution explicitly forbade political alliances between cantons (mostly due to the Sonderbund experience), but this article no longer exists – in fact, the new Article 34(1) allows cantons to form associations among themselves and set up common institutions. The new Article 44 introduces the principle of federal comity, calling for cooperation between the cantons and the federal government, which had been exercised without a constitutional base until then.[10] The revision also provided some tidying up of the constitution, which had become convoluted with the numerous amendments introduced. In this context, Article 3 of the former constitution, which gave the cantons residual powers, became Article 32 in the new constitution. The reforms, however, have brought no constitutional recognition to the linguistic regions of Switzerland.

"Romandie," as the region of French-speakers, has no legal or administrative base. The same is true for German Switzerland. For Italian-speakers the situation is different because they are concentrated in the canton Ticino, thereby allowing for the cantonal boundaries to correspond to the linguistic community for the most part – with the addition of the few Italian-speaking communities in neighboring Grisons. The case of the mountainous canton of Grisons composed of three linguistic communities of German-speakers, Italian-speakers and Romansche-speakers, on the other hand, does not represent a political challenge due to its geographical isolation. In addition to their tiny populations and geographical isolation, both Ticino and Grisons are economically dependent on German Switzerland. This all means that the salient political division in Switzerland is between French-speakers and German-speakers.

In Swiss German, the colloquial expression of the French–German divide is *Röstigraben* (the "Roeshti" ditch), named after the favorite dish of German Switzerland. Swiss Romands, on the other hand, either simply refer to the division as "the ditch" (*le fossé*) or use the phrase *d'outre Sarine* after the river Sarine, which roughly runs along the French–German linguistic divide. Switzerland is officially multilingual, but individuals tend to live unilingual lives. The same can be said about the linguistic communities. According to François Grin:

"Switzerland may be quadrilingual but to most intents and purposes each point of its territory can be viewed as unilingual."[11] The linguistic communities live in relative isolation from one another in a system of mutual cultural ignorance. As the Swiss writer Friedrich Dürrenmatt put it: "We live side-by-side one another but we don't live together. What is missing is dialogue and communication between German Swiss and Swiss Romands."[12] This question of language divisions within Switzerland has attracted recent academic interest. A study on national unity led by Ernest Weibel states that:[13]

> [These researchers] observe a mutation of the linguistic cleavage within the institutional context of Switzerland. The divergences can no longer be resolved through federalism, as it was the case before. All the important questions, with which Switzerland is essentially confronted today, concern its external relations in a number of cases, and these have the tendency to exacerbate the linguistic cleavage.

The Swiss National Research Program on Cultural Diversity and National Identity is one such study. The final report of this program draws attention to the centrality of linguistic communities:[14]

> Various opinion polls confirm the cultural significance of language spaces. Belonging to a linguistic community has a bearing on the choice of employment, on the vacation destination, on the frequency of media consumption, and on the views concerning the relations between the constituent parts of the country. Language spaces determine in high degree the personal relationship circle, the school system, and the corresponding media community. The importance of the linguistic-cultural component is also clear in comparison to the weakening importance of the confessional component.

The linguistic demarcation is not recognized by the constitution, however. It exists in all but name in other aspects of public life. According to Hanspeter Kriesi: "Language has become more important because *the public space is segmented by language*: the members of the major language communities only use television, radio, and the press of their own respective communities."[15] As a reflection of the linguistically demarcated public space, the broadcasts of the Swiss Public Broadcasting Corporation (SRG/SSR) are based on language regions. Uli Windisch's detailed study on the relations between linguistic communities concludes by stating that "Linguistic identity has become a very important, or even the definitive, dimension of social identity and the sentiment of belonging to a community."[16] It has to be noted that historically it was the religious cleavage that mattered more. According to William Martin:[17]

> People are often astonished that Switzerland has managed to survive the centuries despite her linguistic diversities, but this astonishment is based on a misapprehension. Language problems are an entirely modern phenomenon.

Formerly, people hated each other because of their religion rather than the language they spoke.

Language has increasingly become the primary marker of collective identity, especially for the Swiss Romands, who had long been divided along other bases of political allegiance.[18] All six cantons where French-speakers reside joined the confederation under different circumstances: Fribourg joined the Swiss confederation in 1481 as the first French-speaking canton, Geneva was admitted in 1815 after years as a French *département,* and Jura's entry was as late as 1979. Geneva, Vaud and Neuchâtel are Protestant cantons, while Valais, Fribourg and Jura are Catholic. Fribourg and Valais both have German-speaking minorities and are officially bilingual. Cantons of Romandie also range from the alpine Valais to the urban Geneva. According to Hans Amstutz:[19]

> To talk about the Swiss Romand and their region as a linguistic community is both appropriate and accurate. But in every other respect – be it historical, political, economical, geographical, religious, or cultural – Romandie is a fiction, just like the idea of a politically or culturally uniform German Switzerland.

Yet the differences between Swiss Romands and German Swiss are increasingly noticeable in the political sphere. A number of fairly recent electoral studies demonstrate the strong impact the linguistic division has on national voting patterns.[20] The political differences between the two communities became particularly visible during three relatively recent referenda on Switzerland's membership of international organizations. There were stark differences between the internationally oriented Swiss Romands and their isolationist-inclined German-speaking compatriots in the two referenda on UN membership in 1986 and 2001, and in the referendum on joining the European Economic Arena in 1992. For example, in the national vote in 1992, 73.39 percent of Swiss Romands voted in favor of joining the European Economic Area, while the number was only 43.6 percent among German Swiss. In the second round of cantonal voting, only the six cantons of Romandie plus Basel voted in favor of joining.

Probably as a result of a combination of being the dominant ethno-linguistic group in the country along with the heterogeneity of Schwyzertütsch dialects, German Swiss do not entertain the same degree of internal homogeneity as do the Swiss Romands. Thus, occasional calls for a new federal order based on language communities tend to come from the French side. One of the earliest expressions of this ideal came from Pierre Guye in 1937:[21]

> As each cantonal community possesses political powers of representation, each linguistic group or community should also possess the political powers of representation. In other words, one should build a Romand confederation and a German Swiss confederation joined by a federal pact to which Ticino and Grisons would be associates.

Media

Media play an indispensable role for language-based public spaces. As reflected in the divisions within mass media, the constituent linguistic communities of Switzerland are not part of the same public space.[22] In addition to being a reflection of the underlying social structure, the divisions in the media system along linguistic demarcations ensure the perpetuation of these very divisions. The print media are strictly divided between linguistic groups, and the same pattern exists in the radio and television network. As Max Frenkel puts it:[23]

> It is evident that the Swiss linguistic borders certainly present the strongest bulwark against the formation of a unity of ideas for entire Switzerland. Media that are not understood have no effect. What we probably have in Switzerland is uniformization of German Swiss and of Swiss Romand. The same hardly exists for Switzerland in general; and if it exists at all, not to the same extent.

Essentially Switzerland is divided into two large public spaces, those of French-Switzerland and German-Switzerland. The Italian-speaking canton Ticino has its own miniscule public space as well, but being on the south of the Gotthard Pass brings Ticino closer to the socio-cultural sphere of Italy proper. The Romansche speakers who make up less than 1 percent of the Swiss population, on the other hand, are a minority even in their own canton Grisons. As discussed earlier, they speak four different dialects, live in isolated mountain valleys, and are further divided into Protestants and Catholics. It is difficult, therefore, to talk about the Romansche-speakers as a constituent linguistic community of Switzerland. In any case, they have mostly integrated into the cultural life of German Switzerland. German Swiss, Swiss Romands and Ticinesi all have political recognition as linguistic communities, but not as territorial communities. Public and private life, however, reflect the deep divisions. According to Wolf Linder:[24]

> The three linguistic regions of German Switzerland, Romandie, and Ticino are (at present) not only autonomous politically, they are remain relatively closed. A large number of citizens receive media from all languages indeed but they only follow the ones in their mother language.

As mentioned earlier, in print media the divisions are watertight. The main German Swiss newspapers, *Blick*, *Tages-Anzeiger*, *Neue Zürcher Zeitung*, *Berner Zeitung* and *Basler Zeitung*, aim exclusively at German Switzerland in terms of both readership and coverage. The same can be said of the main Swiss Romand newspapers, *24 heures*, *La Suisse*, *Tribune de Genève*, *Le Matin* and *Le Temps*. Furthermore, the recent years have witnessed consolidation of ownership and journalism within language regions. Between 1990 and 2000, the number of different newspapers in Switzerland fell from sixty-seven to forty-three.[25] Many cantonal papers have merged, leading to further homogenization within the linguistic public spheres. According to Meier and Schanne:[26]

> Media consumption lies first and foremost in the mother-tongue ... [There are] no national media; this statement sums up the principal characteristic of the field of Swiss media. In Switzerland there is no such thing as a national media. The focus of journalists remains primarily on their immediate surrounding of their own language, and later on a distant horizon belonging to their own linguistic community. An interest in the other cultural spaces of Switzerland does not follow.

Similar divisions exist in the field of broadcasting, which constitutionally is under federal jurisdiction but in practice is divided into three linguistic communities. Here, language regions form an intermediary position between cantons and the federal level. Divisions in print media are almost preordained in linguistically divided countries, but the devolution of a national public broadcasting corporation to constituent ethno-linguistic communities is a process which can only be explained by the theory of congruence. Similar to a process which took place in Belgium, the nationwide public broadcasting corporation became the first federal institution to recognize the divisions within the social structure and reorganize itself along linguistic lines.[27]

Broadcasting in Switzerland had started with a number of private initiatives for radio studios. The Swiss Broadcasting Society SRG/SSR (*Schweizerische Rundspruch-gesellschaft/Société Suisse de radio et télévision*), set up on 24 February 1931, brought these private stations together under its framework. Broadcasting, however, had an uncertain legal status because, while telecommunications was under federal jurisdiction, culture was under cantonal control. There was no major constitutional review of the issue, as cases were dealt with practically in an ad hoc manner broadly guided by Article 36 of the constitution, which regulated postal and telegraph services.

In 1953, the first television broadcasts were made under the auspices of the SRG/SSR. These first broadcasts were into German Switzerland, carried out by the station in Beromünster. The following year the Sottens station began broadcasts in French, and canton Ticino received its broadcasts in Italian from the Monte Ceneri station. There was a referendum in 1957 on placing broadcasting under exclusive federal jurisdiction, but the proposal was not passed and broadcasting remained organized on a national basis. During the discussions, the financial issues were set on clearer basis as the federal government and major newspapers agreed jointly to subsidize television broadcasts. The SRG/SSR was legally a multilingual public broadcasting corporation, but in practice it was divided into self-contained linguistic sections. A few years later, this system acquired official recognition.

On 1 November 1964 a reform package came into force, which divided the SRG/SSR into three networks and also introduced a major organizational overhaul for the broadcasting system. Accordingly, three new bodies based on the linguistic communities were established. The SRG/SSR acquired a new statute, and its full name was changed to *Schweizerische Radio- und Fernsehgesellschaft/Société Suisse de Radiodiffusion et Télévision*. The French-language SSR (*Société Suisse de Radiodiffusion et Télévision de la Suisse romande*) became the public broadcaster for Swiss Romands, while the German language DRS (*Radio und Fernsehgesellschaft der deutschen und rätoromanischen Schweiz*) became the public broadcaster for the German Swiss. DRS was also responsible for broadcasts in Romansche, through its affiliate *Cumünza Rumantscha Radio e Televisiun*. And finally canton Ticino was given its own Italian-language broadcasting network, the SI (*Società cooperative per la radiotelevisione della Svizzera italiana*). In sum, the SRG/SSR became the only federal institution which explicitly recognized the existence of the federal society. According to André Wuerth:[28]

> The SRG carries the linguistic differentiation even further because in reference to the integration of the linguistic regions, the nationally designed SRG takes an increasingly ambivalent position. At the level of the SRG, the audiovisual media are run according to a clear division along the linguistic border.

This division, however, was not unanimously welcomed by German Switzerland. An example of the critical view is the statement made by the representative of canton Zurich in the Estates Council in 1968 during the discussions on television broadcasting:[29]

> Switzerland does not consist primarily of German-speaking, French-speaking and Italian-speaking parts and not of single regions of East, Central and Northwest Switzerland but of exactly 22 cantons. It is therefore dangerous to divide Switzerland into single blocks, especially when these blocks correspond to linguistic borders.

During the same discussion, a member of the Federal Council explained that in practice the system was divided, and that the institutional structure had to correspond to the divisions: "There are three important regional societies for which three programs with different commissions exist. This aspect of diversity through the relationship of three languages and three channels allows us to practically act like three countries."[30] However, Swiss broadcasting lacked a clear constitutional base until 1984. This was changed with a referendum, on 2 December 1984, on Article 55 of the constitution. As a result, the federation acquired constitutional jurisdiction over broadcasting. The process continued with the Federal Law on Radio and Television (*Radio- und Fernsehgesetz*, RVTG/*loi sur la radio et la television*, LFRT), which was passed by the Federal Council on 28 September 1987. After the usual lengthy process of ratification and national votes, the new law came into force on 16 March 1992 as the new *Bundesgesetz über Radio und Fernsehen*. The law specifically mentions the linguistic regions as a part of the organizational structure of Swiss broadcasting. The law also allows for private television stations, which were set up in due course.

In the meantime, the process of congruence continued, with the SRG/SSR formally being divided into regional associations on 22 November 1991. Language regions now officially constitute the primary basis of Swiss broadcasting. Studies of the Swiss media focus on language regions as the constituent units of Switzerland (*Sprachregionen als Landsteilen*) in their analyses. According to one such study carried out by the SRG/SSR itself, the consumers of broadcasting in Switzerland rarely cross these linguistic borders: 80 percent of German Swiss, 77 percent of Swiss Romands and 73 percent of Ticinesi follow only the programs of their own broadcasting corporations.[31] In another study carried out for the Federal Office of Statistics, Hanspeter Kriesi and his colleagues point out to the role language plays in dividing up the Swiss public sphere:[32]

> Public space is strictly segmented according to the border between linguistic regions. Analysis of the distribution of press and the diffusion of audiovisual media (television and radio) shows that Swiss citizens do not use the media of other linguistic regions. Swiss of all linguistic regions rather turn to the media of neighboring countries who speak their languages.

In sum, the media form a policy area where identity politics play a predominant role. Naturally, the process towards congruence is most visible in this field inextricably tied to the notion of public space. In the field of media, the Swiss public space is divided into linguistic sections which function independently of the structure set up by cantonal demarcations. The preceding section shows that politics in the cultural sphere work separately from the political framework set up by the federal constitution.

Education

A second reflection of the emergence of language as the predominant societal fault-line is in the field of education. However, here the process of congruence has not reached the conclusive strict separation that characterizes the field of mass media. Examination of educational policy in Switzerland shows that a country formerly divided over private education controlled by the Church and secular public education has moved in a direction where linguistic issues have become more prominent. As it is the case in many ethno-linguistically divided societies, education is an increasingly sensitive policy area in Switzerland.[33]

Article 69 of the new federal constitution places education under cantonal jurisdiction, but also allows for federal and cantonal cooperation. This article is identical to the previous Article 27, which regulated education before the 1999 constitutional reform. This article was added in 1872 as a part of a reform increasing the role of the state in public life in order to limit the powers of the Church, particularly the Roman Catholic Church. However, even before 1872 the federal government had made incursions – with the approval of the cantons – into the area of education. The first such example was the establishment of the Federal Technical University (*Eidgenösssische Technische Hochschule*) in Zurich in 1855. In a parallel effort, the cantons also took measures to coordinate aspects of their education policies. On 24 February 1897, they set up the Conference of Cantonal Education Directors (*Eidgenössische Konferenz der Kantonalen Erziehungsdirektoren/Conférence des directeurs cantonaux de l'instruction publique*, EDK/CDIP). Coordination never led to the development of a national education system, however, as educational policies remained cantonal and separate.

After the end of World War II, the federal government increased its involvement in higher education and research. The process started with the establishment of the Swiss National Foundation for the Promotion of Scientific Research (*Schweizerische Nationalfonds zur Förderung der Wissenschaftlichen Forschung*) in 1952, followed by the Swiss Documentation Center for School and Educational Affairs (*Schweizerische Dokumentationsstelle für Schul- und Bildungsfragen/Centre suisse de documentation en matière d'enseignement et d'éducation*, CESDOC) in 1962.[34] The federal government continued to expand into an area constitutionally under cantonal jurisdiction. In 1965, the Swiss Science Council (*Schweizerische Wissenschaftsrat*) was set up to coordinate research projects; this was followed by the Promotion of Universities Law (*Hochschulförderungsgesetz*) in 1968 and the creation of the Swiss Conference of Universities (*Schweizerische Hochschulkonferenz*) the following year. Cantons supported the process of Bund–canton coordination by setting up the Commisson for Intercantonal Cooperation (*Kommission für interkantonale Zusammenarbeit*) in 1967. Cantonal efforts culminated in the 29 October 1970 Intercantonal Concordat on School Coordination (*Konkordat über die Schulkoordination/Concordat sur la coordination scolaire*), which was approved by the Federal Council on 14 December 1970. However, the initiative failed because German Swiss cantons, led by Bern and Zurich, refused to ratify the concordat. This was due partly to fears of strong centralization in the area of education, and partly to a reaction to the close cooperation between Swiss Romand cantons.

By 1970, cantons of French-speaking Switzerland had already undertaken measures towards unification of their education systems. In 1962, the Swiss Romand Pedagogical Society (*Société pédagogique de la Suisse romande*, SPR) had published a proposal entitled Towards a Romand School (*Vers une école romande*). In the coming years, the proposal was widely debated within policy circles. Teachers' unions and parent associations gave strong support to the idea of coordination and, in response to widespread demands, in 1967 the governments of the six French-speaking cantons agreed to coordinate their educational policies.[35] The following year, the Romand Interdepartmental Commission for the Coordination of Education (*Commission interdépartmentale romande de coordination de l'enseignement*, CIRCE) was set up to carry out the implementation of the "école romande."[36] In order to aid the process of coordination, the cantons also established the Romand Institute for Pedagogical Research and

Documentation (*Institut romand de recherche et de documentation péda-gogiques,* IRDP), based in Neuchâtel. The "école romande" initiative led to three successive waves of CIRCE standardization programs, in 1972, 1979 and 1985. According to a public opinion survey carried out during that time, 95.9 percent of Swiss Romands were in favor of the coordination of education among French-speaking cantons.[37] Cantonal governments sought to formalize what came to exist in practice. As Jura's Education Minister, Anita Rion, explained: "It is obvious that common sense calls for a redefinition of competences and political lines in order to reach a better harmonization in the field of educa-tion."[38] However, German Swiss cantons displayed strong opposition to the idea. In the meantime, a federal referendum on standardizing spring as the beginning of the school year failed to survive German Swiss opposition in 1985.

The timing of the beginning of the school year turned out to be a major divid-ing line between German Swiss and Swiss Romands. It also signaled a German Swiss desire to go it alone. During a debate on the issue in the National Council, a member of parliament for the canton Aargau put it as follows: "Let's leave the Swiss Romands and Ticinesi with the fall start for the study year and turn our efforts back again to German Switzerland for inner coordination."[39] During the same debate at the National Council, another member of parliament expressed the all too common dilemma of being torn between the need to recognize differ-ences and the risk of exacerbating them through such recognition:[40]

> We federalists obviously have two souls in our chest.... Of course, one can play down the significance of the rift between Swiss Romands and German Swiss, but after all, we have recently started to draw the thin lines on the map. Thin lines can turn into thick ones over time however.

The line between Swiss Romand and German Swiss has become increasingly thick in the field of education. As Swiss Romands integrated their education systems, the German Swiss intensified their coordination efforts. According to Gunther Hega, German Switzerland has pursued "negative" integration by removing the barriers between cantonal education systems. This is different from the Swiss Romand method of "positive" integration by building common institutions.[41] The differences within German Switzerland account for the slow progress of harmonization. As the dominant ethno-linguistic group, there is also less pressure to seek solidarity among German-speakers and affirm linguistic distinctiveness. In the meantime, the cantons of French Switzerland have moved further in the direction of congruence.

Based on the success of "école romande," Swiss Romand cantons expanded the standardization process to include the fields of secondary education, voca-tional training and higher education. As a result, three new entities were estab-lished; the Romand Commission of Secondary Education (*Commission romande des moyen enseignement,* COROME), the Conference of Cantonal Vocational Training Offices (*Conférence des offices cantonaux de formation professionnelle de la Suisse romand,* CRFP) and the West Swiss University Conference (*Con-*

férence Universitaire de la Suisse Occidentale, CUSO). Most recently, the cantons of French Switzerland merged their polytechnic colleges in 1997, creating the *La haute école specialisée de Suisse occidentale* (HES-SO).

This section demonstrates that the move towards language regions in the field of education has been more visible in French Switzerland than in German Switzerland. It has to be noted, however, that the process of congruence still falls short of the creation of a common educational system for Romandie.[42] Compared to the field of media, a comprehensive system that works above the cantons at the language region level does not yet exist. Nevertheless, educational policy increasingly reflects the constituent ethno-linguistic communities of Switzerland, despite the cross-cutting cantonal demarcations.

Conclusion

Throughout its history, Swiss federalism has acted as an inspiration for those who pondered on federal decentralization, local government and direct democracy. The Swiss constitution has often been seen as a unique experiment in bringing democracy closer to its citizens. According to a prominent Swiss scholar, Herbert Lüthy: "The essential content of [Swiss] federalism is not a division of competences between the federal level and the cantons, but the realization of democracy at all levels of society."[43] However, contemporary Swiss federalism faces a challenge for which it was not designed; linguistic cleavages are increasingly replacing region, class and religion as the main source of collective identity. While this divides linguistic/cultural communities from one another, it also strengthens inner-group cohesion. As a result, cantons within the same linguistic group increasingly pool their resources and act collectively, while their relations with the cantons across the language line continue to diminish. Since Lüthy's times, the workings of Swiss federalism have come to reflect this ethno-linguistic divide. Switzerland is increasingly becoming a federation of two major linguistic communities, together with the smaller Ticinesi and Romansch-speakers. A recent collection of interviews with leading figures in Swiss public life shows how deep the divisions have become.[44] The recurring theme in this collection is the "Röstigraben" or "fossé" between German Swiss and Swiss Romands.

Despite the growing pressures towards congruence, formal change has been moderate. In his incisive study of Swiss politics, Jonathan Steinberg notes that the Swiss political system is not characterized by a propensity for large-scale change; as he puts it, "the system shuns conflict and hence very unwillingly takes hard decisions, and never quickly".[45] Consequently, change comes through the way the federal system functions, not through major institutional reform. Swiss federal institutions are still not fully congruent with the constituent ethno-linguistic communities, and a broad reform in that direction seems unlikely for the time being. However, in the workings of the system, particularly in the fields of education and mass media, congruence is well advanced. As Gonzague de Reynold remarked in 1938: "The principle of Switzerland, its roots, its reason for existence, its value, its originality, is federalism. Switzerland will be federalist, or it will not be."[46] The federalism de Reynold talked about was the territorially decentralized variant designed to disperse political power symmetrically amongst the cantons; the statement still holds, but the federalism in question is now increasingly a multinational one.

7 The political sociology of federalism

The political sociology of federalism

Explaining Federalism is a study that puts society before the state. This brings the approach closer to the political sociology tradition. According to Reinhard Bendix and Seymour Martin Lipset, "political science starts with the state and examines how it affects society, while political sociology starts with society and examines how it affects the state."[1] Giovanni Sartori has also drawn attention to the different approaches that political sociology and political science employ: "The independent variables – causes, determinants, or factors – of the sociologist are, basically, *social* structures, while the independent variables – causes, determinants, or factors – of the political scientist are, basically, *political* structures."[2] Therefore, it is only natural that structuralist approaches are more prevalent in sociology.[3]

Due to its emphasis on how social structures influence politics, one could classify the argument put forward in this five-country study as the political sociology of federalism. From structural-functionalism to Marxism, theoretical perspectives of structuralist persuasion used to be fairly influential in political science. In recent decades, however, they have lost the centrality they once enjoyed in comparative politics. These grand theories came to be seen to suffer from structural determinism, and the literature embraced other approaches that stress "choice" instead. But macro-social work emphasizing structural constraints and opportunities did not entirely disappear. One example is Gregory Luebbert's study on social classes and the origins of political regimes. Luebbert's analysis uses social structure as the key factor in explaining the political differences among European countries. He expresses his findings in unequivocal terms by stating that "leadership and meaningful choice played no role in the outcomes."[4] Outcomes were dependent on the class alliances and not on the choices of the decision-makers: "I have found little evidence that similarly situated leaders responded differently, or at least with different levels of success, to similar inherited inducements and constraints."[5] Stefano Bartolini's study of the European left and the class cleavage is yet another example of structuralist political sociology. Bartolini states that his investigation looks at "the environmental constraints and macrosocial features of the political system and leaves little room, if any, to the study of the individual or collective actors' motivations, choices and strategies."[6] Colin Crouch prefers another term to describe structuralist political sociology: "The sociology of politics ... refers to deeper, less accessible structures within society which impart differential kind and levels of power to different social interests, which tend to be difficult to change through deliberate action."[7]

As a result of their bold claims and generalizations, structuralists frequently come under criticism – mostly on the question of social determinism. In an edited volume on the state of comparative politics, Mark Lichbach scathingly summarizes the shortcomings of structuralism that he identifies:[8]

> Given structure, outcomes follow. Structural causes are so powerful that everything becomes predictable: there are imperatives and not possibilities, dictates and not contingencies. To structuralists, in sum, structure is fate. This perspective leads to historical fatalism, an iron cage determinism, and the absence of voluntarism.

While sharing the same emphasis on social structures, the approach of this book is somewhat softer than in the earlier generation of structuralist works. The preceding case studies demonstrate the choices and the constraints facing political actors that were strongly influenced by the broad societal set-up. The findings show that the societal structure predisposed decision-makers towards demarcating their political communities in line with the ethno-linguistic structure, and thereby not only constraining the options available to them but also providing opportunities. The book tries to avoid iron-cage determinism by bringing in contingency as a way to operationalize the argument on congruence. Social structures need decisions made by actors to be translated into political outcomes; in this context, political actors and contingency play the role of a filter between broad structural pressures and outcomes. In all five cases, evidence shows that options available to political actors were influenced by the ethno-linguistic composition of the society.

The question of empirical evidence brings us to another strategy to deal with the risk of determinism: it is imperative for structuralist studies to carry out extensive and in-depth empirical investigation that would convincingly establish whether or not the political patterns proposed have really taken place. Unless macro-social structural theories are supported by detailed examination, their arguments will remain defenseless against accusations of structural determinism. A related question is that of generalizability: can the political sociology of federalism explain the broad patterns of continuity and change in other federal systems as well?

Does the political sociology of federalism work elsewhere?

The United States

The origins of federalism in the United States date back to the confederation between the thirteen former colonies that followed the 1776 Declaration of Independence. The confederation formally came into being in 1781, but ended up being a short-lived experiment; it was replaced by a new federal constitution in 1787 which allowed for a stronger national government. John Jay – sharing the pseudonym "Publius" with Alexander Hamilton and James Madison – wrote a series of articles supporting the ratification of the new constitution that came to be known as the Federalist Papers. His writings give a clear indication that the framers of the constitution had a unitary understanding of the American nation:[9]

> Providence has been pleased to give this one connected country to one united people, a people descended from the same ancestors, speaking the same language, professing the same religion, attached to the same principles of government, very similar in their manners and customs.

Despite the centralist move, the 1787 constitution allowed the constituent states to retain considerable powers, notably over education and the press. The federal government, on the other hand, acquired stronger powers than its confederal predecessor. For the following 100 years the American federal system remained a "dual" one, where the two levels of government retained separate areas of responsibility over which they enjoyed exclusive jurisdiction.

Starting around the turn of the nineteenth century, the two levels of government entered the phase of "cooperative" federalism, pooling their efforts in order to provide the public services that modern mass politics demanded. The joint efforts increased as the country tried to deal with the problems of the Great Depression and the new responsibilities expected from government. According to Joseph Zimmerman, "the overall trend since the 1930s is in the direction of policy-making centralization in the Congress and administration of national policies by state and local governments."[10] The New Deal program of the 1930s and the creation of national standards brought about uniform national public policies in many areas. Some believe that state governments were simply not equipped to deal with the demands of modern politics.[11] The process towards centralization culminated in President Lyndon B. Johnson's announcement of the "Great Society" program in 1964. National goals and standards were set in all areas of public life, and education was a key element of this program. One of the first initiatives was the Elementary and Secondary Education Act of 1965. Observers at that time interpreted the Great Society program as part of a general move towards a unitary politics. According to James Sundquist, "the nation for decades has been coalescing into a national society."[12] Sundquist saw this not as a presidential initiative, but as a nationwide tendency towards unity: "the Great

Society is, by definition, one society: the phrase is singular, not plural."[13] Even proponents of a more decentralist federal order along Jeffersonian lines acknowledged the broad tendencies. As Morton Grodzins and Daniel Elazar put it: "The role of the national government as an emulator is fostered by the nationwide communication network and the nationwide political process which produce demands for national minimum standards."[14] Mel Dubnick and Alan Gitelson show that the nationalization of American public policies has run parallel to the expansion of federal spending and jurisdiction.[15]

In somewhat abated form, the process towards nationwide policies continued into the 1980s. In the field of education, the 1983 Report of the National Commission on Education, entitled "A Nation at Risk," gave voice to the broad support Americans had for a unitary approach to education. In general terms, however, the centralization process in American federalism slowed down during Ronald Reagan's presidency, although Reagan's advocacy of state rights has been interpreted by some as a partisan attempt to cut down social spending rather than a genuine realignment of federal–state responsibilities.[16] Regardless of differing interpretations, a great deal of de facto harmonization between education and media policies of the states defines the contemporary picture. This renders unnecessary a further push towards *de jure* standardization along German and Austrian lines. Education continues to be seen in nationwide terms. A recent example is the January 2002 Education Bill, which committed 26 billion dollars of new federal spending to education. This federal measure came about through bipartisan activism in Washington, and enjoys widespread support among the states.

Despite the differences between North America and Europe, and despite American "exceptionalism,"[17] it is still possible to see the logic of congruence at play in American politics – in terms of both actual developments and also the observations made by students of American federalism. Thomas Dye points out the importance attached to the content of public polices rather than the issue of jurisdictional control: "Most debates over federalism [in the United States] are only lightly camouflaged debates over policy.... Citizens as well as political leaders consistently subordinate constitutional questions to immediate policy concerns."[18] This observation is echoed by David Nice: "Most people [in the United States] have little interest in abstract debates that argue which level of government should be responsible for a given task. What most people care about is getting the policies they want."[19] The most explicit recognition of the process of congruence comes from Harry Scheiber, who believes that there was an "incongruent fit" of states' authority and the problems to be addressed, which then paved the way for calls for nationwide solutions: "increasingly, the territorial reach of the states' individual jurisdictions was incongruent with the dimensions of the policy problems to be addressed. Over time, this changing situation generated strong pressures for centralization."[20]

Without territorially based ethno-linguistic distinctiveness, the American society is similar to the non-federal German and Austrian societies. As Samuel H. Beer puts it:

The existence of states makes the United States a compound republic. But while the republic is compound, the nation is unitary. The nation is that "one people" who bring the republic into existence and who govern themselves by means of its institutions for the sake of their "increase" as a nation.[21]

There are often bitter conflicts between states and the federal government, but with a satisfactory degree of harmonization between state laws and a fairly strong political centre, it is natural that the question of content rather than control dominates the field of public policy. To quote Samuel H. Beer again:[22]

Overwhelmingly ... most Americans treat federalism – that is, a territorial allocation of authority secured by constitutional guarantees – as a means to an end, not as an end in itself. The question that moves individuals and groups in the political arena is not which government proposes to act, but what action some government proposes to take.

Spain

Federalism in Spain exists without the constitutional form of a federation. However, this should not stop us from examining whether the political sociology of federalism could help us to explain the political patterns in Spain. Regardless of the absence of the constitutional label, there are strong federal characteristics in the 1978 system of the State of Autonomous Communities (*estado de las autonomías*).[23] At the end of the day, according to Michael Burgess, "the *absence* of federation should not blind one to the *presence* of federalism."[24] Thus, it is not uncommon for Spain to be examined through a federal perspective.[25] The brief overview below suggests that the pattern towards congruence between political institutions and the ethno-linguistic social structure can also be seen in the Spanish experience with federalism.

The Spanish federalization process ran parallel to the democratization of the country. Following the death of General Franco, a new constitution was adopted in 1978 which provided the so-called "historical nationalities" with the right of autonomy. Catalonia, the Basque provinces and Galicia had passed autonomy statutes during the second Spanish Republic (1931–36), hence their "historical" claim for autonomy. However, the constitutional right to autonomy led all the Spanish regions to follow the path of the historical nationalities of Catalonia, the Basque provinces and Galicia, and to adopt statutes of autonomy. Some of these Castilian-speaking (those who speak the mainstream Spanish vernacular) Autonomous Communities correspond to historical principalities like Leon and Andalucia; others, like Cantabria, Murcia and La Rioja, are artificial new creations. Currently there are seventeen Autonomous Communities, but their powers are widely different.

In this federal society, there appears to be a process towards congruence between the underlying ethno-linguistic structure and the policy-making in the areas of education and media. Catalonia, the Basque provinces and Galicia run their own educational systems.[26] There is more symmetry among the fourteen remaining Castilian-speaking regions, who have largely standardized many of their educational policies. The same process has also taken place in the field of mass media. On 31 December 1982, the Basque public broadcasting corporation ETB was set up; this was followed by the Catalan TV3 in 1983 and the Galician Broadcasting Corporation on 24 July 1985, while the rest of Castilian-speaking Spain mostly relied on the TVE.[27] These developments led a number of observers to label the Spanish State of Autonomous Communities an asymmetrical system of federalism.[28] The asymmetrical character of Spanish federalism has emerged in piecemeal fashion rather than as a product of a grand constitutional design – in other words, federalism has emerged through an "inductive allocation of resources."[29] At one point, the two largest parties of the Spanish center, the Center Right UCD and the Socialist PSOE, tried to impose uniformity on the Autonomy Statutes in terms of the powers granted to the Autonomous Communities. Consequently, a bill entitled Organic Law on the Harmonization of the Autonomy Process (*Ley Orgánica del Armonización de Process Autonómico*, LOAPA) was tabled in the Cortes in September 1981. However, in its 1983 ruling the Spanish Constitutional Court (*Tribunal Constitucional*) found parts of the Organic Law to be unconstitutional, which led the Spanish government to withdraw the bill. Since then, the Spanish federalization process has moved further in the direction of devising institutions to correspond to underlying ethno-linguistic structures. According to Luis Moreno: "As in other plural states, regional devolution in Spain seeks to articulate a response to the stimuli of diversity and plurality of society, comprising minority nations and regions with differences of language, history or traditions."[30]

Australia

While Spain has elements of a federal society, Australia is closer to Germany and Austria in terms of its ethno-linguistic homogeneity. The Commonwealth of Australia was created in 1901 as result of a process starting with the constitutional convention of 1890 to unite the seven antipodean colonies of the British Crown. During the first meeting of the so-called Australasian Federation Convention, its President, Sir Henry Parkes, proposed a toast to "One People, One Destiny," which later became the slogan of the pro-federation forces. Due to geographic concerns, New Zealand was not included in the final design. After a decade of negotiations, the Commonwealth of Australia was inaugurated on 1 January 1901. The citizens of this new country were almost exclusively of Anglo-Celtic background. One of the forefathers of the Australian Commonwealth and its first Prime Minister, Edmund Barton, declared that for the first time in history there was an opportunity to "have a nation for a continent and a continent for a nation."[31]

Australia has no territorially based diversity which corresponds to the demarcations of the six constituent states of the Commonwealth. For a long time, the most important politically salient social cleavage remained class – which is a nationwide phenomenon. There seems to be little regional identification, and there is a high degree of geographic mobility.[32] Without territorially defined distinctiveness, according to Lawrence Mayer, the Australian political system remains formally federal with nationwide political divisions: "Australia has some [economic and cultural] diversities but they are not territorially defined. Thus, Australia may be classified as a 'relatively homogeneous society.' And the federal system imposed on such a society has been defined as 'formalistic.' "[33] In his comparative study on federalism, William Riker found Australia to be the most homogeneous federal system:[34]

> The divisions in Australian culture seem to be economic and religious with hardly any geographic base. Hence there also seems to be an Australian patriotism unobstructed by loyalties to states. Indeed, of all federations now in existence, Australia seems less in need of appeasing subordinate patriotisms than any other government. One wonders, indeed, why they bother with federalism in Australia.

William Livingston had similar words to say: "Indeed one is sometimes tempted to wonder why the Australians retain their federal system. The Australians often wonder about this also."[35] In the context, it comes no surprise that the workings of the federation are more unitary than the constitution suggests.

Many national policies in Australia were put in place through circumventing the constitution. In their study of the Australian welfare state and federalism, Francis Castles and John Uhr document how the Commonwealth persuaded the states to implement national programs in areas under state jurisdiction.[36] Parallel to this, the ad hoc meetings between premiers and state ministers were gradually formalized, and a working system very similar to the one between the German Länder and the Bund emerged. Ministerial Councils established between state governments pursued standardization around uniform national legislation. For example, the Ministers of Education from both the states and the Commonwealth sat together in the Australian Education Council, which was set up to develop "collective approaches to education policy."[37] Joan Rydon calls this the joint effort of the Commonwealth and states in "getting round the Constitution":[38]

> Commonwealth governments have been able, by agreement with the states, by parallel legislation or by the establishment of joint authorities, to participate in projects and affect developments far outside the limited range of matters on which they have constitutional power to legislate, and have even established ministries in fields such as education and health which appear entirely matters for the state.

Australian political parties, as representatives of class interests, have been instrumental in bringing about nationwide approaches to public policy concerns.

The Australian Labor Party is particularly critical of the federal structure, which they see as incoherent and wasteful.[39] Similar centralist tendencies also exist on the right. The Liberal/National coalition also seeks national policies, but its concern has largely been the establishment of national standards and legislation to minimize the economic costs of federalism in terms of differing state regulations which interfere with the free movement of factors of production.[40] Even if its frame of reference is still a national one, the non-Labor coalition tends to follow a right-wing program of small government, privatization and deregulation which is at odds with the Labor party's vision of national policies. As a result, the nationwide approach to public policy has not been a controversial issue in itself, but the contents of policies have often divided the Australian political landscape.

Australian politics have traditionally revolved around national issues with two political blocks facing one another. In this federation with a "non-federal society," media and education have consequently become nationwide policies despite state jurisdiction over these policy areas. For most Australians, federalism is not a major concern; political issues are national and the constituent states of the Australian Commonwealth are largely seen as intermediary layers of public administration in the implementation of national policies.

The above examination of the three remaining federal experiences in the industrialized world provides some further support for the theory of congruence. The brief overview exposes some of the processes of congruence at play, and also indicates the directions where further research might produce interesting findings concerning federalism and institutional change. The next step could be the construction of a comprehensive study based on all eight cases of federalism in the industrialized West, and policy areas other than education and media.

Notes

Preface

1 William H. Riker (1964), *Federalism: Origin, operation, significance*, Boston: Little, Brown, and Company, p. xii.

1 Federalism and congruence

1 Paul Pierson (1995), "Fragmented Welfare States: Federal Institutions and Development of Social Policy," *Governance*, Vol. 8, No. 4, p. 450; Jan Erk (2006), "Does Federalism Really Matter?" *Comparative Politics*, Vol. 39, No. 1 (2006), p. 116.
2 For a discussion of the prescriptive license in federalism scholarship, see Jan Erk (2007), "Federalism as a Growth Industry," *Publius: The Journal of Federalism*, Vol. 37.
3 Thomas O. Hueglin (1999), *Early Modern Concepts for a Late Modern World: Althusius on Community and Federalism*, Waterloo, Ontario: Wilfrid Laurier University Press.
4 Johannes Althusius (1964) [1614], *The Politics of Johannes Althusius*, translated by Frederick S. Carney, an abridged translation of the Third Edition (1614) of *Politica Methodice Digesta, Atque Exemplis Sacris Et Profanis Illustrata*, Boston: Beacon Press, p. ix.
5 The origins of federalism in the United States date back to the confederation between the thirteen former colonies that followed the 1776 declaration of independence. The confederation was formalized in 1781, but it was replaced by a new federal constitution in 1787 which allowed for a stronger national government. During the ratification process of the new federal constitution, a series of letters supporting federalism were published by Alexander Hamilton, James Madison and John Jay under the pseudonym *Publius*. These letters later came to be known as the "Federalist Papers." See Alexander Hamilton, James Madison and John Jay (1961) [1787], *The Federalist Papers*, Clinton Rossiter (ed.), New York: Mentor.
6 See Daniel Ziblatt (2006), Structuring the State: The Formation of Italy and Germany and the Puzzle of Federalism, Princeton: Princeton University Press.
7 Karl Renner (under the *nom de plume* Rudolf Springer) (1902), *Der Kampf der österreichischen Nationen um den Staat*, Vienna and Leipzig; Otto Bauer (1924) [1907], *Die Nationalitätenfrage und die Sozialdemokratie*, Vienna.
8 A.V. Dicey (1915) [1885], *Introduction to the Study of the Law of the Constitution*, London.
9 Laski wrote the article after a visit to the United States. It is a critical assessment of the federal government's ability to manage the political economy of large-scale capitalism. Harold Laski (1939), "The Obsolescence of Federalism," *New Republic*, Vol. 3, pp. 367–369.
10 Ronald Watts (1994), "Contemporary Views on Federalism," in Bertus de Villiers (ed.), *Evaluating Federal Systems*, Dordrecht, Boston and London: Martinus Nijhoff, p. 2.
11 K.C. Wheare (1946), *Federal Government*, London: Oxford University Press.

12 Pierre-Joseph Proudhon (1863), *Du principe fédératif et de la nécessité de reconstituer le parti de la revolution*, Paris: E. Dentu. For an English translation, see Richard Vernon (ed.) (1979), *The Principle of Federation*, Toronto: University of Toronto Press.

13 The work of Garth Stevenson on Canadian federalism is one example. According to Stevenson, different industrial interests have dominated different levels of government and have therefore shaped the workings of federalism in Canada; Garth Stevenson (1982), *Unfulfilled Union: Canadian Federalism and National Unity*, Toronto: Gage. A similar political economy approach which sees class conflict as central to the workings of federal systems is employed by Alain-G Gagnon and Mary-Beth Montcalm (1990), *Québec: Beyond the Quiet Revolution*, Scarborough, Ontario: Nelson. See also Thomas O. Hueglin (1990), *A Political Economy of Federalism: In Search of a New Comparative Perspective with Critical Intent Throughout*, Kingston, Ontario: Institute of Intergovernmental Relations, Queen's University.

14 William S. Livingston (1952), "A Note on the Nature of Federalism," *Political Science Quarterly*, Vol. 67, p. 84.

15 Michael Stein (1971), "Federal Political Systems and Federal Societies," in J. Peter Meekison (ed.), *Canadian Federalism: Myth or Reality?* Second Edition, Toronto: Methuen, p. 34.

16 Donald V. Smiley (1983), "Federal Society and Federal Government," in Smiley, *Canada in Question: Federalism in the Eighties*, Third Edition, Toronto: McGraw-Hill Ryerson, p. 1.

17 Charles D. Tarlton (1965), "Symmetry and Asymmetry as Elements of Federalism: A Theoretical Speculation," *The Journal of Politics*, Vol. 27, p. 869.

18 Aaron Wildavsky (1967), "Party Discipline under Federalism: Implications of the Australian Experience," in Aaron Wildavsky (ed.), *American Federalism in Perspective*, Boston: Little, Brown and Company, p. 178.

19 Will Kymlicka (1998), *Finding Our Way: Rethinking Ethnocultural Relations in Canada*, Toronto: Oxford University Press, Ch. 10; Philip Resnick (1994), "Towards a Multination Federalism," in Leslie Seidle (ed.), *Seeking a New Canadian Partnership: Asymmetrical and Confederal Options*, Montreal: Institute for Research on Public Policy, p. 71. More recently, Wayne Norman has drawn attention to the different *raison d'êtres* behind territorial and. multinational federalism; Wayne Norman (2006), *Negotiating Nationalism: Nation-Building, Federalism and Secession in the Multinational State*, Oxford: Oxford University Press, p. 87.

20 Thomas Koelble (1995), "The New Institutionalism in Political Science and Sociology," *Comparative Politics*, Vol. 27; Jonas Pontusson (1995), "From Comparative Public Policy to Political Economy: Putting Political Institutions in their Place and Taking Interests Seriously," *Comparative Political Studies*, Vol. 28, p. 1; Sven Steinmo, Kathleen Thelen and Frank Longstreth (eds) (1992), *Structuring Politics: Historical Institutionalism in Comparative Analysis*, Cambridge: Cambridge University Press; Kent Weaver and Steve Rockman (eds) (1993), *Do Institutions Matter? Government Capabilities in the United States and Abroad*, Washington: Brookings Institute.

21 Richard Simeon (1977), "Regionalism and Canadian Political Institutions," in J. Peter Meekison (ed.), *Canadian Federalism: Myth or Reality?* Third Edition, Toronto: Methuen, p. 297.

22 Douglas North (1990), "Institutions and Their Consequences for Economic Performance," in Karen Schweers Cook and Margaret Levi (eds), *The Limits of Rationality*, Chicago and London: University of Chicago Press, p. 383.

23 For example, see Pauline Jones Luong (2002), *Institutional Change and Political Continuity in Post-Soviet Central Asia*, Cambridge: Cambridge University Press.

24 Wolfgang Streeck and Kathleen Thelen (2005), "Introduction: Institutional Change in Advanced Political Economies," in Wolfgang Streeck and Kathleen Thelen (eds), *Beyond Continuity: Institutional Change in Advanced Political Econmies*, New York and London: Oxford University Press, p. 1.

25 Richard Simeon (1989), "We are all Smiley's People: Some Observations on Donald Smiley and the Study of Federalism," in David P. Shugarman and Reg Whitaker (eds), *Federalism and Political Community: Essays in Honor of Donald Smiley*, Peterborough, Ontario: Broadview Press, pp. 418–419.

26 Erik Wibbels (2005), *Federalism and the Market: Intergovernmental Conflict and Economic Reform in the Developing World*, Cambridge and New York: Cambridge University Press, p. 16.

27 Erik Wibbels (2006), "Madison in Baghdad? Decentralization and Federalism in Comparative Politics," *Annual Review of Political Science*, Vol. 9, p. 167.

28 J. Pontusson (1995), "From Comparative Public Policy to Political Economy," pp. 137–138.

29 Ibid., p. 142.

30 William H. Riker (1969), "Six Books in Search of a Subject or Does Federalism Exist and Does it Matter?" *Comparative Politics*, Vol. 2, No. 1, p. 146.

31 Carl J. Friedrich (1968), *Trends of Federalism in Theory and Practice*, New York: Praeger, p. 54.

32 The most important study on political cleavages was carried out by Seymour Martin Lipset and Stein Rokkan. The authors identified four sets of cleavages which left a mark on European politics. Two of these, state–church and center–periphery cleavages, resulted from national revolutions. The remaining two, land–industry and employer–worker cleavages, resulted from the industrial revolution; see: Seymour Martin Lipset and Stein Rokkan (1967), "Cleavage Structures, Party Systems, and Voter Alignments: An Introduction," in Seymour M. Lipset and Stein Rokkan (eds), *Party Systems and Voter Alignments: Cross-National Perspectives*, New York: Free Press, pp. 1–64. See also Douglas Rae and Michael Taylor (1970), *The Analysis of Political Cleavages*, New Haven, Connecticut: Yale University Press; Alan Zuckerman (1975), "Political Cleavages: A Conceptual and Theoretical Analysis," *British Journal of Political Science*, Vol. 5, No. 2, pp. 231–248.

33 Terry Nichols Clark and Seymour Martin Lipset (2001), *The Breakdown of Class Politics: A Debate on post-Industrial Stratification*, Baltimore: Johns Hopkins University Press; Geoffrey Evans (ed.) (1999), *The End of Class Politics: Class Voting in Comparative Context*, Oxford: Oxford University Press; Walter Korpi (1983), *The Democratic Class Struggle*, London: Routledge and Kegan Paul.

34 David Martin (1978), "The Religious Condition in Europe," in Salvador Giner and Margaret Scotford Archer (eds), *Contemporary Europe: Social Structure and Cultural Patterns*, London: Routledge and Kegan Paul, pp. 228–287; Hans Mol (ed.) (1972), *Western Religion: A Country by Country Sociological Inquiry*, The Hague: Mouton.

35 For a discussion of the increasing political role of language, see Jan Erk (2007), "Real Constitution, Formal Constitution, and Democracy in the European Union," *Journal of Common Market Studies*, Vol. 45, No. 3, pp. 633–652.

36 "La langue est un marqueur ethnique, mais c'est aussi l'instrument essentiel par lequel s'instaure et se maintient la vie démocratique," Dominique Schnapper (1994), *La communauté des citoyens: Sur l'idée moderne de nation*, Paris: Gallimard, p. 141.

37 Dominique Schnapper (2004), "Linguistic Pluralism as a Serious Challenge to Democratic Life," in Philippe van Parijs (ed.), *Cultural Diversity versus Economic Solidarity: Proceedings of the Seventh Franqui Colloqium*, Brussels: De Boeck Université, pp. 219–220.

38 Margaret Moore (2001), *The Ethics of Nationalism*, Oxford: Oxford University Press, p. 49.

39 Brian Barry (1991), *Democracy and Power: Essays in Political Theory I*, Oxford: Clarendon Press, p. 178.

40 Jeremy Webber (1994). *Reimagining Canada: Language, Culture, Community and the Canadian Constitution*, Montreal and Kingston: McGill-Queen's University Press, p. 200.

41 Ibid., p. 204.

42 European integration literature has produced works that employ the same logic to suggest that the lack of such a pan-European democratic base caps the extent of how far integration can proceed. This view is often known as the "no demos" argument. For the application of this concept to multinational societies, see: Philip Resnick (2003), "Un ou plusieurs Demos? Impératifs fédéraux ou confédéraux dans les États multinationaux," in Jules Duchastel (ed.), *Fédéralismes et mondialisation: l'avenir de la démocratie et de la citoyenneté*, Montreal: Athéna, pp. 199–214; Dieter Grimm (1995), "Does Europe Need a Constitution?" *European Law Journal*, Vol. 1, No. 3, pp. 282–302.

43 Gabriel A. Almond and Sidney Verba (1963), *The Civic Culture: Political Attitudes and Democracy in Five Nations*, Princeton: Princeton University Press, p. 21.

44 Harry Eckstein (1961). *A Theory of Stable Democracy*, originally published as Research Monograph Number 10 by the Center of International Studies, Princeton University, reprinted as appendix in H. Eckstein (1966), *Division and Cohesion in Democracy. A Study of Norway*, Princeton: Princeton University Press.

45 Ibid., p. 283.

46 Harry Eckstein (1966), *Division and Cohesion in Democracy: A Study of Norway*, Princeton: Princeton University Press, pp. 186–192, 232–241.

47 Ibid., p. 186.

48 For criticism of Eckstein's work, see in particular: Ronald Rogowski (1998), "Eckstein and the Study of Private Governments: An Appreciation, Critique, and Proposal," *Comparative Political Studies*: Special Issue: A Tribute to Harry Eckstein, Vol. 31, p. 4.

49 The work that comes closest to a general theory of congruence is one that Eckstein co-authored with Robert Ted Gurr. Harry Eckstein and Ted Robert Gurr (1975), *Patterns of Authority: A Structural Basis for Political Inquiry*, New York and Toronto: Wiley. See also Harry Eckstein (1973), "Authority Patterns: A Structural Basis for Political Inquiry," *American Political Science Review*, Vol. 68, p. 4.

50 Ernest Gellner (1983), *Nations and Nationalism*, New York: Cornell University Press, p. 1.

51 Writing on the limits of educational reform, Martin Carnoy and Henry M. Levin argue that, regardless of reforms, the educational system ultimately reflects the larger socio-economic context. The authors call this the "correspondence principle," and argue that education is embedded in the broader structure of corporate capitalism; Martin Carnoy and Henry M. Levin (1976), *Limits of Educational Reform*, New York and London: Longman, p. 23. A similar argument is put forward by Fred Siebert *et al.* in the field of media. The authors believe mass media always takes on the form of the socio-economic structure within which it operates, Fred S. Siebert, Theodore Peterson and Wilbur Schramm (1956), *Four Theories of the Press*, Urbana, Chicago and London: University of Illinois Press, p. 1.

52 Stefano Bartolini (2000), *The Political Mobilisation of the European Left 1860–1980: The Class Cleavage*, Cambridge: Cambridge University Press, p. 49.

53 Gregory M. Luebbert (1991), *Liberalism, Fascism, or Social Democracy: Social Classes and the Political Origins of Regimes in Interwar Europe*, New York and Oxford: Oxford University Press, pp. 306–307.

54 In his study on nationalism and citizenship in Germany and France, Rogers Brubaker notes the increasing centrality of identity politics in modern democracies. Rogers Brubaker (1992), *Citizenship and Nationhood in France and Germany*, Cambridge: Harvard University Press, p. 182.

55 Margaret Levi and Michael Hechter (1985), "A Rational Choice Approach to the Rise and Decline of Ethnoregional Political Parties," in Edward A. Tiryakian and Ronald Rogowski (eds), *New Nationalisms of the Developed West: Towards an Explanation*, Boston: Allen and Unwin; Donald Horowitz (1985), *Ethnic Groups in Conflict*,

Berkeley: University of California Press. Agency-based rational action models are prominent in other areas of comparative politics as well. For example, see Christoph Knill and Andrea Lenschow (2001), "Seek and Ye Shall Find: Linking Different Perspectives on Institutional Change," *Comparative Political Studies*, Vol. 34, No. 2; Joseph Colomer (ed.) (1991), *Journal of Theoretical Politics*, Special Issue, "The Strategy of Institutional Change," Vol. 13, No. 3; Rudra Sil (2000), "The Foundation of Eclecticism: The Epistemological Status of Agency, Culture, and Structure in Social Theory," *Journal of Theoretical Politics*, Vol. 12, No. 3.

56 According to Thomas Koelble, once ethnic identities congeal, it is very difficult to unmake them: "Once mobilized, ethnicity and nationalism can take on a quite independent character.... Once nationalism becomes an organizing principle, it has the ability to shape its environment and is capable of altering the context within which it arose." Thomas Koelble (1995), "Towards a Theory of Nationalism," *Nationalism and Ethnic Politics*, Vol. 1, No. 4, p. 85.

57 For a discussion of the theoretical tools used by macro-social perspectives, see: David D. Laitin (1998), "Towards a Political Science Discipline: Authority Patterns Revisited," *Comparative Political Studies*, Vol. 31, No. 4, p. 438.

58 Claus Offe (2003), *Herausforderungen der Demokratie: Zur Integrations und Leistungsfähigkeit politischer Institutionen*, Frankfurt: Campus Verlag, p. 8.

59 Giovanni Sartori (1969), "From the Sociology of Politics to Political Sociology," in Seymour Martin Lipset (ed.), *Politics and the Social Science*, New York: Oxford University Press, pp. 65–100; Colin Crouch (2001), "Breaking Open Black Boxes: The Implications for Sociological Theory of European Integration," in Anand Menon and Vincent Wright (eds), *From the Nation State to Europe? Essays in Honour of Jack Hayward*, Oxford: Oxford University Press, p. 197; S. Bartolini (2000), *The Political Mobilisation of the European Left*, p. 6.

60 All citations and quotations from primary sources are translated into English in the text, but the original forms in German, French and Dutch are provided in the footnotes for verification. All translations, including those from secondary sources, are the author's. In cases where the English equivalent fails to fully capture the meaning of a term, the original word is provided in brackets.

61 Theda Skocpol (1984), "Emerging Agendas and Recurrent Strategies in Historical Sociology," in Skocpol (ed.), *Vision and Method in Historical Sociology*, New York: Cambridge University Press.

62 Alexander George (1979), "Case Studies and Theory Development: The Method of Structured Focused Comparison," in Paul Gordon Lauren (ed.), *Diplomacy: New Approaches in History, Theory and Policy*, New York: Free Press.

63 Donald N. McCloskey (1991), "History, Differential Equations, and the Problem of Narration," *History and Theory*, Vol. 30, p. 22.

64 Robert H. Bates, Avner Grief, Margaret Levi, Jean Laurent Rosenthal, Barry R. Weingast (1998), *Analytic Narratives*, Princeton: Princeton University Press; Margaret Levi (1997), *Consent, Dissent and Patriotism*, Cambridge: Cambridge University Press.

65 M. Levi (1997), *Consent, Dissent and Patriotism*, p. 6.

66 This is point is made by Kiser as he refers to Philip Abrams (1982), *Historical Sociology*, Somerset: Open Books, pp. 211–212; in Edgar Kiser (1996), "The Revival of Narrative in Historical Sociology: What Rational Choice Theory Can Contribute," *Politics and Society*, Vol. 24, No. 3, p. 256.

67 M. Levi (1997), *Consent, Dissent and Patriotism*, p. 14.

68 Donald Green and Ian Shapiro (1994), *Pathologies of Rational Choice Theory*, New Haven and London: Yale University Press, p. 10.

69 John R. Bowen and Roger Petersen (1999), "Introduction: Critical Comparisons," in John R. Bowen and Roger Petersen (eds), *Critical Comparisons in Politics and Culture*, Cambridge: Cambridge University Press, p. 1.

70 William Riker (1990), "Political Science and Rational Choice," in James E. Alt and Kenneth A. Shepsle (eds), *Perspectives on Positive Political Economy*, Cambridge: Cambridge University Press, pp. 170–171.
71 Miriam Golden (1999), "Case Studies in Contemporary Job Loss," in John R. Bowen and Roger Petersen (eds), *Critical Comparisons in Politics and Culture*, Cambridge: Cambridge University Press, p. 116.

2 Austria

1 Josef Werndl (1984), *Die Kompetenzverteilung zwischen Bund und Ländern: Ihre Ausgangslage, Entwicklung und Bedeutungsverschiebung auf der Grundlage des Bundesverfassungsgesetzes von 1920*, Vienna: Wilhelm Braumüller, p. 13; Ludwig K. Adamovich and Bernd-Christian Funk (1984), *Österreichisches Verfassungrecht*, Second Edition, New York and Vienna: Springer, pp. 110–111; Karl Ucakar (1991), "Verfassung: Geschichte und Prinzipien," in Herbert Dachs, Peter Gerlich, Herbert Gottweis, Franz Horner, Helmut Kramer, Volkmar Laubner, Wolfgang C. Müller and Emerich Tálos (eds), *Handbuch des Politischen Systems Österreichs*, Third Edition, Vienna: Mansche, p. 92.
2 For example, see Ludwig K. Adamovich, Bernd-Christian Funk and Gerhart Holzinger (1997), *Österreichisches Staatsrecht, Bands I und II*, New York and Vienna: Springer, pp. 129, 161; Anton Pelinka and Sieglinde Rosenberger (2000), *Österreichische Politik: Grundlagen, Strukturen, Trends*, Vienna: WUV, p. 25.
3 The author has used the social structure-based perspective in the examination of Austrian federalism before, see Jan Erk (2004), "Austria: A Federation without Federalism," *Publius: The Journal of Federalism*, Vol. 34, No. 1, pp. 1–20.
4 Quoted in Josef Langer (1999), "Last in, First out? – Austria's Place in the Transformation of National Identity," in Hanspeter Kriesi, Klaus Armingeon, Hannes Siegrist and Andreas Wimmer (eds), *Nation and National Identity: The European Experience in Perspective*, Zurich and Chur: Ruegger, p. 153.
5 Some of these crown lands, however, were divided at the Saint Germain peace treaty at the end of World War I. The region of South Tyrol was given to Italy, while the region of Lower Styria was given to the new Yugoslav state. The two German-speaking regions of Moravia and Bohemia became part of the new Czechoslovakia. The region of Carinthia was also created by the Saint Germain treaty as the former province of Klagenfurt was carved up. Most of Burgenland, which joined the federation in 1922, historically belonged to the Hungarian side of the Habsburgs. Vienna was part of the province of Lower Austria until 29 December 1921.
6 For an overview of the anti-Vienna sentiments in the rest of the country, see Charles A. Gulick (1948), *Austria: From Habsburg to Hitler, Volume I: Labor's Workshop of Democracy*, with a foreword by Walter Federn, Berkeley and Los Angeles: University of California Press, p. 94.
7 For detailed accounts of the constitutional settlement, see Robert Walter (1984), *Die Entstehung des Bundesverfassungsgesetzes 1920 in der Konstituierenden Nationalversammlung*, Vienna: Mansche; Reinhard Owerdieck (1987), *Parteien und Verfassungsfrage in Österreich: Die Entstehung des Verfassungsprovisoriums der Ersten Republik 1918–1920*, Munich: R. Oldenbourg; Felix Ermacora (1989), *Materialen zur österreichischen Bundesverfassung: Die Länderkonferenzen 1919/20 und die Verfassungsfrage*, Vienna: Wilhelm Braumüller; Felix Ermacora (1967), *Quellen zum österreichischen Verfassungsrecht (1920)*, Vienna: Ferdinand Berger und Söhne. In English see Rudolf Schlesinger (1945), *Federalism in Central and Eastern Europe*, London: Kegan Paul, pp. 248–274, and C. Gulick (1948), *Austria: From Habsburg to Hitler*, pp. 84–111.
8 Among students of Austrian federalism there is a long-standing disagreement as to whether the Länder were created by devolving the powers of the central government

or whether the collective action of the Länder created the Bund. These two approaches are respectively referred to as the decentralization theory of the Vienna School, and the compact theory closer to the point of view of the Länder. Classic texts for the decentralization school are: Hans Kelsen (1925), *Allgemeine Staatslehre*, Berlin: Julius Springer, p. 207; and Hans Kelsen (1970) [1923], *Österreichisches Staatsrecht: Ein Grundriss Entwicklungsgeschichtlich Dargestellt*, Tübingen: Scientia. A contemporary example of this approach is Robert Walter and Heinz Mayer (2000), *Grundriß des österreichischen Bundesverfassungsrechts*, Ninth Edition, Vienna: Manzche, pp. 54–55, 78–79. Examples of the opposing interpretation are: Peter Pernthaler (1992), "Zum Begriff von Föderalismus und Bundesstaat in Österrreich," in Herbert Schambeck (ed.), *Föderalismus und Parlamentarismus in Österreich*, Vienna: Österreichische Staatsdruckerei, pp. 47–49; Felix Ermacora (1976), *Österreichischer Föderalismus: Vom patrimonialen zum kooperativen Bundesstaat*, Vienna: Wilhelm Braumüller; and Herbert Schambeck (1984), "Entwicklungstendenzen und Perspectiven des Föderalismus in Österreich," in Stephan Koren, Karl Pisa and Kurt Waldheim (eds), *Politik für die Zukunft*, Vienna and Cologne: Herman Böhlaus, pp. 139–154.

9 In addition to the Länder question, the federal constitution of 1920 also reflects the compromise between the two political parties and the respective Lager they represented. The strength of Socialists in Vienna and Christian-Socials in the remaining Länder accentuated the federal dynamics. See: Bernd-Christian Funk (1996), *Einführung in das österreichische Verfassungsrecht*, Graz: Leykam, p. 78. Rainer Nick believes that party politics lie at the core of the initial compromise: Rainer Nick (1988), "Die Bundesländer und das österreichische Parteiensystem," Anton Pelinka and Fritz Plasser (eds), *Das österreichische Parteiensystem*, Vienna, Cologne and Graz: Böhlau, pp. 402–403. This point is also made by Herbert Schambeck (1992), "Zum Werden und zu den Aufgaben des österreichischen Föderalismus," in Herbert Schambeck (ed.), *Föderalismus und Parlamentarismus in Österreich*, Vienna: Österreichische Staatsdruckerei, pp. 18–19. Felix Ermacora, on the other hand, believes that federalism was about political parties more than the Länder; F. Ermacora (1976), *Österreichischer Föderalismus*, p. 52.

10 The National Assembly is now composed of 183 members elected for four years. Before 1970, the number was 165. Since 1992, political parties have to exceed a 4 percent national threshold to be represented. The Federal Chancellor heads the parliamentary government, while the Federal President fulfills a largely ceremonial role as the head of state.

11 Members of the Bundesrat are elected by provincial parliaments. The smallest Land has three seats at the Bundesrat while the most populous Land has twelve seats. All other Länder have between three and twelve seats in proportion to their populations. Currently, the Bundesrat is composed of 64 seats.

12 There was also a much smaller third Lager representing Liberal-Nationalists. Initially the Liberal-Nationalist camp was the smallest, and represented anticlerical middle-class views with strong pan-German leanings. They later gained strength and as the Großdeutsche Volkspartei became the main force behind the push to join Nazi Germany. After World War II, the Liberal-Nationalists re-emerged as the union of Independents (*Verband der Unabhängigen*), and in 1955 they renamed themselves the Austrian Freedom Party (*Freiheitliche Partei Österreichs*, FPÖ). For further information, see: Adam Wandruszka (1977) [1954], "Östrreichs Politische Struktur. Die Entwicklung der Parteien und politischen Bewgungen," in Heinrich Benedikt (ed.), *Geschichte der Republik Österreich*, Vienna: Verlag für Geschichte und Politik, pp. 289–348.

13 The SPÖ (*Sozialistischepartei Österreichs*) was set up as the continuation of the *Sozialdemokratische Arbeiterpartei* created in 1874. In 1991, the party was renamed the *Sozialdemokratische Partei Österreichs*.

14 The ÖVP (*Österreichische Volkspartei*) was created in 1945 as a continuation of the *Christlich-Soziale Partei*. Along Catholic corporatist principles, it is composed of three estates (*Bünde*): the *Österreichischer Arbeiter- und Angestelltenbund*, the *Österreichischer Bauernbund*, and the *Österreichischer Wirtschaftbund*. See Wolfgang C. Müller (1997), "Die Österreichische Volkspartei," in Herbert Dachs, Peter Gerlich, Herbert Gottweis, Franz Hormer, Helmut Kramer, Volkmar Lauber, Wolfgang C. Müller and Emmerich Tálos (eds), *Handbuch des politischen System Österreich*, Third Edition, Vienna: Manzche, p. 908.

15 The theory of consociational democracy seeks to explain political stability in divided societies by using the notions of an elite cartel, proportional representation, grand coalitions, and depoliticisation. For Austria, see Gerhard Lehmbruch (1967), *Proporzdemokratie: Politisches System und politische Kultur in der Schweiz und in Österreich*, Tübingen: J.C.B. Mohr; Kurt Richard Luther and Wolfgang C. Müller (1992), "Consociationalism and the Austrian Political System," *West European Politics*, Vol. 15, No. 1, pp. 1–15.

16 Fried Esterbauer (1976), *Kriterien föderativer und konföderativer Systeme unter besonderer Berücksichtigung Österreichs und der Europäischen Gemeinschaften*, Vienna: Wilhelm Braumüller, p. 87.

17 "Die politischen Subsysteme der Parteien, Verbände, Kommunicationsmedien und der öffentlichen Meinung setzen sich in Österreich mehr als in anderen Bundesstaaten aus überwiegend antiföderalistischen Kräften zusammen," Ibid. p. 87.

18 For further information on Vienna's unique position, see Herbert Obinger (2005), "Austria: Strong Parties in a Weak Federal Polity," in Herbert Obinger, Stephan Leibfried and Francis G. Castles (eds), *Federalism and the Welfare State: New World and European Experiences*, Cambridge: Cambridge University Press, p. 193

19 An interesting point to note is that Austrian voters often prefer to vote for different parties in Land elections than for the one they vote in federal elections. For example, during the three-term Socialist majority government between 1971 and 1983, voters opted for ÖVP majorities in seven of the Länder.

20 Bundesrat members are not directly elected but are appointed by provincial parliaments (*Landtage*). Despite its *raison d'être* as the assembly for Länder representatives, Fried Esterbauer argues that the Bundesrat quickly became an institution representing political party interests instead; F. Esterbauer (1976), *Kriterien föderativer und konföderativer Systeme*, p. 91; Wolfgang C. Müller (1992), "Austrian Governmental Institutions: Do They Matter?" *West European Politics*, Vol. 15, No. 1, pp. 123–124.

21 Riker argued that the dynamics of a federal system can be best explained by the political party structure. According to Riker, federations where unified political parties exist at both levels of government face centralizing tendencies – in contrast with federations, where different political parties exist at the two levels; William H. Riker (1964), *Federalism: Origin, Operation, Significance*, Boston and Toronto: Little, Brown and Company.

22 From Gottfried Heindl, *Die Republik und ihr Rundfunk* (unpublished manuscript), cited in Norbert Feldinger (1990), *Nachkriegsrundfunk in Österreich: Zwischen Föderalismus und Zentralismus von 1945 bis 1957*, Munich: Saur, p. 168.

23 "Ein Vergleich des politischen Ist-Zustandes mit der Verfassung führt notwendigerweise zur Feststellung einer Diskrepanz, eines Spannungsverhältnisses zwischen Verfassung und politischer Wirklichkeit," Anton Pelinka (1971), "Parteien und Verbände," in Herbert Dachs, Peter Gerlich, Herbert Gottweis, Franz Hormer, Helmut Kramer, Volkmar Lauber, Wolfgang C. Müller and Emmerich Tálos (eds), *Demokratie und Verfassung in Österreich*, Vienna, Frankfurt and Zurich: Europa, p. 326.

24 Theo Öhlinger, "Centralizing and Decentralizing Trends in the Austrian Constitution," C. Lloyd Brown-John (ed.), *Centralizing and Decentralizing Trends in Federal States*, Lanham, New York: University Press of America, p. 231.

25 "Obgleich die Länder sehr verschiedene historische Erfahrungen gemacht haben und ihre Bevölkerung ein recht ausgeprägtes Landesbewußtsein besitzt, konnte im Überblick gesehen, eine weitgehende substantielle Gleichartigkeit der Bevölkerung, der Parteien und der Interessenvertretungen festgestellt werden. Diese starke soziale und politische Homogenität fand ihren Niederschlag in der Ausgestaltung der föderativen Ordnung von 1920, die in der Folgezeit den Verfahrenrahmen für den föderalen Prozeß in Österreich absteckte," Christa Altenstetter (1969), *Der Föderalismus in Österreich, unter besonderer Berücksichtigung der politischen Verhältnisse von 1945–1966*, Heidelberg: Quelle and Meyer, p. 124.

26 "Die Homogenität der österreichischen Bevölkerung, die Überlagerung der Länderinteressen durch Partei- und Sachinteressen, vor allem aber der Trend zur großräumigen, einheitlichen Regelung waren nach 1945 der bundesstaatlichen Entwicklung in Österreich nicht günstig," Friedrich Koja (1975), *Entwicklungstendenzen des österreichischen Föderalismus*, St Pölten and Vienna: Niederösterreichische Juristische Gesellschaft, p. 30.

27 For a discussion of the Austria's highly centralized party system, see H. Obinger (2005), "Austria: Strong Parties in a Weak Federal Polity," p. 189.

28 The composition of the constitutional court is clearly tilted towards the center as most of its members are appointed by the Federal President, based on nominations by the National Assembly and the federal government. The only substate input is the Bunderat's right to nominate of three members to this fourteen-member court. According to Fried Esterbauer, the court is predisposed towards the Bund perspective; F. Esterbauer (1976), *Kriterien föderativer und konföderativer Systeme*, pp. 80–86. Adamovich also argues that the Court has failed to protect Länder prerogatives; Ludwig K. Adamovich (1973), "Die Zukunft des Föderalismus in Österreich," Heinz Laufer and Frank Pilz (eds), *Föderalismus: Studientexte zur bundesstaatlichen Ordnung*, Munich: Wilhelm Goldman, p. 362; a similar point is made by Kurt Richard Luther (1997), "Bund–Länder Beziehungen: Formal- und Realverfassung," in Herbert Dachs, Peter Gerlich, Herbert Gottweis, Franz Hormer, Helmut Kramer, Volkmar Lauber, Wolfgang C. Müller and Emmerich Tálos (eds), *Handbuch des politischen System Österreich*, Third Edition, Vienna: Manzche, p. 908.

29 For discussion of the principle of duty for federal consideration in Austrian federalism, see Sigrid Lebitsch-Buchsteiner (2001), *Die bundesstaatliche Rücksichtnahmepflicht*, Vienna: Wilhelm Braumüller; Ulrike Davy (1986), "Zur Bedeutung des bundesstaatlichen Rücksichtnahmegebotes für Normenkonflickte," *Österreichische Juristen-Zeitung*, Vol. 41, No. 8, pp. 225–234; Heinz Mayer (1986), "Neue Wege der Kompetenz interpretation?" *Österreichische Juristen-Zeitung*, Vol. 41, No. 17, pp. 513–520; Siegbert Morscher (1985), "Weschselseitige Rücksichtnahmepflicht Bund-Länder," *Juristische Blätter*, Vol. 107, No. 15/16, pp. 479–481.

30 "... der Föderalismus nicht bei den Ländern enden darf," from "Mensch und Demokratie: Parteiprogramm der Sozialistischen Partei Österreichs, Beschlossen am Bundesparteitag vom 18. bis 20. Mai 1978 in Wien," in Bernd Stampfer (1981), "Zur Situation des Föderalismus in Österreich," Andreas Khol and Alfred Stirneman (eds), *Österreichischen Jahrbuch für Politik 1980*, Munich: R. Oldenbourg and Vienna: Verlag für Geschichte und Politik, p. 24.

31 Kurt Wedl (1969), *Der Gedanke des Föderalismus in Programmen Politischer Parteien Deutschland und Österreichs*, Munich and Vienna: Günter Olzag, pp. 196–200 for the ÖVP.

32 "Ein Haupthindernis für echte Reformen dürfte in einem fehlenden föderalistischen Bewusstsein bei maßgeblichen politischen Akteuren und den Massenmedien liegen," Institut für Föderalismus (2002), *26. Bericht über den Föderalismus in Österreich*, Vienna: Wilhelm Braumuller, p. 50.

33 In May 1919, Vorarlbergers had held a referendum to join Switzerland. More than 80 percent voted in favor, but their overture was turned down by Switzerland. The Swiss

were hesitant to accept a new German-speaking Catholic canton into a federal system based on a delicate balance between French speakers and German speakers on the one hand, and Catholics and Protestants on the other. For a discussion of Vorarlberg's role in the Austrian federation, see Richard Luther (1986), "The Revitalization of Federalism and Federation in Austria," Michael Burgess (ed.), *Federalism and Federation in Western Europe*, London: Croom and Helm, pp. 154–186.

34

    Angelegenheiten, die vom Land selbst besorgt werden können, sollen in seine Zuständigkeit fallen, um so die Bedürfnisse der Bevölkerung und die Verhältnisse im Land besser berücksichtigen zu können, die kulturelle Vielfalt zu gewährleisten und die Staatstätigkeit möglichst kostengünstig zu gestalten. In Anwendung dieses Grundsatzes ist eine Stärkung der Zuständigkeiten bzw. der Mitbestimmungsrechte des Landes insbesondere in folgenden Angelegenheiten herbeizuführen: ... Schulwesen (z.B. Mitsprache bei der Gestaltung von Lehrplänen und Schulbüchern), Erwachsenenbildung, Rundfunk (bessere Berücksichtigung der Landesbelange, stärkere Regionalisierung), Denkmalschutz.

From 10 Punkte zur Stärkung der Stellung des Landes (der Länder) und der Gemeinden im Rahmen des österreichischen Bundesstaates, Vorarlberger Landtage, XXIII. Sitzungsbericht, in Siegbert Morsch (1981), "Pro Vorarlberg," in Andreas Khol and Alfred Stirneman (eds), *Österreichischen Jahrbuch für Politik 1980*, Munich: R. Oldenbourg and Vienna: Verlag für Geschichte und Politik, p. 48.

35 Two notable exceptions are Tyrol and Lower Austria. In 1983, the Tyrolean Landtag passed a similar "Pro-Tirol" motion; the Landtag of Lower Austria also followed suit in 1985.

36 F. Esterbauer (1976), *Kriterien föderativer und konföderativer Systeme*, p. 79.

37 In Vienna, the School Board was called the *Stadtschulrat*.

38 Helmut Engelbrecht (1988), *Geschichte des österreichischen Bildungswesens; Erziehung und Unterricht auf dem Boden Österreichs, Band V, Von 1918 bis zur Gegenwart*, Vienna: Österreichischer Bundesverlag, p. 474.

39 See Suzanne Dermutz (1983), "Bildungspartnerschaft. Historische Entwicklung und Merkmale des bildungspolitischen Systems in Österreich," *Österreichische Zeitschrift für Politikwissenschaft*, Vol. 1, pp. 19–32; Gertraud Wollansky (1983), "Schulpolitik in Österreich: Ein Überblick," *Österreichische Zeitschrift für Politikwissenschaft*, Vol. 1, pp. 5–18.

40 F. Ermacora (1976), *Österreichischer Föderalismus*, pp. 86–99.

41 "Es waren sehr schwierige Kompetenzfragen zwischen dem Bund und dem Ländern zu lösen, vor allem die Frage, ob das Schwergewicht des Einflusses auf des Schulwesen mehr auf der Länderebene verlagert bleiben oder ob nicht dem Bund angesichts bestimmter Notwendigkeiten ein größerer Einfluß auf die Schulverwaltung eingeräumt werden sollte," Karl Kummer (ÖVP), *106. Sitzung des Nationalrates der Republik Österreich, Mittwoch, 18 Juli 1962, Stenographische Protokolle über die Sitzungen des Nationalrates, 1962, IX. Gesetzgebungperiode, V. Band*, Vienna: Druck der österreichischen Staatsdruckerei, p. 4692.

42 "Sicherlich ist – und nehme ich auf die Verteilung der Kompetenzen Bezug – eine möglichst einheitliche Gestaltung des Schulwesens ein dringendes Gebot der Verantwortung für die kommenden Generationen, damit sie sich in einer Großraumwirtschaft unserer allernächsten Zukunft leichter behaupten können." Otto Winter (SPÖ), Ibid., p. 4695.

43 "Mit diesem Gesetz werden wir das Provisorium und Transitorium Österreich, des Staates, der zu Zeiten durch die Schwäche des Glaubens seiner eigenen Staatsbürger in seiner Existenz bedrängt war, ja sie sogar verloren hat, beenden. Wir werden uns auf kulturpolitischem Gebiet endlich in einer Gemeinsamkeit treffen." Heinrich Drimmel, Ibid., p. 4706.

44 "Diese Schulgesetze eröffnete vor kurzem die Novellierung des Hochschul-Organisations-gesetzes. Dies war besonders für die Bundesländer erfreulich, weil sie durch die Gründung von neuen Hochschulen einen verstärkten Anteil am Geistesleben unseres Vaterlandes bekommen sollen." Franz Fruhstorfer (SPÖ), representative of Upper Austria, *194. Sitzung des Bundesrates der Republik Österreich, Freitag, 20 Juli 1962, Stenographische Protokolle über die Sitzungen des Bundesrates 1959 bis 1962, IX. Gesetzgebungperiode der Republik Österreich, V. Band*, Vienna: Druck der österreichischen Staatsdruckerei, p. 4692.

45 "Der extreme Föderalismus führt zur Zersplitterung und Auflösung, er übersieht, daß wir doch in einem gemeinsamen Haus wohnen," Ibid., p. 4695.

46 Reinhard Rack (1995), "Federalism: Making the Community More Attractive to Europeans: The Austrian Point of View," in C. Lloyd Brown-John (ed.), *Federal-Type Solutions and European Integration*, Lanham, New York, London: University Press of America, p. 400.

47 "[Die 1962 Verfassunggesetznovelle] bedeutet die vollständige Zerstörung der Hoheit der Länder auf dem Gebiet des Schulwesens, was wohl einen der stärksten Rückschläge des österreichischen Föderalismus darstellt." Felix Ermacora (1970), "Vorstellungen und Wirklichkeit im österreichischen Föderalismus 1848–1970," Felix Ermacora, Heinrich Koller, Hans Klecatsky, Gertrude and Manfried Welan (eds), *Föderalismus in Österreich*, Munich and Salzburg: Anton Puslet, p. 88.

48 "Die intensive Zentralisation, Konzentration und Steuerung des gesamten Bildungsinhaltes aller österreichischen Schulen und Universitäten durch den Bund hat eine weit über den Sachbereich hinauswirkende Schwächung des Föderalismus im Bewußtsein und der politische Bildung des Lehrer und Schüler – und damit im weiteren Gefolge des *Gesamtbevölkerung* – zur Folge" [italics in original], Peter Pernthaler (1988), "Kulturpolitik in Österreich." Verfassungsrechtliche und verfassungspolitische Rahmenbedingungen," in Peter Pernthaler (ed.), *Föderalistische Kulturpolitik*, Vienna: Wilhlem Braumüller, p. 17.

49 Peter Bußjäger (2000), "Modernisierungsprobleme im österreichischen föderalen System," *Zeitschrift für Politik*, Vol. 49, No. 2, p. 158.

50 "Salzburger Programm der österreichischen Volkspartei, 1 Dezember 1972," quoted in B. Stampfer (1981), "Zur Situation des Föderalismus in Österreich," p. 24.

51 "Wie können die Länder in ihrer Selbständigkeit zusammenarbeiten, so daß die gemeinsame Aufgabe und, die Durchlässigkeit des österreichischen Schulwesens' erhalten bleibt und keine umzumutbaren Mehrkosten entstehen?" Markus Juranek (1999), *Schulverfassung und Schulverwaltung in Österreich und in Europa, Volume I*, Vienna: Verlag Österreich, p. 488.

52 F. Esterbauer (1976), *Kriterien föderativer und konföderativer Systeme*, pp. 97–80.

53 *Stenographische Protokoll, 116. Sitzung des Nationalrates der Republik Österreich, V. Gesetzgebungsperiode, Mittwoch 13 July 1949*, Vienna: Druck der österreichische Staatsdruckerei, pp. 3302–3303.

54 *Stenographische Protokolle, 46. Sitzung des Bundesrates der Republik Österreich, Freitag 15. Juli 1949*, Vienna: Druck der österreichische Staatsdruckerei, pp. 803–804.

55 For a detailed account of Vorarlberg's and Tirol's short-lived activism, see Norbert Feldinger (1990), *Nachkriegsrundfunk in Österreich: zwischen Föderalismus and Zentralismus von 1945 bis 1957*, Munich: Saur, pp. 91–94.

56 During debates at the National Assembly, both the Federal Minister for Instruction, Erich Kolb, and the Federal Minister for Traffic, Karl Waldbrunner, made cases for broadcasting to remain within the exclusive control of their respective ministries. *Stenographische Protokolle des Nationalrates der Republik Österreich, VI. Gesetzgebungsperiode, 15 October 1952, Anfragebeantwortung 494/A.B. vom 3. September 1952, 1. und 2. Beiblatt*, Vienna: Druck der österreichische Staatsdruckerei, p. 98.

57 "Ich trete nicht für einen 'zentralistischen', sondern für einen 'gemeinsamen'

österreichischen Rundfunk ein. Das heißt, es soll weder ein 'verstaatlicher' noch ein 'verländerter' Rundfunk sein. Im übrigen hat die 'öffentliche Verwaltung' ihre Funktion längst erfüllt. Der nächste Schritt kann nur ein Rundfunkgesetz sein," Alfons Übelhör, cited in F. Ermacora (1976), *Österreichischer Föderalismus*, p. 96.

58 "Eine gewisse Zentralisierung ist die einzige Möglichkeit, um einen Rundfunk wirtschaftlich zu lenken. Der Österreichische Rundfunk wird bereits heute bei weitem föderalistischer geführt als etwa bis zum Jahre 1938," Wilhelm Füchsl, cited in Ibid., pp. 96–97.

59 "Die Länder sind von der Möglichkeit eigene Rundfunkanlagen zu errichten und zu betreiben, keineswegs ausgeschlossen, da es sich bleiben nicht um Akte der Hoheitsverwaltung, sondern um eine Betätigung im Rahmen der Privatwirtschaftsverwaltung handelt, die der Kompetenz verteilung des B-VG nicht unterliegt. Sie bedürfen aber hierzu – so wie jedes andere Rechtsubjekt-infolge des zugunsten des Bundes gesetzlich aufgestellten Vorbehaltes der Konzession der zuständigen Fernmelde behörde." Verfassungsgerichthof (1996) [1954], "Fernmeldegesetz slg. 2721, 1954," *Die Judicatur des Verfassungsgerichthofes 1919–1964, I. Band*, Vienna: Druck und Verlag der Österreichischen Staatsdruckerei, p. 497.

60 A notable exception is the work of scholars affiliated with the Institute of Federalism (*Institut für Föderalismus*, formerly *Institut für Föderalismusforschung*) based in Innsbruck, Tyrol. The Institute publishes yearly reports on the state of federalism in Austria.

61 Johannes Grießer (1989), *Der Österreichische Rundfunk als Thema der Parlamentarische Auseinandersetzung von 1970 bis 1983*, Vienna: Universität Wien, p. 13.

62 Hans Magenschab (1973), *Demokratie und Rundfunk: Hörfunk und Fernsehen im politischen Prozeß österreichs*, Vienna and Munich: Herold, p. 179. For a detailed discussion of the 1964 public petition for a referendum see Ibid., pp. 172–243.

63 "Die Reform muß in jeden Fall gewährleisten, daß die Österreichische Rundfunkgesellschaft aus einem parteipolitischen Proporzinstrument der schwarz-roten Koalition zu einer Kultureinrichtung des ganzen Volkes umgewandelt wird ...," Emil van Tongel (FPÖ), *20. Sitzung des Nationalrates der Republik Österreich, Freitag, 8. Juli 1966, Stenographische Protokolle über die Sitzungen des Nationalrates, XI. Gesetzgebungsperiode, II. Band*, Vienna: Druck der Österreichischen Staatsdruckerei, p. 1548.

64 "Das neue Rundfunkgesetz ist ein Beginn. Möge es die Erwartungen erfüllen, die es bei seinem Entstehen begleiten. Für Volk und Staat sollen Rundfunk und Fernsehen als Kulturinstrument unserem Vaterland dienen." Ibid., p. 1553.

65 *244. Sitzung des Bundesrates der Republik Österreich, Freitag 22 Juli 1966, Stenographische Protokolle über die Sitzungen des Bundesrates der Republik Österreich, 1966 bis 1967, XI Gesetzgebungsperiod, 1967*, Vienna: Druck der Österreichischen Staatsdruckerei, pp. 5968–6001.

66 "Meine Damen und Herren! Der Föderalismus ist wahrscheinlich für mich und auch für meine Freunde im Klub der ÖVP die Notwendigkeit, den Differenzierungen in den Bundesländern nach demographischen, geographischen, wirtschaftlichen und sozialen Verhältnissen eine entsprechende Struktur zu geben, um damit den Bundesländern ihr Bewußtsein für ihr Bundesland und für ihr Landesvolk zu geben," from *111. Sitzung des Nationalrates der Republik Österreich, Mittwoch 10 Juli 1974, Stenographische Protokolle über die Sitzungen des Nationalrates, XIII. Gesetzgebungsperiode, 8. Band*, Vienna: Druck der österreichischen Staatsdruckerei, p. 11037.

67 "Meine Damen und Herren! Problematisch ist auch die Frage in bezug auf den Föderalismus, wobei wir sagen können: der Föderalismus hat hier nicht zugenommen, sondern abgenommen," Herbert Schambek (ÖVP), representative of Lower Austria, *334. Sitzung des Bundesrates der Republik Österreich, Dienstag 16. und Mittwoch 17. Juli 1974, Stenographische Protokolle über die Sitzungen des Bundesrates der Republik Österreich, 1974 bis 1975, XIII. Gesetzgebungsperiode*, Vienna: Druck der Österreichischen Staatsdruckerei, p. 10322.

68 "Österreich lebt als Bundesstaat aus der Einheit des Gesamtstaates und aus der Kraft seiner Gliedstaaten, das heißt, daß ein wesentliches Prinzip der staatlichen Ordnung der Föderalismus ist," Hans Schickelgruber (SPÖ) representative of Lower Austria, *334. Sitzung des Bundesrates der Republik Österreich, Dienstag 16. und Mittwoch 17. Juli 1974, Stenographische Protokolle über die Sitzungen des Bundesrates der Republik Österreich, 1974 bis 1975, XIII. Gesetzgebungsperiode*, Vienna: Druck der Österreichischen Staatsdruckerei, p. 10289.

69 The recent ORF-Law (*Aufgaben und die Einrichtung des Österreichischen Rundfunks BGBl lNr 83/2001*), which came into force on 1 August 2001, restores some of powers to the Länderstudios; Institut für Föderalismus (2002), *26. Bericht über den Föderalismus in Österreich*, Vienna: Wilhelm Braumüller, p. 48.

3 Belgium

1 For the role linguistic/cultural differences play in Belgian public policies, see Jan Erk (2003), "'Wat We Zelf Doen, Doen We Beter': Belgian Substate Nationalisms, Congruence and Public Policy," *Journal of Public Policy*, Vol. 23, No. 2, pp. 201–224.

2 Robert Senelle with Edgard Van de Velde and Emiel Clement (1999), *Kronieken van de Vlaamse Staatswording, Over de Identiteit van het Vlaming-Zijn*, Lannoo: Tielt, p. 46.

3 The origins of Walloon nationalism can be traced to the nineteenth century labor movements. For example, see Marinette Bruwier, Nicole Caulier-Mathy, Claude Desame and Paul Gerin (1990), *1886 La Wallonie née de la grève?*, Bruxelles: Editions Labor.

4 Hervé Hasquin estimates the Francophone population of Brussels to be less than 15 percent in 1780, quoted in Kas Deprez (1992), "The Dutch Language in Flanders," in Theo Hermans, Louis Vos and Lode Wils (eds), *The Flemish Movement, A Documentary History 1780–1990*, London and Atlantic Highlands: Athlone, p. 420. Kenneth McRae cites a study which estimates the number of Brussels francophones in 1788 as a trifling 5 percent. Kenneth McRae (1986), *Conflict and Compromise in Multilingual Societies: Belgium*, Waterloo: Wilfrid Laurier University Press, p. 294. In 1846, 60 percent of the inhabitants of the city were Dutch-speakers, in 1910 the number had decreased to 46 percent; Wilfried Dewachter (1992), *De duelistische identiteit van de Belgische maatschappij*, Amsterdam: Koninklijke Nederlandse Akademie van Wetenschappen, p. 15.

5 "De unitaire Staat, met zijn structuur en zijn werkwijze zoals die thans door de wetten nog geregeld zijn, is door de gebeurtenissen achterhaald. De gemeenschappen en de gewesten moeten hun plaats innemen in vernieuwde staatstructuren die beter aangepast moeten aan de eigen toestanden van het land," from Prime Minister Eysken's "Communication du Gouvernement," Séance du mercredi 18 février 1970/Vergadering van woensdag 18 februari 1970, *Annales Parlementaire de Belgique, Chambre des Répresentants, Session Ordinaire 1969–1970/Parlementaire Handelingen van België, Kamer der Volksvertegenwoordigers, Gewone Zitting 1969–1970*, Dewarichtet: Brussels, p. 3.

6 Kris Deschouwer (2002), "Causes and Effects of Constitutional Changes in Multilingual Belgium," in Stephen Brooks (ed.), *The Challenge of Cultural Pluralism*, Westport: Praeger, p. 132.

7 Flemish nationalist parties were divided between the Social-Democrat and moderate Volksunie (VU) and the far-right anti-immigrant Vlaams Blok (VB). Marijke Breuning (1997), "Nationalism and Nationalist Parties: A Comparison of the Flemish Volksunie and Vlaams Blok," *Nationalism and Ethnic Politics*, Vol. 3, No. 1, pp. 1–27. Recently, Volksunie has splintered into two factions which have then allied themselves with other parties.

8 OESE (Doorlichting van het Educatief Overheidsbeleid) (1991), Ministerie van de

Vlaamse Gemeenschap, Department Onderwijs, Ministère de l'Education, de la Recherche et de la Formation; Verwaltung de Deutschsprachigen Gemeinschaft, Abteilung Unterricht, *Het Educatief Bestel in België: Van Convergentie naar Divergentie*, Brussels.

9 Els Witte, Jan De Groof and Jeffrey Tyssens (eds) (1999), *Het Schoolpact van 1958: Onstaan, graondlijnen en toepassing van een Belgisch compromis/Le pacte scolaire de 1958: Origines, principes et application d'un compromis belge*, Brussels: Vrije Universiteit Brussels.

10 "Il voit dans la création de conseil culturel, dotés de compétences réelles, le meilleur moyen d'encourager le développement des deux communautés, dans le respect de leur caractère propre. C'est dans le même esprit qu'a été reconnue, dans la structure même du gouvernement, la nécessité d'une transformation profonde des départements de l'Instruction publique et des Affaires culturelles en fonction de l'existence de deux culture dans le pays." From the declaration of the government during the discussion on the law proposals "emploi des langues en matière administrative" and "Régime linguistique dans l'enseignement," Séance du jeudi 27 juin 1963/Vergadering van donderdag 27 juni 1963, *Chambre des Réprésentants, Annales Parlementaires/Kamer der Volksvertegenwoordigers, Parlementaire Handelingen*, Dewarichtet: Brussels, p. 4.

11 "Een gemeenschap die niet het recht heeft te zeggen dat zij aan onderwijs en/of aan ondergeschikte besturen meer of minder wil besteden is geen gemeenschap die autonoom is op die terreinen. Zij wordt een uitbetalings organisme, een loket, een beambte van de centale Staat," Séance du mercredi 30 juillet 1980/Vergadering van woensdag 30 juli 1980 (discussion on "Project de loi ordinaire des réformes institutionelles" and "Projet de loi spéciale des réformes institutionelles"), *Annales Parlementaire de Belgique, Chambre des Réprésentants, Session Ordinaire 1979–80/Parlementaire Handelingen van België, Kamer der Volksvertegenwoordigers, Gewone Zitting 1979–80*, Dewarichtet: Brussels, p. 2782.

12 "En réalité, le projet éducatif constitue toujours un choix de caractère politique, un choix de société intimement lié, en l'occurrence, à l'avenir de noter Communauté française." FDF-RW member Brasseur during the reading of the Council Executive's declaration, Conseil de la Communauté Française, Session 1980–81, Séance du Mardi 4 Novembre 1980, *Compte Rendu Intégral*, p. 45.

13 "Notre problème ... c'est de garder notre dignité de francophones, c'est d'être capables d'assumer correctement nos autonomies avec les moyens qui sont les notres." Minister Hansenne, from the Déclaration de l'Exécutif, Conseil de la Communauté Française, Session 1980–81, Séance du Mardi 4 Novembre 1980, *Compte Rendu Intégral*, p. 62.

14 Vlaamse Executieve (1983), Standpuntbepaling van de Vlaamse Executieve i.v.m. "de communautarisering van het onderwijs," 27 April 1983, reproduced in Jan de Groof (ed.) (1990), *De Schoolpactwet: Coördinatie en annotatie*, Brussels: Story Scienta Scienta and Centrum voor Politieke, Economische en Sociale Studies CEPESS.

15 Ibid., Art. 1.1.

16 Ibid., Art. 2.1.

17 *Overeenkomst van 8 februari 1984 betreffende de onderwijsaangelegenheden die krachtens de Grondwet niet tot de bevoegheid van de Gemeenschappen behoren*, reproduced in J. De Groof (ed.) (1990), *De Scholpactwet*, p. 103.

18 "Waarom is de communautarisering van het onderwijs nu zo belangrijk? ... De geschiedenis van de Vlaamse Beweging is vooral de geschiedenis van de strijd om culturele autonomie. De verschillende stappen in de vernederlandsing van ons onderwijs zijn evenvele stappen op weg naar culturele autonomie voor het Vlaamse volk. Wat is meer evident dan dat een Gemeenschap haar onderwijs beheert?" From the speech of CVP Deputy Moors, Séance Plenieres jeudi 7 juillet 1988/Plenaire Vergadering van donderdag 7 juli 1988 (1989), *Annales Parlementaire et Rapports nomi-*

natifs des Commissions, Chambre des Réprésentants de Belgique, Session Extraordinaire 1988, Dewarichtet: Brussels, p. 946.

19 Xavier Mabille (1997), *Histoire politique de la Belgique: Facteurs et acteurs de changement*, reviewed and updated new edition, Brussels: Crisp, p. 388.

20 For example, Destatte puts it in the following terms: "[La dénonciation] a pourtant pris l'acuité des espoirs déçus depuis la communitarisation de l'enseignement en 1989," Philippe Destatte (1998), "La Wallonie dans l'enseignement de l'histoire," in Jean-Claude Van Cauwenberghe (ed.), *Oser être Wallon!*, Editions Quorum: Gerpinnes, p. 45.

21 "Onderwijs blijft een essentiële pijler van het Vlaamse beleid. Het blijft immers onze eerste zorg éénieder.," Ministrie van de Vlaamse Gemeenschap (1995), *Een regering voor de Vlamingen*. Brussels, p. 41.

22 The Autonomous Board for Community Education, ARGO (*Autonome Raad voor het Gemeenschaps-onderwijs*), set up in 1988, is responsible for what was formerly called state education. The provincial system of public schools has its own peak organ called the Unit for Flemish Provincial Education, CVPO (*Cel voor Vlaams Provinciaal Onderwijs*). The Catholic educational system, on the other hand, has had its own board VSKO (*Vlaams Secretariat van het Katholiek Onderwijs*) since 1957. All these organizations, together with unions and interest groups, cooperate within the peak association of the Union of Formation and Education Organisations, BVVO (*Bond van Vorming -en Ontwikkelings Organisaties*). In addition to the three educational boards, an overarching non-political advisory body, the Flemish Educational Council, VLOR (*Vlaamse Onderwijsraad*), was created with the law of 31 July 1990. VLOR is responsible for all levels of education, including universities.

23 "La scission entre le pays 'légal' et le pays 'réel' jointe à la distanciation progressive des deux communauté éducatives, faisait apparaître le caractère artificiel d'une législation nationale en la matière. La responsabilité partagé et donc différenciée, par excellence en matière d'enseignement, ne pouvait être corrigée que par l'unicité des interventions après transfert intégral." Jan De Groof (1996), "Les Sociaux-Chrétiens et l'enseignement," in Wilfried Dewachter, Georges-Henri Dumont, Michel Dumoulin, Manu Gérard, Emiel Lamberts, Xavier Mabille and Mark Van den Wijngaert (eds), *Un Parti Dans l'Histoire 1945–1995, 50 Ans d'Action du Parti Social Chrétien*, Ducolot: Louvain-la-Neuve, p. 595.

24 Jan Erk (2005), "From Vlaams Blok to Vlaams Belang: The Belgian Far-Right Renames Itself," *West European Politics*, Vol. 28, No. 3, pp. 493–502.

25 Wilfried Dewachter (1998), "Belgique: La Déchirure," *Politique internationale*, Vol. 78, p. 185.

26 One of the most prolific observers of Belgian media, Jan Servaes, concludes that viewers of the Francophone channels RTBF and RTL-TVi never watch the Flemish channels BRT and VTM, and vice versa. Jan Servaes (1998), "Médias et politique," in Marco Martiniello and Marc Swyngedouw (eds), *Où va la Belgique? Les soubresauts d'une petite démocratie européenne*, Paris: L'Harmattan, pp. 167–168.

27 "Het communicatiebestel in België – en daarmee slaat men de brug tussen economie en cultuur- is duidelijk opgedeeld in twee aparte netten … Er zijn de Nederlandstalige kranten, radio, televisie, weekbladen en er zijn de Franstaligen. Zij penetreren nauwelijks elkaars taalgebied." W. Dewachter (1992), *De duelistische identiteit van de Belgische maatschappij*, p. 22.

28 "Pour radiodiffusion et la télévision, un Conseil de gestion wallon et un Conseil de gestion flamand devraient êtres créés." Quoted in Hugues Dumont and Georges-Henri Dumont (1996), "La Politique Culturelle Sociale-Chrétienne sous le Signe de l'autonomie et du pluralisme," in Wilfried Dewachter, Georges-Henri Dumont, Michel Dumoulin, Manu Gérard, Emiel Lamberts, Xavier Mabille and Mark Van den Wijngaert (eds), *Un Parti Dans l'Histoire 1945–1995, 50 Ans d'Action du Parti Social Chrétien*, Ducolot: Louvain-la-Neuve, p. 556.

29 The cultural autonomy law of 8 August 1980 did not include competence over government communications and commercial advertisements. The 1988 reform added commercial advertisements, print press, regulatory and financial control over mass media to Community competence, as well as the right to provide public funds to media. The 1993 state reform finally gave the Communities full jurisdiction, removing the federal government from the picture entirely.

30 "La loi Harmel (du 18 mai 1960), née à l'issue de langues négociations portant sur la réforme du statut de l'INR, a ouvert – et c'était la première fois dans le contexte belge – des perspectives sur l'autonomie culturelle." Christian Carette, Jan de Groof, Patrick Peeters and Jan Vermeire (1993), *La Legislation des Media, Le cadre normatif général, Les normes administratives et techniques relatives aux radio- et télécommunications*, Cepess: Brussels, p. 14.

31 K. McRae (1986), *Conflict and Compromise in Multilingual Societies: Belgium*, p. 239.

32 Article 3.1. of Vlaamse Gemeenschap en Gewest, Decreten betreffende de radio-omroep ende televisie, gecoördineerd bij Besluit van de Vlaamse Regering van 25 January 1995, Belgische Staatsblad May 1995, zoals bekrachtigd bij Decreet 8 March 1995, Belgische Staatsblad, 31 May 1995, eer Belgische Staatsblad, 31 October 1995, reproduced in Leo Neels, Dirk Voorhoof and Hans Maertens (eds) (1996), *Medialex: Selectie van bronnen van de media- en informatie wetgeving*, Fourth Edition, Kluwer: Antwerp, p. 154.

33 "De programma's moeten bijdragen tot de vereder ontwikkeling van de diversiteit van de Vlaamse cultuur en van een democratische en verdraagzame samenleving." Vlaamse Gemeenschap en Gewest, Decreten betreffende de radio-omroep ende televisie, gecoördineerd bij Besluit van de Vlaamse Regering van 25 January 1995, b.s. May 1995, zoals bekrachtigd bij Decreet 8 March 1995, b.s., 31 May 1995, eer b.s., 31 October 1995, reproduced in Ibid., p. 154.

34 "Pour assurer le développement culturel, notamment par la mise en valeur et la promotion des activités culturelles de la Communauté française, son patrimoine en Wallonie, à Bruxelles et à l'étranger ainsi que la valorisation appropriée des spécificités régionales." Quoted in François Jongen (1998), "Radiodiffusion et Culture en Droit Belge," in Hugues, Dumont and Strowel (eds), *Politique culturelle et droit de la radio-télévision*, Brussels: Publications des Facultés universitaire Saint-Louis.

35 "Le choix institutionnel doit donc être lié au choix médiatique: il faut construire des espaces de communication qui correspondent aux structures politiques," Philippe Destatte and Jacky Morael interviewed by Henri Goldman, in Christophe Derenne and Colette De Troy (eds) (1997), *Belgique: Disparition d'une nation européennes*, Brussels: Éditions Luc Pire, p. 169.

36 The French Community first formed a Commission for Audiovisual Affairs under the Ministry of Culture in 1984. This body was replaced by the High Council for Audiovisual Affairs (*Conseil supérieur de l'audiovisuel*) in 1987. However, the RTBF is by far the most important actor in the heavily regulated Francophone media. On the Flemish side, VRT does not have a similarly central role. The private channels in Flanders are under the supervision of the Flemish Media Council (*Vlaamse Mediaraad*). The Council's competences cover radio and television broadcasting, print press, and all other means of communication and information. Another such public body is the Flemish Arbitration Board for Radio and Television (*Vlaamse Geschillenraad voor Radio en Televisie*) established in 1996.

37 "Sur le plan des médias, il est clair que la société belge n'existe plus," W. Dewachter (1998), "Belgique: La Déchirure," p. 185.

38 For the role of religion in fostering the left–right divide between Wallonia and Flanders, see Jan Erk (2005), "Substate Nationalism and the Left-Right Divide: Critical Junctures in the Formation of Nationalist Labour Movements in Belgium," *Nations and Nationalism*, Vol. 11, No. 4, pp. 551–570.

4 Canada

1 This article draws upon material first published in Jan Erk (2006), "'Uncodified Workings and Unworkable Codes': Canadian Federalism and Public Policy," *Comparative Political Studies*, Vol. 39, No. 4, pp. 441–462.
2 Quoted in Colin H. Williams (1995), "A Requiem for Canada?" in Graham Smith (ed.), *Federalism: The Multiethnic Challenge*, London and New York: Longman.
3 From P.B. Waite (1963), *The Confederal Debates in the Province of Canada, 1865*, p. 40; quoted in Roger Gibbins (1987), "Federal Societies, Institutions, and Politics," in Herman Bakvis and William Chandler (eds), *Federalism and the Role of the State*, Toronto, Buffalo and London: University of Toronto Press.
4 See Jennifer Smith (2003), "The Constitutional Debate and Beyond," in François Rocher and Miriam Smith (eds), *New Trends in Canadian Federalism*, Second Edition, Peterborough: Broadview, pp. 45–66; James Ross Hurley (2002), "Canadian Federalism: Idiosyncratic Characteristics, Evolution and Lessons Learned," in Jürgen Rose and Johannes Traut (eds), *Federalism and Decentralisation: Perspectives for the Transformation Process in Eastern and Central Europe*, Hamburg and New York: Palgrave, p. 149; Alain-G. Gagnon (1991), "Everything Old is New Again: Canada, Québec and Constitutional Impasse," in Frances Abele (ed.), *How Ottawa Spends. The Politics of Fragmentation 1991–92*, Ottawa: Carleton University Press, p. 63.
5 Keith Banting (1987), *The Welfare State and Canadian Federalism*, Second Edition, Montreal and Kingston: McGill-Queen's University Press, pp. 171–182.
6 Will Kymlicka (1998), "Multinational Federalism in Canada: Rethinking the Partnership," in Roger Gibbins and Guy Laforest (eds), *Beyond the Impasse, Toward Reconciliation*, Montreal: Institute for Research on Public Policy, p. 37.
7 Even in Alberta – where the provincial government tends to distance itself from federal initiatives – more than 60 percent of the respondents expressed support for a stronger federal government; Figure 2 "Strong Federal Government vs. More Power to the Provinces," in Citizens' Forum on Canada's Future (1991), *Report to the People and Government of Canada*, Ottawa: Ministry of Supply and Services, p. 158.
8 Andrew Petter (1989), "Federalism and the Myth of the Federal Spending Power," *The Canadian Bar Review*, Vol. 68, No. 3, p. 449–455.
9 Fred Cutler and Matthew Mendelsohn (2001), "What Kind of Federalism do Canadians (outside Québec) want?" *Policy Options*, Vol. 22, No. 8, p. 29. The survey results can be accessed at qsilver.queensu.ca/~mattmen/mediaroom/index.html.
10 Fred Cutler and Matthew Mendelsohn, "Canadians Can't Make Sense of Intergovernmental Disputes: Institutions of Federalism are Outdated," *Globe and Mail*, July 31, 2001, p. A-11.
11 W. Kymlicka (1998), "Multinational Federalism in Canada: Rethinking the Partnership," pp. 31–32 [italics in original].
12 Kenneth McRoberts (1997), "Trudeau and the New Federal Orthodoxy: Denying the Quebec Question," in M. McRoberts, *Misconceiving Canada: The Struggle for National Unity*, Toronto: Oxford University Press, p. 55–76.
13 Marc Raboy (1990), *Missed Opportunities: The Story of Canada's Broadcasting Policy*, Montreal and Kingston: McGill-Queen's University Press, p. 52.
14 "Dans le domaine de la radiodiffusion, le Québec considère que la centralization de la audiodiffusion entre les mains de la bureaucratie fédérale va à l'encontre des principes fondamentaux ratifies par la Constitution canadienne et les Pères de la Confédération …" Maurice Duplessis (1948), quoted in Gilles Proulx (1986), *La Radio: d'hier à aujourd'hui*, Québec: Libre expression, p. 116.
15 Austin Weir (1965), *The Struggle for National Broadcasting in Canada*, Toronto: McClelland and Stewart, p. 294.
16 "Nous comprenons que le gouvernement federal recherché à la fois l'uniformité administrative et l'uniformité des services à la population à la grandeur du pays. Je

répondrai à cela que le souci de l'uniformité administrative ne pas justifier la centralisation et les decisions unilatérales.... Le Québec ne tient pas à ce genre d'uniformité, car dès que l'on accepte que notre communauté nationale a le droit de s'épanouir comme elle l'entend.... Il faut logiquement que les decisions administratives du gouvernement du Québec ne soient pas nécessairement identiques à celles des governments des autres provinces." Jean Lesage (1965), quoted in in Gilles Proulx (1976), *L'Aventure de la Radio*, Montreal: Édition la, pp. 59–60.

17 "Un autre domaine, affirma-t-il, auquel le gouvernement du Québec attaché la plus haute importance concerne les instrument d'éducation et de culture, notemment, la radio et la television.... Le Québec ne peut tolérer plus longtemps d'être tenu à l'écart d'un domaine où son intérêt vital est aussi evident, surtout si l'on tient compte des perspectives d'avenir des moyens audio-visuels de communication de masse." Quoted in G. Proulx (1976), *L'Aventure de la Radio*, p. 60.

18 *Le Devoir*, "Jean-Paul L'Allier expose sa politique: la culture ou rien," 29 May 1976, pp. 1 and 20.

19 *Le Soleil*, "O'Neill craint l'intervention d'Ottawa dans le contôle de la radiodiffusion," 7 April 1977, p. F-1.

20 "A manqué d'intérêt de chacun des réseaux envers l'autre groupe linguistique, s'ajoutent des differences marquees entre les journalists de langue anglaise et ceux de langue française quant aux point de vue, à l'attitude et aux methods de travail," excerpt published in *Le Droit*, "Radio, television et unité nationale," 25 July 1977, p. 7.

21 "Mais le dualisme des réseux, present dès l'origine, a survécu à tous les changement. Cela ne saurait être le fruit du hazard ou de l'entêtement, mais d'un souci de fidelité au reel," Claude Ryan, "Les deux solitudes à Radio Canada," *Le Devoir*, 30 July 1977, p. 4.

22 "Reconnaître la specificité du système télévisuel francophone dans l'ensemble du Canada, ce qui pourrait signifier la mise en place de deux politiques de télédiffusion differentes au pays," from the report "L'avenir de la television francophone au Canada," *La Presse*, 22 May 1985, p. C-1.

23 "La radio-télévision française au Canada, productions, stations et auditoire, est presque entièrement québécoise. Le contenu canadien y est, pour essential, un contenu québécois," from Gerald Caplan and Florian Sauvageau (1986), *Rapport du Groupe de travail sur la politique de la radiodiffusion*, Ottawa: Ministère des Approvisionnement et Services, p. 225.

24 Gerald Caplan and Florian Sauvageau (1986), *Report of the Task Force on Broadcasting Policy*, Ottawa, p. 161.

25 Clare Beckton and A. Wayne Mackay (1986), "Institutional and Constitutional Arrangements: An Overview," in Clare Beckton and Wayne Mackay (eds), *Recurring Issues in Canadian Federalism*, Toronto: University of Toronto Press, p. 4. For discussions of Quebec's de facto special status, see also Alain-G. Gagnon and Joseph Garcea (1988), "Quebec and the Pursuit of Special Status," in Martin Westmacott and R.D. Olling (eds), *Perspectives on Canadian Federalism*, Scarborough: Prentice Hall; Jacques Brossard (1974), "Fédéralisme et status particulier," in Adrian Popovici (ed.), *Problèmes de droit contemporain: Mélanges Louis Baudoin*, Montreal: Les Presses de l'Université de Montréal.

26 Mary Jane Miller (1995), "Will English-Language Television Remain Distinctive," in Kenneth McRoberts (ed.), *Beyond Quebec: Taking Stock of Canada*, Montreal and Kingston: McGill-Queen's University Press, p. 191.

27 Greg Marc Nielsen (1994), *Le Canada de Radio-Canada: Sociologie critique et diagolisme culturel*, Toronto: Éditions du Gref; Alain Laramée (ed.) (1993), *Les communications au Québec*, Montréal: Saint-Martin; Frederick J. Fletcher and Martha Fletcher (1989), "Federalism and Communication Policy: Communications and Confederation Revisited," in David P. Shugarman and Reg Whitaker (eds), *Federalism*

and Political Community: Essays in Honour of Donald Smiley, Peterborough, Ontario: Broadview Press; D.E. Smith (1989), "Broadcasting in the Federation: National Power, Divided Purpose," in David P. Shugarman and Reg Whitaker (eds), *Federalism and Political Community: Essays in Honour of Donald Smiley*, Peterborough, Ontario: Broadview Press; Jonathan Rose (1998), "Federalism, Broadcasting, and the Search for Community," in Martin Westmacott and Hugh Mellon (eds), *Challenges to Canadian Federalism*, Scarborough: Prentice Hall, pp. 129–143.

28 Rowland Lorimer (1995), "The Future of English-Language Publishing," in Kenneth McRoberts (ed.), *Beyond Quebec: Taking Stock of Canada*, Montreal and Kingston: McGill-Queen's University Press, p. 202; this is a point echoed by François Demers (1993), "La presse écrite: fin de cycle, fin de siècle," in Alain Laramée (ed.); *Les communications au Québec*, Montréal: Saint-Martin, pp. 35–54.

29 Arthur Siegel (1983), *Politics and the Media in Canada*, Toronto: McGraw-Hill, pp. 209–210.

30 Marc Raboy (1997), "Media, Nationalism and Identity in Canada and Quebec," *Res Publica*, 1997, Vol. 2, p. 318.

31 Keith Banting notes the support in English-speaking provinces for broader federal engagement; Keith Banting (2005), "Canada: Nation-Building in a Federal Welfare State," in Herbert Obinger, Stephan Leibfried and Francis G. Castles (eds), *Federalism and the Welfare State: New World and European Experiences*, Cambridge: Cambridge University Press, p. 103.

32 While the 1867 British North America Act gave Québec the prerogative to protect French language and Roman Catholicism in the province itself, the key issue here is the asymmetrical relationship Québec has with the federal government which sets it apart from other provinces.

33 Whether the British North America Act was based on a compact between English and French Canada or whether it was a compact between four provinces has historically divided the students of Canadian federalism. As an explanation for the differences in interpretation, some observers have drawn attention to the ambiguity in certain parts of the BNA Act; see Alain-G. Gagnon and Jan Erk (2001), "Legitimacy, Effectiveness and Canadian Federalism; On the Benefits of Ambiguity," in Herman Bakvis and Grace Skogstad (eds), *Canadian Federalism: Performance, Effectiveness and Legitimacy*, Toronto: Oxford University Press, pp. 317–330; David M. Thomas (1997), *Whistling Past the Graveyard: Constitutional Abeyances, Quebec, and the Future of Canada*. Toronto: Oxford University Press; Michael Foley (1989). *The Silence of Constitutions: Gaps, "Abeyances" and Political Temperament in the Maintenance of Government*, London: Routledge.

34 "Depuis la Confédération, le sentiment québécois et canadien-français en général ne s'est pas dementi: la jurisdiction exclusive des provinces sur l'éducation est l'un des point cardinaux du compromise confédératif, elle doit être jalousement gardée et demeurer aussi intégrale que possible," Arthur Tremblay (1955), *Contribution à l'étude des problèmes et des besoins de l'enseignement dans la province de Québec, Commission Royale d'Enquête su le Problèmes Constitutionnels*, Québec, p. 381.

35 David M. Cameron documents the various opt-outs by Québec; David M. Cameron (1991), *More Than an Academic Question: Universities, Government and Public Policy in Canada*, Halifax: Institute for Research on Public Policy, pp. 85–86, 117, 122.

36 Michael Behiels (1985), "Quebec Confronts the New Federalism," in Behiels, *Prelude to Québec's Quiet Revolution: Liberalism versus Neo-nationalism 1945–1960*, Montréal and Kingston: McGill-Queen's University Press, p. 208.

37 From Daniel Johnson's critique of Jean Lesage's budget, delivered on 23 April 1963. English translation in Frank Scott and Michael Oliver (eds) (1964), *Quebec States Her Case: Speeches and Articles from Quebec in the Years of Unrest*, Toronto: Macmillan, p. 33.

38 John Saywell (ed.) (1969), *Canadian Annual Review for 1968*. Toronto: University of Toronto Press, pp. 60–61.

39 Organisation for Economic Cooperation and Development (1976), *Reviews of National Policies for Education – Canada*, Paris: OECD, pp. 96–97, 102–103.

40 "Pourquoi alors n'ont-ils pas fondé leur rapport sur l'indéniable réalité de deux identités 'nationales'? Ne l'ont-ils pas perçu en touchant le filon de la volonté politique du Québec ou en voyant la nécessité de developer les deux cultures majoritaires?" Jean-Marie Beauchemin (1976), "Perception francophone du rapport ou Alice au pays merveilles," in *Reactions to the OECD Review – Canada, 1976 Conference of the Canadian Education Association*, Toronto: The Canadian Education Association, p. 26.

41 From John Roberts' address to the conference "The Humanities in Society: Towards a New Coalition," Ottawa, 22 November 1978; quoted in Susan Hargraves (1981), "Federal Intervention in Canadian Education," in J.W. George Ivany and Michael E. Manley-Casimir (eds), *Federal-Provincial Relations: Education Canada*, Toronto: Ontario Institute for Studies in Education, p. 24.

42 The Constitutional Committee of the Québec Liberal Party (1980), *A New Canadian Federation*, Montreal, p. 77.

43 Francis M. Cox (1981), "The Federal Interest," in J.W. George Ivany and Michael E. Manley-Casimir (eds), *Federal–Provincial Relations: Education Canada*, Toronto: Ontario Institute for Studies in Education, p. 54.

44 Brian R. D. Smith (1981), "The Need for Intergovernmental Cooperation," in J.W. George Ivany and Michael E. Manley-Casimir (eds), *Federal–Provincial Relations: Education Canada*, Toronto: Ontario Institute for Studies in Education, p. 58.

45 *The Globe and Mail*, "For a Federal Role in Education," 14 April 1993, p. A-16.

46 *Maclean's*, "Special Report: What's Wrong at School," 11 January 1993, p. 4.

47 Kymlicka cites the report of the *Citizen's forum on Canada's future* (1991), p. 158; Will Kymlicka (2001), "Minority Nationalism and Multination Federalism," in Will Kymlicka (ed.), *Politics in the Vernacular: Nationalism, Multiculturalism and Citizenship*, Oxford and New York: Oxford University Press, p. 103.

48 Alain Noël (2000), "General Study of the Framework Agreement," Alain-G. Gagnon and Hugh Segal (eds), *The Canadian Social Union Without Quebec*, Montreal: Institute for Research on Public Policy, p. 17.

49 Ibid., pp. 17–18

50 Richard Simeon (2004), "Canada: Federalism, Language, and Regional Conflict," in Ugo M. Amoretti and Nancy Bermeo (eds), *Federalism and Territorial Cleavages*, Baltimore and London: The Johns Hopkins University Press, p. 117.

51 Richard Simeon (1972), *Federal–Provincial Diplomacy: The Making of Recent Policy in Canada*, Toronto: University of Toronto Press, p. 175.

52 Ibid., pp. 232–233.

53 W. Kymlicka (2001), "Minority Nationalism and Multination Federalism," p. 113.

5 Germany

1 Konrad Hesse (1962), *Der unitarische Bundesstaat*, Karlsruhe: C.F. Müller.

2 "Die Crux deutscher Bundesstaatlichkeit besteht demnach von Anbeginn in der mangelnden Deckungsgleichheit von Form und Inhalt. In föderalistischen Institutionen betätigen sich unitarische Akteure, geprägt (überwiegend) von unitarischem Denken und von Interessen/die eher zufällig mit Regionalinteressen koinzidieren." Heidrun Abromeit (1992), *Die verkappte Einheitsstaat*, Opladen: Leske und Budrich, p. 9.

3 Peter Katzenstein (1987), *Policy and Politics in Western Germany: The Growth of a Semi-Sovereign State*, Philadelphia: Temple University Press, p. 15.

4 "[D]as Wesen der Frage ist die Aufgabe der Dekonzentration der Macht, d.h. der Abgrenzung der Gebiete ... gegen die unitarischen Tendenzen des gesellschaftlichen

Lebens in Deutschland." Hermann Brill (1950), "Der Typ des künftigen deutschen Bundeslands," in H.L. Brill, E. Scheu and C.W. Aubin (eds), *Die Bundesländer: Beiträge zur Neugliederung der Bundesrepublik*, Frankfurt am Main: Institut zur Förderung öffentlicher Angelegenheiten, p. 14.

5 Fritz W. Scharpf, Bernd Reissert and Fritz Schnabel (1976), *Politikverflechtung: Theorie und Empirie des kooperativen Föderalismus in der Bundesrepublik*, Kronberg: Scriptor Verlag.

6 Geoffrey Pridham (1973), "A 'Nationalization' Process? Federal Politics and State Elections in West Germany," *Government and Opposition*, Vol. 8, No. 4, pp. 455–473.

7 "Die Regierungen," Elisabeth Noelle and Erich Peter Neumann (eds) (1956), *Jahrbuch der öffentlichen Meinung 1947–1955*, Allensbach: Institut für Demoskopie, p. 280.

8 Ibid., p. 280.

9 Bundesverfassungsgericht (1952), "Urteil vom 20. Februar 1952 'Finanzausgleich'," *Entscheidungen des Bundesverfassungsgerichts*, Tübingen: J.C.B. Mohr, p. 131; Bundesverfassungsgericht (1952), "Urteil vom 21. Mai 1952, Verteilung von Bundeswohnungbaumitteln an die Länder," *Entscheidungen des Bundesverfassungsgerichts*, Tübingen: J.C.B. Mohr, p. 315.

10 Bundesverfassungsgericht (1956), "Urteil vom 1. December 1954, Schranken der Befugnis des Bundes zur Rahmengesetzgebung gemäß Art. 75 GG, Besolddunggesetz für das Land Nordrhein-Westfalen 9. Juni 1954," *Entscheidungen des Bundesverfassungsgerichts*, Tübingen: J.C.B. Mohr, p. 140; also Bundesverfassungsgericht (1957), "Urteil vom 26. März 1957. Reichskonkordat vom 20. Juli 1933. Niedersächsisches Gesetz über das öffentliche Schulwesen vom 14. September 1954," *Entscheidungen des Bundesverfassungsgerichts*, Tübingen: J.C.B. Mohr, p. 361.

11 "Co-operative federalism" was first introduced by the Report of the Troeger Commission set up by the Federal and Länder governments to propose reforms to the financial structure. The Chair of the Commission, Troeger, was the former Finance Minister of the Land Hesse and the Vice-President of the Bundesbank at the time. The recommendations of the Commission for joint Bund–Länder tasks were adopted by the Christian Democrat–Social Democrat grand coalition in 1966.

12 Bundesverfassungsgericht (1959), "Urteil vom 30. Juli 1958," *Entscheidungen des Bundesverfassungsgerichts*, Tübingen: J.C.B. Mohr, p. 138.

13 Philip Blair (1981), *Federalism and Judicial Review in West Germany*, Oxford: Clarendon, p. 209.

14 The Basic Law originally established a separate financial system (*Trennsystem*) for individual Länder and the Bund through Article 109(1). Starting with the 1955 reforms, however, this system of separate finances was gradually replaced by a mixed system (*Mischsystem*) of financial equalization. Accordingly, income, corporate and value added taxes were shared horizontally among the Länder, and vertically between the Länder and the Bund, in a way to channel resources to poorer Länder. For further information on financial equalization, see Hans Mackenstein and Charlie Jeffery (1999), "Financial Equalization in the 1990s: On the Road Back to Karlsruhe?" in Charlie Jeffery (ed.), *Recasting German Federalism: The Legacies of Unification*, London: Pinter; Rüdiger Voigt (1989), "Financing the German Federal System in the 1980s," *Publius: The Journal of Federalism*, Vol. 19; Ulrich Exler (1992), "Financing German Federalism: Problems of Financial Equalization in the German Unification Process," *German Politics*, Vol. 1; Gisela Färber (1992), "Länderfinanzausgleich und Gemeindefinanzen – Anmerkungen zu einigen häufig übersehenen Tatsachen," in Kurt Bohr (ed.), *Föderalismus, Demokratische Struktur für Deutschland und Europa*, Munich: C.H. Beck, pp. 85–122.

15 "Es ist richtig zu sehen, dass Unitarisierung in der Bundesrepublik keineswegs ausssschließlich aus der Zentralisierung von legislativen Kompetenzen beim Bund resul-

tierte, sondern zu einem ganz erheblichen Teil ein Ergebnis der umfangreichen Selbstkoordinierungsaktivitäten der Länder war," Ludger Helms (2002), "Das föderative System der Bundesrepublik Duetschland im internationalen Vergleich," Zeitschrift für Politik, Vol. 49, No. 2, p. 133.

16 "... den in einem homogenen Lande wie der alten Bundesrepublik populären Druck zugunsten einheitlicher und als solcher bereits häufig vorteilhafter Lösungen durch eine solche Selbstkoordinierung aufzufangen, bevor er eine Kompetenzverlagerung auf den Bund erzwingen könnte," Wolfgang Rudzio (1991), *Das politische System der Bundesrepublik Deutschland*, Third Edition, Opladen: Leske und Budrich, p. 354.

17 For a detailed anlaysis of German federalism and media policy, see Jan Erk (2003), "Federalism and Mass Media Policy in Germany," *Regional and Federal Studies*, Vol. 13, No. 2, pp. 107–127.

18 "... ich würde diese Geschichte mit den Sendeanlagen und den Anstalten des öffentlicchen Rechts doch nicht hier hineinnehmen denn das ist die Vorwegnahme einer Gesetzgebung, die heute sehr bunt durcheinander geht und die wir selbstverständlich in die Hand des Bundes bekommen wollen. Wir wollen nicht drei -oder vierlei Radiorecht." From the 32. meeting of the Grundsatzausschuss of the Parlementarische Rat, 11 December 1949, quoted in Carl-Heinz Lüders (1953), *Die Zuständigkeit zur Rundfunkgesetzgebung*, Bonn: Köllen Verlag, p. 40.

19 John Sanford (1976), *The Mass-Media of the German-Speaking Countries*, London: Oswald Wolff, p. 53.

20 Kurt Rebmann, Martin Ott, Werner Storz (1964), *Das baden-württembergische Gesetz über die Presse (Landespressegesetz) vom 14. Januar 1964 nebst dem Modellenentwurf eines Landespressegesetzes*, Kohlhammer: Stuttgart, p. 5.

21 "Mit dem LPrG [*Landespressegesetz*] für Baden-Württemberg konnte deshalb auch ein wesentliche Beitrag zur Rechtseinheit im Bundesgebiet geleistet werden," Ibid., p. 25.

22 "Wahrnehmung der gemeinsamen Interessen der Rundfunkanstalten bei der Ausübung von Hoheitsrechten auf dem Gebiet des Rundfunks," in *Satzung der Arbeitgemeinschaft der öffentlich-rechtlichen Rundfunkanstalten der Bundesrepublik Deutschland (9/10.6.1950)*, Günther Hermann (ed.), *Rundfunkgesetze: Fernsehen und Hörfunk Textsammlung*, Second Edition, Köln, Berlin, Bonn and Munich: Carl Heymanns, p. 300.

23 As a result, ARD included all the broadcasting corporations of the Länder (Bayerischer Rundfunk, Hessischer Rundfunk, Norddeutscher Rundfunk, Radio Bremen, Saarländischer Rundfunk, Sender Freies Berlin, Süddeutscher Rundfunk, Südwestfunk, Westdeutscher Rundfunk). The two federal broadcasting corporations (Deutsche Welle, Deutschlandfunk) and RIAS Berlin (the broadcasting corporation of the American Zone in Berlin) were also to participate in an advisory capacity.

24 "Auch für den Rundfunkbereich liegt der Nutzen vereinten Auftretens auf der Hand, so daß es keiner weiteren Begründung bedarf, daß z.B. das gemeinsame Auftreten aller Rundfunkanstalten in der und durch die ARD gegenüber (insbesondere zentrale Institutionen) effizienter ist als verschiedene Einzelaktivitäten einzelner Rundfunkanstalten," in Günther Hermann (1994), *Rundfunkrecht; Fernsehen und Hörfunk mit neuen Medien*, Munich: C.H. Beck, p. 384.

25 *Gesetz über die Errichtung von Rundfunkansstalten des Bundesrechts vom 29.11.1960*, in G. Hermann (ed.), *Rundfunkgesetze: Fernsehen und Hörfunk Textsammlung*.

26 "... die Länder und nicht der Bund für die Regelung von Organisations-und Programmfragen auf dem Gebiet des Rundfunks zuständig seien." Bundesverwaltungsgericht (1966), "Gültigkeit des Staatsvertrag über die Errichtung des Zweiten Deutsches Fernsehens," *Entscheidungen des Bundesverwaltungsgerichts*, Band 22, Berlin: Carl Heymanns, p. 205.

27 Ibid., p. 229.

28 J. Sanford (1976), *The Mass-Media of the German-Speaking Countries*, p. 105.

29 "Es gibt aber keine Vorschrift im Grundgesetz, nach der Staatsgewalt eines Landes nur in seinem Gebiet ausgeübt werden könnte und bei einer Ausdehnung der Zuständigkeit auf das ganze Bundesgebiet nur der Bund zuständig wäre." Bundesverwaltungsgericht (1966), "Gültigkeit des Staatsvertrages über die Errichtung des Zweiten Deutschen Fernsehens," *Entscheidungen des Bundesverwaltungsgerichts*, Band 22, Berlin: Carl Heymanns, pp. 306–307.

30 "Es kommt hinzu, daß im Hinblick auf Art 30 GG neue, nicht vorhergesehene staatliche Aufgaben nicht ausgeschlossen werden können, die nur einheitlich geregelt oder von einer zentralen Stelle für das Bundesgebiet erfüllt werden können, für die aber der Bund nicht zuständig ist und -jedenfalls in der gebotenen Zeitkürze- auch nicht zuständig gemacht werden kann. Dies nötigt zu einer Auslegung und Handhabung des Grundgesetz, die den Ländern sowohl übereinstimmende einheitliche Regelungen wie die Einrichtung zentraler Stellen für die Erfüllung einer solchen Aufgabe ermöglicht." In Bundesverwaltungsgericht (1966), "Gültigkeit des Staatsvertrag über die Errichtung des Zweiten Deutschen Fernsehens," p. 308.

31 "Viele Schwierigkeiten, die sich im deutschen Rundfunkwesen dadurch ergeben haben, daß überregionale Aufgaben nicht immer entsprechend ihrer Bedeutung gelöst wurden, sind sicher auf diesen organisatorischen Wirrwar zurückzuführen," in Klaus Furchner (1960), *Von der Notwendigkeit der Rundfunkneuordnung in der Bundesrepublik Deutschland*, Würzburg: Johan Wilhelm Nauman, p. 29.

32 "Es ist einer der großen Fehler der föderativen Struktur unseres Grundgesetzes, daß es nur eine Trennung der Zuständigkeiten und eine Aufteilung der Aufgaben auf Bund und Länder kennt, daß es aber nichts von gemeinsamen Aufgaben weiß, die gemeinsam -von Bund und von den Ländern- ausgeführt werden müssen." In Friedrich von der Heydte (1960), "Föderalismus und Rundfunkordnung," from Deutsche Tagespost, 27 January 1969, reproduced in K. Furchner (1960), *Von der Notwendigkeit der Rundfunkneuordnung in der Bundesrepublik Deutschland*, p. 50.

33 "Föderalismus kann auch Verzicht auf Zuständigkeiten um der gemeinsamen Sache willen, er kann Abtrennung von Hoheitsrechten -vermeintlichen und echten Hoheitsrechten – an den Foedus, an den Bund bedeuten," Ibid., p. 52.

34 J. Sanford (1976), *The Mass-Media of the German-Speaking Countries*, p. 130.

35 "Daß die Länder überhaupt zur Koordinierung und Harmonisierung ihrer Aufgaben befugt sind ist wohl keine Frage mehr, über die ernsthaft diskutiert werden muß.... Das Bundesstaatsprinzip gewährt den Ländern zwar die Möglichkeit zu einer sachlich divergierenden Behandlung der ihnen durch die Verfassung zugewiesenen Aufgabenbereiche. Diesem Recht zur abweichenden Handhabung der ihnen eingeräumten Kompetenzen korrespondiert aber keine Pflicht der Länder zur Uneinigkeit." In Klaus Stern (1969), "Föderative und unitarische Aspekte im deutschen Rundfunkwesens," in Hans R. Klecatsky, Klaus Stein, Ulrich Weber, Svente Bergström, *Rundfunkrecht und Rundfunkpolitik: Referate und Reden aus wissenschaftlichen Veranstaltungen des Instituts Rundfunkrecht an der Universität zu Köln*, Munich: C.H. Beck, p. 33.

36 "Es ist nämlich ganz und gar nicht sicher, daß wir mit dem föderalistischen System, so wie wir es heute institutionell haben, die Aufgaben der Zukunft bewältigen können. Das gilt für die Länder in ihrer Form gegenüber dem Verfassungsauftrag, den sie kulturell, wirtschaftlich, sozial und administrativ und auf anderen Gebieten ihren Bürgern gegenüber zu erfüllen haben, das gilt für die Rundfunkanstalten und ihre spezielle Aufgabe der kommunikativen Versorgung der Bevölkerung durch Rundfunk," in Heinz Kühn (1971), *Rundfunkneuordnung und bundesstaatliche Struktur*, Düsseldorf: Landesregierung Nordrhein-Westfalen, p. 8.

37 "Bund und Länder haben sich am 1. Juli 1996 darauf verständigt, im Rahmen der Zuständigkeitsverteilung des Grundgesetzes einen in der Sache einheitlichen Rechtsrahmen in Form eines Bundesgesetzes und eines Länderstaatsvertrags zu schaffen.

Es bestand Einigkeit darüber, die notwendigen Regelungen nicht an unterschiedlichen Auffassungen in Kompetenzfragen scheitern zu lassen." From the *Staatsvertrag über Mediendienste (Mediendienste-Staatsvertrag) vom 20. Januar-12. Februar 1997*, published in *Media Perspectiven Dokumentation* 1996, Vol. 1, p. 25.

38 For a detailed analysis of German federalism and education policy, see Jan Erk (2003), "Federal Germany and its Non-Federal Society: Emergence of an all-German Educational Policy in a System of Exclusive Provincial Jurisdiction," *Canadian Journal of Political Science*, Vol. 36, No. 2, pp. 295–317.

39 Die Ständige Konferenz der Kultusminister der Länder in der Bundesrepublik Deutschland (Kultusministerkonferenz) behandelt Angelegenheiten der Kulturpolitik von über-regionaler Bedeutung mit dem Ziel einer gemeinsamen Meinungs- und Willensbildung und der Vertretung gemeinsamer Anliegen," *Geschäftsordnung der Ständigen Konferenz der Kultusminister der Länder in der Bundesrepublik Deutschland*, according to the resolution dated 19.11.1955, 1.

40 Hessischer Minister für Erziehung, Volksbildung und Justiz, Dr. Edwin Stein: "Die Kultusminister werden durch ihre Zusammenarbeit dazu beitragen, daß bei aller Anerkennung der Länder bedingten Eigenartigen die Einheit des deutschen Geistesleben gewahrt bleibt und gefördert wird," in Bernard Vogel, "Auf dem Weg zur Inneren Einheit: KMK Reflex und Impuls kultureller Identität," Sekretariat der Ständige Konferenz der Kultusminister der Länder in der Bundesrepublik Deutschland (ed.) (1998), *Einheit in der Vielfalt: 50 Jahre Kultusministerkonferenz 1948–1998*, Neuwied, Kniffel and Berlin: Luchterhand, p. 92.

41 "Die KMK hat es verstanden … das erforderliche Mindestmaß an Einheitlichkeit des Bildungswesens in der bundesstaatlichen Verfassungsordnung zu koordinieren und die geistige Einheit Deutschlands zu erhalten." From KMK's fortieth anniversary meeting on 19 February 1988, quoted in Christoph Führ (1996), *Deutsches Bildungswesen seit 1945; Grundzüge und Probleme*, Bonn: Inter Nationes, p. 38.

42 "[Die KMK] hat in Deutschland zu einer Vergleichbarkeit im Bildungswesen geführt, die kein anderer föderalistischer Staat aufweisen kann." Bernard Vogel, "Auf dem Weg zur Inneren Einheit: KMK Reflex und Impuls kultureller Identität," in Sekretariat der Ständige Konferenz der Kultusminister der Länder in der Bundesrepublik Deutschland (ed.) (1998), *Einheit in der Vielfalt*, p. 93.

43 Ibid., p. 93.

44 "Vor allem in der staatlichen Zersplitterung und Teilung nach dem Zweiten Weltkrieg hielt man an dem fest, was nationale Einheit zu verbürgen schien, an der verbinden den Macht von Geschichte, Sprache, Literatur, Musik … wenn man sich schon in einem gemeinsamen Staat, einer gemeinsamen Verfassung aller Deutschen nicht mehr treffen konnte." Hans Maier, "Die Kultusministerkonferenz im Föderalen System," in Sekretariat der Ständige Konferenz der Kultusminister der Länder in der Bundesrepublik Deutschland (ed.) (1998), *Einheit in der Vielfalt*, p. 22.

45 "In Deutschland nämlich erwartet man vom Kulturföderalismus paradoxerweise nicht nur, wie anderswo, die Bewahrung föderaler Eigenheiten der Länder, sondern auch, und fast im selben Atemzug, die Stiftung kultureller Einheit und politischer Homogenität im Gesamtstaat." Ibid., p. 23.

46 "… eine bessere Zusammenarbeit von Bund und Ländern [ist] im Interesse der deutschen Jugend, der deutschen Wissenschaft und Forschung, der deutschen Kultur und des deutschen Volkes." Ständige Konferenz der Kultusminister der Länder in der Bundesrepublik Deutschland, "Die Kultusministerkonferenz und ihre Arbeit von 1952 bis 1955," from *Niederschriften über die Sitzungen des Plenums vom 28–29.4.1955/18.19.1955, 46–49 Sitz*, Bonn: KMK, p. 12.

47 Arthur Hearnden (1974), *Education in the Two Germanies*, Boulder: Westview Press, 1976; first published Oxford: Basil Blackwell, 1974, p. 69.

48 "Die Selbstkoordination der Länder … hat verhindert, daß der Kulturföderalismus zu einer völligen Zersplitterung des Schulrechts führte." Hans Heckel and Herman Ave-

narius, with Helmut Fetzer (1986), *Schulrechtskunde: Ein Handbuch für Praxis, Rechtsprechung und Wissenschaft*, Sixth Edition, Neuwied and Dramstadt: Luchterhand, p. 17.

49 Ibid., p. 16.

50 "Unterricht," Elisabeth Noelle and Erich Peter Neumann (eds) (1956), *Jahrbuch der öffentlichen Meinung 1947–1955*, Allensbach: Institut für Demoskopie, p. 223.

51 Sixteen percent of the respondents were undecided. Ibid., p. 225.

52 For example, see Joachim Tiburtius (1959), "Kulturpolitik: Sache der Länder oder des Bundes," in Ossip K. Flechtheim (ed.), *Bund und Länder*, Berlin: Colloqium Verlag, p. 73.

53 "Vater versetzt, Sohn sitzenbleiben," quoted in Ludwig von Friedeburg (1989), *Bildungsreform in Deutschland: Geschichte und gesellschaftlicher Widerspruch*, Frankfurt am Main: Suhrkamp Verlag, p. 319.

54 Der Ausschuß ist davon überzeugt, daß die geistige Einheit unseres Volkes, die über alle weltanschaulichen und sozialen Unterschiede hinaus besteht und gestärkt werden muß, eine Erziehung fordert, die von allen Schularten gemeinsam zu leisten ist und sie mit einander verbindet. Das kann aber nicht allein durch die Organisation eines für alle Bildungseinrichtungen und Begabungen verbindlichen äußeren Aufbaus erreicht werden. Vielmehr muß eine Besinnung auf den innneren Zusammenhang aller berechtigen Bildungsbedürfnisse unserer Zeit führen …" In "The Frameworkplan for the Remodelling and Standardization of the General Education School System of the German Committee for the Upbringing and Education System," Deutscher Ausschuss für das Erziehungs- und Bildungwesen (1959), *Empfehlungen und Gutachten des Deutschen Ausschuss für das Erziehungs- und Bildungswesen; Rahmenplan zur Umgestaltung und Vereinheitlichung des allgemeinbildendenden öffentlichen Schulwesens*, Stuttgart: Ernst Klett Verlag, p. 2.

55 "Der Schulaufbau muß das Seinige dazu beitragen, die geistige Einheit des Volkes in den elementaren Grunderfahrungen, Übungen und Einsichten kräftig zu erhalten und für das Bewußtsein dieser Einheit einen breiten gemeinsamen Grund zu legen." Ibid., p. 16.

56 "Wissenschaftsrat," Elisabeth Noelle and Erich Peter Neumann (eds) (1967), *Jahrbuch der öffentlichen Meinung 1965–67*, Allensbach and Bonn: Institut für Demoskopie, p. 358.

57 "Wir brauchen … ein Bundeskultusministerium und eine zentrale Kulturverwaltung. Wir brauchen deshalb ein Änderung des Grundgesetz." The article "Die deutsche Bildungskatastrophe" first appeared in *Christ und Welt*. It also appears in Georg Picht (1964), *Die deutsche Bildungskatastrophe, Analyse und Dokumentation*, Olten and Freiburg im Breisgrau: Walter Verlag, p. 45.

58 An example is the April 1964 Baden-Württemberg *Law for the Standardization and Ordering of the School System*. Baden-Württemberg is one of the most powerful German Länder, with sufficient resources to take independent action, but instead of protecting its exclusive jurisdictions from outside encroachment Baden-Württemberg enthusiastically participated in the building of a nationwide educational policy. See Herbert Hochstetter (1972), *Gesetz zur Vereintlichung und Ordnung des Schulwesens in Baden-Württemberg (Schulverwaltunggesetz)*, Fourth Edition, Stuttgart: Kohlhammer, p. 13.

59 "Unsere Kritik richtet sich dagegen, daß dem Bund keine ausreichenden Kompetenzen gegeben werden, die für eine dringend notwendige Reform im Bildungswesen erforderlich sind, um unserer Jugend im internationalen Wettbewerb eine gesicherte Zukunft zu ermöglichen und dadurch das Unbehagen an unserem Staat zu nehmen," quoted from the speech of FDP representative Mishnik at the Bundesrat, Karin S. Poeppelt (1978), *Zum Bildungsgesamtplan der Bund-Länder-Kommission: Die Einfügung des Artikels 91b in das Grundgesetz und der Prozeß der Bildungsplannung für den Elementar-, Primer- und Sekunderbereich in der Bund-Länder-Kommission für Bildungsplanung*, Weinheim and Basel: Beltz Verlag, p. 76.

60 Der Bundesminister für Bildung und Wissenschaft (1970), *Bildungsbericht '70, Report of the Federal Government on Education, The Federal Government's Concept for Educational Policy*, English version, Bonn: 1970, p. 5.

61 Ibid., p. 224.

62 Arthur Gunlicks (1989), Introduction to the special issue "Federalism and Intergovernmental Relations in West Germany: A Fortieth Year Appraisal," *Publius: The Journal of Federalism*, Vol. 19, No. 4, p. 9.

63 "Wenn es überhaupt einen kurzfristigen Ausweg aus dem Dilemma des Kulturföderalismus gibt, hier bahnt er sich an! Die Schaffung der Bund-Länder-Kommission ist ein Ereignis von großer politischer Tragweite- und der hoffnungsvolle Beginn einer neue Aera in der bildungspolitischen Entwicklung unseres Lands." Quoted in Karin S. Poeppelt (1978), *Zum Bildungsgesamtplan der Bund-Länder-Kommission: Die Einfügung des Artikels 91b in das Grundgesetz und der Prozeß der Bildungsplannung für den Elemantar-, Primar- und Sekundarbereich in der Bund-Länder-Kommission für Bildungsplannung*, Weinheim and Basel: Beltz Verlag, pp. 3–4.

64 Bundesverfassungsgericht (1972), "Absoluter Numerus Clausus für Medizinstudium," *Entscheidungen des Bundesverfassungsgericht*, Band 33, Tübingen: J.C.B. Mohr, p. 304.

65 "Entscheidungsbefugnis," Elisabeth Noelle and Erich Peter Neumann (eds) (1974), *Jahrbuch der öffentlichen Meinung 1968–1973*, Allensbach and Bonn: Institut für Demoskopie, p. 171.

66 See Erhard Denninger with Peter Becker, Ulrich Hammer, Andreas Kehler, Jürgen Lüthje, Peter Hauck, Hans-Albert Lennartz, Henning Schrimpf and Bernard Nagel MCL (1984), *Hochschulrahmengesetz: Kommentar*, Münich: C.H. Beck, p. v.

67 "Wie weit nämlich Zentralisierung, Unitarisierung und Koordinierung überhaupt noch getrieben werden können, ohne die in Artikel 79 iii GG verankerte absolute Garantie für den Bundesstaat zu verletzen." Ulrich Karpen (1976), "Plannung des Hochschulwesens und Grundgesetz," in Ulrich Karpen and Franz-Ludwig Knemeyer (eds), *Verfassungsprobleme des Hochschulwesens*, Paderborn: Ferdinand Schöningh, p. 25.

68 "Die Diskrepanz zwischen sachlich Notwendigem und verfassungrechtlich Möglichem bei der Neuordnung der beruflichen Bildung ist einfach unerträglich," Helga Schuhardt, "Auf mehr Bundeskompetenz in der Beruflichen Bildung kann auf die Dauer nicht verzichtet werden," *Frei demokratische Korrespondenz*, 26 September 1975, reproduced in Der Bundesminister für Bildung und Wissenschaft (1978), *Bericht der Bundesregierung über die strukturellen Probleme des föderativen Bildungssystem*, Bonn, p. 124.

69 "Die von diesen Entscheidungen in erster Linie Betroffenen – die Schüler, Auszubildenden und Studenten, die Eltern und Lehrer -erwarten zu Recht, daß auch in einem Bundesstaat ein Mindestmaß an notwendiger Einheitlichkeit im Bildungswesen als Voraussetzung für Freizügigkeit, Mobilität und Chancengleichheit im Bildungwesen und Beschäftigungssystem gesichert wird," Der Bundesminister für Bildung und Wissenschaft (1978), *Bericht der Bundesregierung über die strukturellen Probleme des föderativen Bildungssystem*, Bonn, p. 5.

70 Jürgen Baumert and Dietricht Goldschmidt (1980), "Centralization and Decentralization as Determinants of Educational Policy in the Federal Republic of Germany," *Social Science Information*, Vol. 19, p. 1046.

71 For further details, see Ständige Konferenz der Kultusminister der Länder in der Bundesrepublik Deutschland (1995), "Hohenheimer Memorandum zur Bildungs-, Wissenschafts- und Kulturpolitik im geeinten Deutschland," in *Handbuch für die Kultusminister-Konferenz*, Bonn: KMK.

72 "Der Föderalismus und die Kulturhoheit der Länder sind eine unaufgebbare Voraussetzung für Vielfalt und Wettbewerb unterschiedlicher Ansätze und Wege. Die Länder stehen aber auch in der besonderen Verantwortung, nicht nur die grundsät-

zliche Gleichwertigkeit der Bildungsgänge, sondern vor allem ein gleichwertiges Niveau in den Abschlüssen unterschiedlicher Bildungsgänge zu gewährleisten.... Schulabschlüsse sind Schritte, Marksteine auf dem Weg jedes einzelnen." Christlich-Demokratische Union (CDU), *Erziehung, Ausbildung und Bildung in unserer frei-heitlichen Demokratie: Für die humane Leistungsschule und ein leistungfähiges Hochschulsystem* (1993), reproduced in Berthold Michael and Heinz-Herman Schepp (eds) (1993), *Die Schule in Staat und Gesellschaft; Dokumente zur deutschen Schulgeschichte im 19. und 20. Jahrhundert*, Göttingen and Zürich: Muster-Schmidt Verlag, p. 484.

73 Sozialdemokratische Partei Deutschlands (SPD), *Grundsatzprogramm der SPD* (1989), reproduced in Ibid.

74 "Um die Einheit des Bildungswesens im zukünftigen Reichsgebiet vorzubereiten, sind die in den einzelnen Ländern vorhandenen Organisationsformen durch eine bun-deseinheitliche Regelung einander anzugleichen." From the FDP 1950 Basic Points on Cultural Policy, quoted in K. Poeppelt (1978), *Zum Bildungsgesamtplan der Bund-Länder-Kommission*, p. 41.

75 "Die FDP will den Grundsatz der Länderkompetenz insoweit erhalten, als sie der Kompatibilität von Ausbildungsgängen innerhalb Deutschlands nicht entgegensteht. Dazu muß der Bund mit den notwendigen Rahmenkompetenzen ausgestattet werden. Mobilität von Lehrenden und Lernenden darf im europäische Integrationprozeß nicht an den Grenzen von Bundesländern scheitern." Frei Demokratische Partei (FDP), *Soziale Chancen durch liberale Marktwirtschaft* (1991), reproduced in Berthold Michael and Heinz-Herman Schepp (eds) (1993), *Die Schule in Staat und Gesellschaft; Dokumente zur deutschen Schulgeschichte im 19. und 20. Jahrhundert*, Göttingen and Zürich: Muster-Schmidt Verlag, p. 501.

76 A recent initiative was led by the Land of North Rhine-Westphalia. A report commis-sioned in 1995 by its Minister-President at the time, Johannes Rau – who later became the President of the Federal Republic – renews calls for a major reform of education. This report, entitled "Future of Education – Schools of the Future," deals with the themes of harmonization and efficiency in German national education. Min-isterpräsidenten des Landes Nordrhein-Westfalen/Bildungskommission Nordrhein-Westfalen (1995), *Zukunft der Bildung-Schule der Zukunft: Denkschrift der Kommission "Zukunft der Bildung-Schule der Zukunft*, Neuwied: Luchterhand.

77 "Zusammenarbeit der Länder ist in der Bundesrepublik Deutschland tägliche Selb-stverständlichkeit. Und weiterhin bleibt kooperativer Föderalismus ein Gebot des Grundgesetzes -und der Vernunft!" Günther Hermann (1994), *Rundfunkrecht; Fernsehen und Hörfunk mit neuen Medien*, Munich: C.H. Beck, p. 155.

78 Gerhard Lehmbruch (1996), "German Federalism and the Challenge of Unification," in Joachim Jens Hesse and Vincent Wright (eds), *Federalizing Europe? The Costs, Benefits and Preconditions of Federal Political Systems*, Oxford: Oxford University Press, p. 173.

79 Steffen Schneider (2004), "Labour Market Policy and the Unemployment Crisis in the Federal Republic of Germany: Institutional Sclerosis or Corporatist Renewal?" in Alain Noël (ed.) (2004), *Federalism and Labour Market Policy: Comparing Different Governance and Employment Strategies*, Montréal and Kingston: McGill-Queen's University Press, p. 88.

6 Switzerland

1 For an earlier application of this line of inquiry, see Jan Erk (2003), "Swiss Federal-ism and Congruence," *Nationalism and Ethnic Politics*, Vol. 9, No. 2, pp. 50–74. André Bächtiger and Jürg Steiner have also drawn attention to the limits of explaining Swiss federalism through institutions; André Bächtiger and Jürg Steiner (2004), "Switzerland: Territorial Cleavage Management as Paragon and Paradox," in Ugo M.

Amoretti and Nancy Bermeo (eds), *Federalism and Territorial Cleavages*, Baltimore and London: The Johns Hopkins University Press, p. 28.

2 The emergence of language as the primary social cleavage at the expense of religion is documented by Uli Windisch in his study of the two bilingual cantons of Fribourg and Valais. Windisch's study shows that in the linguistically and confessionally mixed areas of canton Fribourg (Courgevaux, Cressier, Courtepin and Morat), religion used to be the main social cleavage historically. This pattern has changed in the direction of linguistic communities becoming the primary social collectivity. Uli Windisch (1992), *Les relations quoditiennes entre Romands et Suisse allemande: Les cantons bilingues de Fribourg et du Valais*, Volume 1, Lausanne: Payot, pp. 607–608.

3 The population of seven million includes 1,318,000 foreign residents, who make up 18.8 percent of the population and 27 percent of the work force. Jonathan Steinberg (1996), *Why Switzerland?* Second Edition, Cambridge: Cambridge University Press, pp. 124–127.

4 Six of the half-cantons are: Appenzell-Inner-Rhoden and Appenzell-Outer-Rhoden, Basel-City and Basel-Land, Obwalden and Nidwalden. The remaining twenty are Zurich, Bern, Luzern, Uri, Schwyz, Glarus, Zug, Fribourg, Solothurn, Schaffhausen, St Gallen, Grisons, Thurgau, Aargau, Ticino, Vaud, Valais, Neuchâtel, Geneva and Jura.

5 "Die Schweiz ist kein Nationalstaat, kein Einheitstaat, kein Staat, der sich als homogene Einheit postuliert; in dem Maße, in dem ihre heutigen Strukturen ohne Bruch der Kontinuität die alten Gemeindefreiheiten des Mittelalters bewahrt haben, ist sie sogar die Antithese des modernen Staates, wie ihn das kontinentale Europa seit dem 19. Jahrhundert begriffen hat. In Ihrer Entstehung und in ihrem historischen Selbstbewusstsein ist die Schweiz nicht anderes als jene Allianz mittelalterlicher Partikularismen gegen die historischen Tendenz zur Vereintlichung zentral gelenkter territorialer, dynastischer, administrativer oder nationaler Staaten, und dieses Geschichtsbewusstsein hat ihre politische Zivilisation begründet." Herbert Lüthy (1966), "Politische Probleme der Mehrsprachigkeit in der Schweiz," *Civitas*, Vol. 22, p. 40.

6 J. Steinberg (1996), *Why Switzerland*, p. 88.

7 Women gained the right to vote in federal elections only in 1971. In the canton of Appenzell, they had to wait until 1990.

8 For further discussion on the weaknesses of the court, see A. Bächtiger and J. Steiner (2004), "Switzerland: Territorial Cleavage Management as Paragon and Paradox," p. 49.

9 The French-speaking and Catholic Jura was a part of the Bern canton dominated by German-speaking Protestants. The linguistic tensions underscored by the religious divide always existed, but the so-called *l'Affaire Moeckli*, named after the Francophone bureaucrat denied a public works position by the cantonal government in 1947, became a turning point for the Jurassian autonomy movement. The first initiative for the establishment of a new Jura canton was defeated in 1959. In 1963, the *Front de liberation du Jura* was formed, around which the autonomist movement was organized. Finally, in 1974, seven districts of the Jura voted for a new canton, with 51.9 percent of the vote in favor. In 1975, the districts which had voted against the proposal voted in another referendum on whether or not to remain attached to Bern. In 1979, Jura officially became a new member of the Swiss confederation.

10 The principle of federal comity (*Bundestreue*) is alternatively referred to as the "federal duty of comity" (*Bundestaatliche Treupflicht*), "duty of consideration" (*Rücksichtpflicht*) or "federal trust" (*fidelité confédérale*). Federal comity is often considered together with the related notions of cooperative federalism (*kooperativer föderalismus*) and executive federalism (*Vollzugföderalismus/fédéralisme de la mise en oeuvre*).

11 François Grin (1999), "Language Policy in Multilingual Switzerland: Overview and

Recent Developments," *ECMI Brief* No. 2, Flensburg: European Centre for Minority Issues, p. 6.

12 "Nous vivons les uns à côté des autres, mais pas ensemble. Ce qui manque, c'est le dialogue, la communication entre Alémaniques et Romands." Quoted in Ernest Weibel with Cordélia Monnier and Marie-Laure Bégin (1997), *La cohesion nationale menacée?/Ist der nationale Zusammenhalt in Frage gestellt?* Neuchâtel: Université de Neuchâtel, p. 37.

13 "Ils constatent une mutation du clivage linguistique dans le contexte institutionnel de la Suisse. Les divergences ne peuvent plus, comme c'était le cas naguerre, être conciliées grace au fédéralisme. Toutes les questions importantes auxquelles la Suisse est confrontées aujourd'hui concernent également, dans de nombreux cas, ses relations extérieurs; ce qui a tendance à accentuer le clivage linguistique." Ibid., p. 55.

14 "Die verschiedenen Befragungen bestätigen die kulturelle Bedeutung der Sprachräume. Die Sprachraumgehörigkeit hat Einfluss auf die Berufswahl, auf die Ferienorte, auf die Häufigkeit des Medienkonsums, auf die Einschätzung der Beziehungen zwischen der Landesteilen. Die Sprachräume bestimmen in hohem Mass das persönliche Beziehungsfeld und das Schulwesen, sie bilden auch eigene Mediengemeinschaft. Die Wichtigkeit der sprachkulturellen Komponente wird auch im Vergleich mit der geringen Prägewirkung der konfessionellen Komponente deutlich." Georg Kreis (1993), *Die Schweiz unterwegs: Schlussbericht des Nationales Forschungsprogramm 21 "Kulturelle Vielvalt und Nationale Identität,"* Basel: Helbing and Lichtenhahn, p. 98.

15 Hanspeter Kriesi, "State Formation and Nation Building in the Swiss Case," in Hanspeter Kriesi, Klaus Armingeon, Hannes Siegrist and Andreas Wimmer (eds) (1999), *Nation and National Identity: The European Experience in Perspective*, Zurich and Chur: Ruegger, p. 21. Italics in original.

16 "L'identité linguistique devient une dimension plus importante, voire determinante, de l'identité social, du sentiment d'appartenance à une communauté." Uli Windisch (1992), *Les relations quoditiennes entre Romands et Suisse allemande: Les cantons bilingues de Fribourg et du Valais*, Vol. 2, Lausanne: Payot, p. 444.

17 William Martin (1971), *Switzerland: From Roman Times to the Present*, New York: Praeger, p. 243.

18 Henry Kerr has written about stronger linguistic identity among Swiss Romands. Henry H. Kerr Jr. (1974), *Switzerland: Social Cleavages and partisan Conflict*, London and Beverly Hills: Sage, p. 24.

19 "Von der welschen Schweiz zu reden ist angebracht und zutreffend, wenn damit die Region als Sprachgemeinschaft wird. In jeder anderen Hinsicht aber – ob historisch, politisch, wirtschaftlich, geographisch, religiös, kulturell – ist *die* Romandie ebenso eine Fiktion, wie wenn man von einer politisch oder kulturell uniformen Deutschschweiz reden wollte." Hans Amstutz (1996), *Das Verhältnis zwischen deutscher und französischer Scwhweiz in den Jahren 1930–1945*, Aargau, Frankfurt am Main, Salzburg: Sauerländer, p. 46.

20 Alexandre Trechsel's study of federal elections is an example of such studies which find strong relationship between linguistic divisions and voting patterns: "En conclusion, nous devons nous rendre à l'évidence que nos données montrent incontestablement que les trois électorats linguistiques en Suisse se distinguent quant à leurs choix politiques lors des élections fédérales," Alexandre H. Trechsel (1995), *Clivages en Suisse: Analyse des impact relatifs des clivages sur l'électorat suisse lors des élections fédérales*, Geneva: Université de Genève, p. 47. René Knüsel has also shown the prevalence of the linguistic cleavage in federal elections; René Knüsel (1994), *Les minorités ethnolinguistique autochtones à territoire: L'exemple du cas helvétique*, Lausanne: Payot, pp. 261–289. The divergence between Swiss Romand and German Swiss voting patterns is also noted in Thomas Widmer and Christof Buri (1992), "Brüssel oder Bern: schlägt das Herz der 'Romands' eher für

Europa?" *Annuaire Suisse de science politique*, Vol. 32, pp. 363–388, especially p. 385.

21 "... de même que chaque communauté cantonal possède son pouvoir politique qui la représente, il faut que chaque communauté ou groupement linguistique possède aussi son pouvoir politique qui la représente. Autrement dit, il faut constituer une confédération romande et une confédération alémanique, qui seront réunies entre elles par une pacte fédérale, auquel s'adjoindront le Tessin et les Grisons." From Pierre Guye (1937), *Le pays romand et la civilisation latin*, quoted in Hans Amstutz, op. cit., p. 112.

22 For example, Uli Windisch stresses to the role media plays in Swiss politics as the provider of the basis for democratic deliberation. Uli Windisch (1998), "Médias et communication politique en démocratie directe: quinze theses," in U. Windisch (ed.), *La Suisse: clichés, délire, réalité*, Lausanne: L'Age d'homme, pp. 79–94. See also Andreas Wuerth (1999), *Die SRG und ihr Integrationsauftrag: Wandel-Gründe-Konsequenzen*, Bern, Stuttgart and Vienna: Paul Haupt.

23 "Es is offensichtlich, dass die schweizerischen Sprachregionen das wohl stärkste Bollwerk gegen die Ausformung einer gesamtschweizerischen Einheitlichkeit der Vorstellungen bilden. Medien, die man nicht versteht, haben keine Wirkung. Wir haben in der Schweiz vielleicht ein deutschschweizerische Uniformisierung und eine welsche, aber kaum, jedenfalls nicht im gleichen Masse, eine schweizerische." From Max Frenkel's presentation in Eric Golaz, Moritz Gubler, François Logez, Olivier Meuwly, Jean Paschoud, Olivier Weniger (eds) (1990), *Perspectives Media: Fédéralisme et concentration des médias/Media Perspectiven: Föderalismus und Medienkonzentration*, Lausanne: Société d'étudiants Helvetica, p. 155.

24 "Die drei Sprachräume der Deutschschweiz, der Romandie und des Tessins sind bis heute politisch nicht nur autonom, sondern auch relative geschlossen bleiben. Der grösste Teil der Bürgerinnen und Bürger verfügt zwar über elektronische Medienangebote aller Sprachen, nutzt aber nur diejenigen der Muttersprache." Wolf Linder (1999), "Politische Kultur," in Ulrich Klöti, Peter Knoepfel, Hanspeter Kriesi, Wolf Linder and Yannis Papadopoulos (eds), *Handbuch der Schweizer Politik/Manuel de la politique suisse*, Zurich: Verlag Neue Zürcher Zeitung, p. 18.

25 European Media Landscape, www.ejc.nl/jr/emland/switzerland.html (accessed 3 June 2003).

26 "L'usage qui est fait des medias est d'abord et avant tout lié à la langue maternelle.... "Aucun media national". Cette constation suffit à faire apparaître la caractéristique principale du paysage médiatique helvétique.... La Suisse ne connaît donc pas l'existence d'un média national. L'attention des journalistes se concentre avant tout sur le proche environnement de même langue, puis sur un horizon plus lointain, mais appartenant à la même communauté linguistique. L'intérêt porté aux autres espaces culturels de Suisse ne vient qu'ensuite.' Werner A. Meier and Michael Schanne (1995), *La paysage médiatique Suisse*, Zurich: Pro Helvetia, p. 36.

27 For Belgian broadcasting and linguistic nationalism, see Jan Servaes (1998), "Médias et politique," in Marco Martiniello and Marc Swyngedouw (eds), *Où va la Belgique? Les soubresauts d'une petite démocratie européenne*, Paris: L'Harmattan; Christian Carette, Jan de Groof, Patrick Peeters, Jan Vermeire (1993), *La Législation des Media, Le cadre normatif général, Les normes administratives et techniques relatives aux radio- et télécommunications*, Cepess: Brussels.

28 "[der SRG] treibt die linguistische Differenzierung immer mehr voran, denn in bezug auf die sprachregionale Integration nimmt die national konzipierte SRG eine zunehmend ambivalente Position ein, verläuft doch bei den audiovisuellen Medien und insbesondere eben bei der SRG die Trennung zusehends entlang den Sprachgrenzen." André Wuerth (1999), "Mediensystem und politische Kommunikation," in Ulrich Klöti, Peter Knoepfel, Hanspeter Kriesi, Wolf Linder and Yannis Papadopoulos (eds), *Handbuch der Schweizer Politik/Manuel de la politique suisse*, Zurich: Verlag Neue Zürcher Zeitung, p. 344

29 [Note: Stucki counts the half cantons together, and since the statement was made before the creation of the canton Jura, the number of cantons is 22]. "Die Schweiz besteht nicht primär aus einem deutschsprachigen, französischsprachigen und italienischsprachigen Teil und auch nicht aus einzelnen Regionen, Ost-, Zentral und Nordwestschweiz, sondern eben aus den 22 Kantonen.... Es ist aber gefährlich, wenn die Schweiz in einzelne Blöcke aufgeteilt werden sollte, besonders wenn diese Blöcke mit den Sprachgrenzen zusammenfallen." Ständerat Stucki, *Schweizerische Volkspartei* representative from Zurich, Sitzung vom 17. December 1968/Séance du 17 décembre 1968, Ständerat-Conseil des États (1968), *Amtliches Bulletin der Bundesversammlung/Bulletin officiel de l'Assemblée fédérale*, Bern: Verbandsdruckerei AG, 1968, p. 305.

30 "... il y a trois sociétés régionales importantes, que chacun d'elles pour les trois programmes, ait des commissions de programmes différentes. C'est cet aspect de la diversité des trois chaînes par rapport aux trois langues, qui nous a permis d'être traité pratiquement comme trois pays." Conseiller fédérale Bonvin, *Christlichsoziale Volkspartei*, Sitzung vom 17. December 1968/Séance du 17 décembre 1968, Ständerat-Conseil des États (1968), *Amtliches Bulletin der Bundesversammlung/Bulletin officiel de l'Assemblée fédérale*, Bern: Verbandsdruckerei AG, p. 306.

31 The study is based on opinion polls carried out in 1998 and 1999. Matthias Steinman, Sabine Zaugg and Roman Gattlen (2000), *Medien und Identität: Eine Studie zum Beitrag von Radio- und Fernsehprogrammen zur gesellschaftlichen und kulturellen Integration in der Schweiz*, Bern: SRG/SSR, p. 189. For divisions particularly in television, see Adrienne Corboud Fumagalli (1996), "Une Suisse ou trios regions?" *Medienwissenschaft Schweiz*, Vol. 1, pp. 11–17.

32 "De plus, l'espace public s'avère strictement segmenté selon des frontières entre les régions linguistiques: tant l'analyse de la distribution de la presse, que celle de la diffusion des médias audiovisuels (télévision et radio) ont montré que les citoyens suisses n'utilisent pas les médias des autres régions linguistiques. Les Suisses de toutes les régions linguistiques se tournent plutôt vers les médias des pays voisins parlant la même langue." Hanspeter Kriesi, Boris Wernli, Pascal Sciarini and Matteo Gianni (1996), *Le clivage linguistique: Problèmes de compréhension entre les communautés linguistiques en Suisse*, Berne: Office fédéral de la statistique, p. 7.

33 For the Belgian case, for example, see OESE (Doorlichting van het Educatief Overheidsbeleid), Ministerie van de Vlaamse Gemeenschap, Department Onderwijs, Ministère de l'Education, de la Recherche et de la Formation; Verwaltung de Deutschsprachigen Gemeinschaft, Abteilung Unterricht (1991), *Het Educatief Bestel in België: Van Convergentie naar Divergentie*, Brussels.

34 In fact, at the time of establishment the name of the institution was the "Central Office for Information on School and Education Question" (*Zentrale Informationstelle für Fragen des Schul- und Erziehungs-wesens*). The name was changed to CESDOC later in 1971.

35 At the time of the agreement, the unilingual French-speaking canton Jura did not exist. The sixth canton to the agreement is the bilingual canton of Bern, which had joined the initiative because of its French-speaking inhabitants in the Jura.

36 The secretariat of the CIRCE was initially in Neuchâtel; it has since moved to Lausanne.

37 Tschoumy cites the ISOPUBLIC poll; Jacques-A. Tschoumy (1985), 'L'innovation scolaire en suisse romande', in Giovanni Busino (ed.), *Les politiques scolaire des Cantons Romands et du Tessin*, Special Issue of *Revue Européene des sciences sociales*, Vol. XXIII, No. 70, p. 163.

38 "Ce sont incontestablement la mise en commun de compétences ainsi que la ligne politique à définir afin d'arriver à une meilleure harmonisation en matière scolaire," in Conférence intercantonale de l'instruction publique de la Suisse romande et du Tessin, CIIP (1999), *Politiques de l'Éducation et Chemin de traverse: 125 ans de collaboration intercantonale en Suisse romand*, Neuchâtel: CIIP, p. 29.

39 "Lassen wir doch der welschen Schweiz und dem Tessin den Herbstschulbeginn und bemühen wir uns in der deutschen Schweiz wieder mehr um die innere Koordination," Nationalrat Müller, *Schweizerische Volkspartei* representative for canton Aargau, Nationalrat-Conseil national, *Amtliches Bulletin der Bundesversammlung/ Bulletin officiel de l'Assemblée fédérale*, 21 March 1984, p. 299.

40 "Selbstverständlich haben wir als Föderalistischen alle zwei Seelen in unserer Brust. ... Natürlich kann man den Graben Welsch-/Deutschschweiz in seiner Bedeutung herunterspielen, aber wir sind in letzter Zeit doch dazu übergegangen, dünne Linien auf der Landeskarte zu ziehen. Aus diesen dünne Linie kann eben doch mit der Zeit einmal ein dicker Strich warden." Nationalrat Keller, *Christlichdemokratische Volkspartei* representative for canton Aargau, Nationalrat-Conseil national, *Amtliches Bulletin der Bundesversammlung/Bulletin officiel de l'Assemblée fédérale*, 21 March 1984, p. 304.

41 Gunther Hega (2000), "Federalism, Subsidiarity and Educational Policy in Switzerland," *Regional and Federal Studies*, Vol. 10, No. 1, p. 6.

42 In particular, canton Vaud has been reluctant to give up certain aspects of its historically distinct educational system. For more information on Vaud's educational system, see, Geneviève Heller, "L'école vaudoise: entre l'identité Suisse et l'identité cantonale," in François de Capitani and Georg Germann (eds) (1987), *Auf dem Weg zu einer schweizerischen Identität 1848–1914*, Fribourg: Universitätsverlag Freiburg Schweiz, pp. 245–271.

43 "Der lebendige Inhalt des Föderalismus [ist] nicht die Kompetenzordnung zwischen Bund und Kantonen, sondern die Verwirklichung der Demokratie auf allen Ebenen der Gesellschaft," quoted in Dorothee Starck (1999), *Föderalismus in der Schweiz: Darstellung der Strukturen und der praktischen Erfahrungen*, Speyer.

44 The collection includes interviews with over twenty prominent Swiss from various fields ranging from politics to business. The interviews originally appeared on the pages of the newspaper *Journal de Genève et Gazette de Lausanne*. Daniel-S. Miéville (ed.) (1996), *"La Suisse est-elle soluble dans l'Europe?" Journal de Genève et Gazette de Lausanne.*

45 J. Steinberg (1996), *Why Switzerland?* p. 127.

46 "Le principe de la Suisse, sa racine, sa raison d'être, sa valeur, son originalité, c'est le fédéralisme. La Suisse sera fédéraliste ou elle ne sera pas." Gonzague de Reynold (1938), *Conscience de la Suisse*, Neuchâtel.

7 The political sociology of federalism

1 Reinhard Bendix and Seymour Martin Lipset (1957), "Political Sociology: An Essay," *Current Sociology*, Vol. VI, No. 2, p. 87.

2 Giovanni Sartori (1969), "Sociology of Politics and Political Sociology," in Seymour Martin Lipset (ed.), *Politics and the Social Sciences*, New York: Oxford University Press, p. 67.

3 Barry Wellman and S.D. Berkowitz (eds) (1988), *Social Structures: A Network Approach*, Cambridge: Cambridge University Press, pp. 332–358.

4 Gregory M. Luebbert (1991), *Liberalism, Fascism, or Social Democracy: Social Classes and the Political Origins of Regimes in Interwar Europe*, New York and Oxford: Oxford University Press, p. 306.

5 Ibid., p. 307.

6 Stefano Bartolini (2000), *The Political Mobilisation of the European Left, 1860–1980: The Class Cleavage*, Cambridge: Cambridge University Press, p. 49.

7 Colin Crouch (2001), "Breaking Open Black Boxes: The Implications for Sociological Theory of European Integration," in Anand Menon and Vincent Wright (eds), *From the Nation State to Europe? Essays in Honour of Jack Hayward*, Oxford: Oxford University Press, p. 197.

8 Mark I. Lichbach (1997), "Social Theory and Comparative Politics," in Mark Irving Lichbach and Alan S. Zuckerman (eds), *Comparative Politics: Rationality, Culture, and Structure*, Cambridge: Cambridge University Press, p. 258.

9 From the *Federalist* No. 2, which is one of the letters supporting the new constitution printed in newspapers under the pseudonym "Publius" during 1787–88. From Alexander Hamilton, James Madison and John Jay (1961), *The Federalist Papers*, Mentor: New York, p. 38.

10 Joseph Zimmerman (1992), *Contemporary American Federalism: The Growth of National Power*, New York: Praeger, p. 189.

11 Joseph F. Zimmerman (1981), "Frustrating National Policy: Partial Federal Preemption," in Jerome J. Hanus (ed.), *The Nationalization of State Government*, Lexington: D.C. Heath; see also Felix Morley (1959), *Freedom and Federalism*, Chicago: Henry Regnery.

12 James Sundquist (1969), *Making Federalism Work*, Washington, DC: Brookings Institution, p. 10.

13 Ibid., p. 12.

14 Morton Grodzins and Daniel Elazar (1974), "Centralization and Decentralization in the American Federal System," in Robert A. Goldwin (ed.), *A Nation of States: Essays on the American Federal System*, Second Edition, Chicago: Rand McNally, p. 19.

15 Mel Dubnick and Alan Gitelson (1981), "Nationalizing State Policies," in Jerome J. Hanus (ed.), *The Nationalization of State Government*, Lexington: D.C. Heath, pp. 39–74.

16 See Robert B. Hawkins Jr. (1982), *American Federalism: A New Partnership for the Republic*, San Francisco: Institute for Contemporary Studies, p. 5; also Samuel Beer (1988), "Introduction," in Timothy Conlan, *New Federalism: Intergovernmental Reform from Nixon to Reagan*, Washington, DC: The Brookings Institution, pp. ix–xxii.

17 Louis Hartz (1955), *The Liberal Tradition in America: An Interpretation of American Political Thought Since the Revolution*, New York: Harcourt, Brace and World; Seymour Martin Lipset (1967), *The First New Nation: The United States in Historical and Comparative Perspective*, New York: Doubleday; Seymour Martin Lipset (1996), *American Exceptionalism: A Double Edged Sword*, New York and London: W.W. Norton.

18 Thomas R. Dye (1990), *American Federalism, Competition Among Governments*, Lexington: Lexington Books, pp. 184–185.

19 David C. Nice (1988), *Federalism: The Politics of Intergovernmental Relations*, New York: St Martin's Press, p. 24.

20 Harry N. Scheiber (2002), "American Federalism as a Working System and as a Constitutional Model," in Jürgen Rose and Johannes Ch. Traut (eds), *Federalism and Decentralization: Perspectives for the Transformation Process in Eastern and Central Europe*, Hamburg: Lit Verlag, and New York: Palgrave, p. 57.

21 Samuel H. Beer (1993), *To Make a Nation: The Rediscovery of American Federalism*, Cambridge: Belknap.

22 Samuel H. Beer (1988), "Introduction," in Timothy Conlan, *New Federalism: Intergovernmental Reform from Nixon to Reagan*, Washington, DC: Brookings Institution, p. xii.

23 The omission of the word "federal" from the Constitution was mainly done to prevent a conservative nationalist reaction against the democratic reforms. Despite the lack of a *pro forma* label, the political structure of Spain is sufficiently federal to allow comparisons with federal experiences elsewhere.

24 Michael Burgess (1995), "Federalism and the European Union: Political Change and Continuity in the European Community," in C. Lloyd Brown-John (ed.), *Federal Type Solutions and European Integration*, Lanham and London: University Press of America, p. 68. Italics in original.

25 For example, see Robert Agranoff (2005) "Federal asymmetry and intergovernmental relations in Spain," Institute for intergovernmental studies, Kingston: Queens' Uni-

versity Working Paper; Ferran Requejo (2005), *Multinational Federalism and Value Pluralism: the Spanish Case*, London: Routledge.

26　Basque and Catalan governments assumed these powers in 1985; Galicia followed suit two years later. Wilfried Swenden (2001), "Comparative Federalism and Higher Education: Some Thoughts for Reflection," *European Journal of Education Law and Policy*, Vol. 5, p. 154.

27　Anna Melich (1990), *Identité Nationale et Media Contemporains: Les Suisses, la pluriculture et les plurimedia*, Lausanne: LEP, pp. 118–121.

28　Robert Agranoff (1994), "Asymmetrical and Symmetrical Federalism in Spain: An Examination of Intergovernmental Policy," in Bertus de Villiers (ed.), *Evaluating Federal Systems*, Dordrecht, Boston and London: Martinus Nijhoff; Josep Ma Valles and Montserrat Cuchilllo Foix (1988), "Decentralisation in Spain: A Review," *European Journal of Political Research*, Vol. 16; Luis Moreno (1994), "Ethnoterritorial Concurrence and Imperfect Federalism in Spain," in Bertus de Villiers (ed.), *Evaluating Federal Systems*, Dordrecht, Boston and London: Martinus Nijhoff; Luis Moreno (1999), "Asymmetry in Spain: Federalism in the Making," in Robert Agranoff (ed.), *Accommodating Diversity: Asymmetry in Federal States*, Baden-Baden: Nomos.

29　Robert Agranoff and Juan Antonio Ramos Gallarín (1997), "Toward Federal Democracy in Spain: An Examination of Intergovernmental Relations," *Publius: Journal of Federalism*, Vol. 27, No. 4, p. 38

30　Luis Moreno (2001), *The Federalization of Spain*, London and Portland, Oregon: Frank Cass, p. 154.

31　Winston Gregory McMinn (1994), *Nationalism and Federalism in Australia*, Melbourne: Oxford University Press, p. 1.

32　Brian Galligan (1989), "Federal Theory and Australian Federalism: A Political Science Perspective," in Brian Galligan (ed.), *Australian Federalism*, Melbourne: Longman Chesire, pp. 43–45.

33　Lawrence Mayer (1970), "Federalism and party behavior in Australia and Canada," *The Western Political Quarterly*, Vol. 23, No. 4, p. 798.

34　William H. Riker (1964), *Federalism; Origin, Operation, Significance*, Boston and Toronto: Little, Brown and Company, p. 113.

35　William S. Livingston (1968), "Canada, Australia and the United States: Variations on a Theme," in Valerie Earle (ed.), *Federalism: Infinite Variety in Theory and Practice*, Itasca: Peacock, p. 140.

36　Francis G. Castles and John Uhr (2005), "Australia: Federal Constraints and Institutional Innovations," in Herbert Obinger, Stephan Leibfried and Francis G. Castles (eds), *Federalism and the Welfare State: New World and European Experiences*, Cambridge: Cambridge University Press, p. 61.

37　Painter quotes the Australian Education Council Charter from Andrew Spaull (1987), *A History of the Australian Education Council, 1936–1986*, Sydney: Allen and Unwin, p. 315, in Martin Painter (1998), *Collaborative Federalism: Economic Reform in Australia in the 1990s*, Melbourne: Cambridge University Press, p. 106.

38　Joan Rydon (1993), "The Australian Tradition of Federalism and Federation," in Michael Burgess and Alain-G. Gagnon (eds), *Comparative Federalism and Federation; Competing Traditions and Future Directions*, Toronto: University of Toronto Press, p. 233.

39　Brian Galligan (1995), "Labor and the Australian Constitution," in Galligan, *A Federal Republic: Australia's Constitutional System of Government*, Melbourne: Cambridge University Press, pp. 91–109; see also Andrew Parkin and Vernon Marshall (1994), "Federalism and the Australian Labour Party," in Campbell Sharman (ed.), *Parties and Federalism in Australia and Canada*, Canberra: Federalism Research Centre, The Australian National University.

40　Martin Painter (1998), *Collaborative Federalism: Economic Reform in Australia in the 1990s*, Melbourne: Cambridge University Press, pp. 1–9.

Bibliography

General references

Books

Abrams, Philip (1982), *Historical Sociology*, Somerset: Open Books.

Almond, Gabriel A. and Sidney Verba (1963), *The Civic Culture: Political Attitudes and Democracy in Five Nations*, Princeton: Princeton University Press.

Althusius, Johannes (1964) [1614], *The Politics of Johannes Althusius*, translated by Frederick S. Carney, an abridged translation of the Third Edition (1614) of *Politica Methodice Digesta, Atque Exemplis Sacris Et Profanis Illustrata*, Boston: Beacon Press.

Barry, Brian (1991), *Democracy and Power: Essays in Political Theory I*, Oxford: Clarendon.

Bartolini, Stefano (2000), *The Political Mobilisation of the European Left 1860–1980: The Class Cleavage*, Cambridge: Cambridge University Press.

Bates, Robert H., Avner Grief, Margaret Levi, Jean Laurent Rosenthal and Barry R. Weingast (1998), *Analytic Narratives*, Princeton: Princeton University Press.

Bauer, Otto (1924) [1907], *Die Nationalitätenfrage und die Sozialdemokratie*, Vienna.

Beer, Samuel H. (1993), *To Make a Nation: The Rediscovery of American Federalism*, Cambridge: Belknap.

Brubaker, Rogers (1992), *Citizenship and Nationhood in France and Germany*, Cambridge: Harvard University Press.

Carnoy, Martin and Henry M. Levin (1976), *Limits of Educational Reform*, New York and London: Longman.

Clark, Terry Nichols and Seymour Martin Lipset (2001), *The Breakdown of Class Politics: A Debate on Post-Industrial Stratification*, Baltimore: Johns Hopkins University Press.

Colomer, Josep (ed.) (1991), *Journal of Theoretical Politics*, Special Issue: *The Strategy of Institutional Change*, Vol. 13, No. 3.

Dicey, A.V. (1915) [1885], *Introduction to the Study of the Law of the Constitution*, London.

Dye, Thomas R. (1990), *American Federalism, Competition Among Governments*, Lexington: Lexington Books.

Eckstein, Harry (1966), *Division and Cohesion in Democracy: A Study of Norway*, Princeton: Princeton University Press.

Eckstein, Harry and Ted Robert Gurr (1975), *Patterns of Authority: A Structural Basis for Political Inquiry*, New York and Toronto: Wiley.

Evans, Geoffrey (ed.), *The End of Class Politics: Class Voting in Comparative Context*, Oxford: Oxford University Press.

Friedrich, Carl J. (1968), *Trends of Federalism in Theory and Practice*, New York: Praeger.

Gellner, Ernest (1983), *Nations and Nationalism*, New York: Cornell University Press.

Green, Donald and Ian Shapiro (1994), *Pathologies of Rational Choice Theory*, New Haven and London: Yale University Press.

Hamilton, Alexander, James Madison and John Jay (1961) [1787–88], *The Federalist Papers*, Clinton Rossiter (ed.), New York: Mentor.

Hartz, Louis (1955), *The Liberal Tradition in America: An Interpretation of American Political Thought Since the Revolution*, New York: Harcourt, Brace and World.

Hawkins, Robert B. Jr (1982), *American Federalism: A New Partnership for the Republic*, San Francisco: Institute for Contemporary Studies.

Horowitz, Donald (1985), *Ethnic Groups in Conflict*, Berkeley: University of California Press.

Hueglin, Thomas O. (1990), *A Political Economy of Federalism: In Search of a New Comparative Perspective with Critical Intent Throughout*, Kingston: Institute of Inter-governmental Relations, Queen's University.

Hueglin, Thomas O. (1999), *Early Modern Concepts for a late Modern World: Althusius on Community and Federalism*, Waterloo: Wilfrid Laurier University Press.

Katznelson, Ira and Aristide R. Zolberg (eds) (1986), *Working-Class Formation: Nineteenth-Century Patterns in Western Europe and the United States*, Princeton: Princeton University Press.

Korpi, Walter (1983), *The Democratic Class Struggle*, London: Routledge and Kegan Paul.

Levi, Margaret (1997), *Consent, Dissent and Patriotism*, Cambridge: Cambridge University Press.

Lipset, Seymour Martin (1967), *The First New Nation: The United States in Historical and Comparative Perspective*, New York: Doubleday.

Lipset, Seymour Martin (1996), *American Exceptionalism: A Double Edged Sword*, New York and London: W.W. Norton.

Luebbert, Gregory M. (1991), *Liberalism, Fascism, or Social Democracy: Social Classes and the Origins of Regimes in Interwar Europe*, New York: Oxford University Press.

Luong, Pauline Jones (2002), *Institutional Change and Political Continuity in Post-Soviet Central Asia*, Cambridge: Cambridge University Press.

McMinn, Winston Gregory (1994), *Nationalism and Federalism in Australia*, Melbourne: Oxford University Press.

Mol, Hans (ed.) (1972), *Western Religion: A Country by Country Sociological Inquiry*, The Hague: Mouton.

Moore, Margaret (2001), *The Ethics of Nationalism*, Oxford: Oxford University Press.

Moreno, Luis (2001), *The Federalization of Spain*, London and Portland: Frank Cass.

Morley, Felix (1959), *Freedom and Federalism*, Chicago: Henry Regnery.

Nice, David C. (1988), *Federalism: The Politics of Intergovernmental Relations*, New York: St Martin's Press.

Offe, Claus (2003), *Herausforderungen der Demokratie: Zur Integrations – und Leistungsfähigkeit politischer Institutionen*, Frankfurt: Campus Verlag.

Painter, Martin (1998), *Collaborative Federalism: Economic Reform in Australia in the 1990s*, Melbourne: Cambridge University Press.

Proudhon, Pierre-Joseph (1863), *Du principe fédératif et de la nécessité de reconstituer le parti de la revolution*, Paris: E. Dentu.

Rae, Douglas and Michael Taylor (1970), *The Analysis of Political Cleavages*, New Haven: Yale University Press.

Renner, Karl (under the *nom de plume* Rudolf Springer) (1902), *Der Kampf der österreichischen Nationen um den Staat*, Vienna and Leipzig.

Requejo, Ferran (2005), *Multinational Federalism and Value Pluralism: the Spanish Case*, London: Routledge.

Riker, William H. (1964), *Federalism: Origin, Operation, Significance*, Boston and Toronto: Little, Brown and Company.

Schnapper, Dominique (1994), *La communauté des citoyens: Sur l'idée moderne de nation*, Paris: Gallimard.

Siebert, Fred S., Theodore Peterson and Wilbur Schramm (1956), *Four Theories of the Press*, Urbana, Chicago and London: University of Illinois Press.

Spaull, Andrew (1987), *A History of the Australian Education Council, 1936–1986*, Sydney: Allen and Unwin.

Steinmo, Sven, Kathleen Thelen and Frank Longstreth (eds) (1992), *Structuring Politics: Historical Institutionalism in Comparative Analysis*, Cambridge: Cambridge University Press.

Sundquist, James (1969), *Making Federalism Work*, Washington, DC: Brookings Institution.

Vernon, Richard (ed.) (1979), *The Principle of Federation*, Toronto: University of Toronto Press.

Weaver, Kent and Steve Rockman (eds) (1993), *Do Institutions Matter? Government Capabilities in the United States and Abroad*, Washington, DC: Brookings Institute.

Wellman, Barry and S.D. Berkowitz (eds) (1988), *Social Structures: A Network Approach*, Cambridge: Cambridge University Press.

Wheare, Kenneth C. (1946), *Federal Government*, London: Oxford University Press.

Wibbels, Erik (2005), *Federalism and the Market: Intergovernmental Conflict and Economic Reform in the Developing World*, Cambridge and New York: Cambridge University Press.

Wildavsky, Aaron (ed.) (1967), *American Federalism in Perspective*, Boston: Little, Brown and Company.

Ziblatt, Daniel (2006), *Structuring the State: The Formation of Italy and Germany and the Puzzle of Federalism*, Princeton: Princeton University Press.

Zimmerman, Joseph (1992), *Contemporary American Federalism: The Growth of National Power*, New York: Praeger.

Articles and chapters

Agranoff, Robert (1994), "Asymmetrical and Symmetrical Federalism in Spain: An Examination of Intergovernmental Policy," in Bertus de Villiers (ed.), *Evaluating Federal Systems*, Dordrecht, Boston and London: Martinus Nijhoff, pp. 61–89.

Agranoff, Robert (2005), "Federal asymmetry and intergovernmental relations in Spain," Institute for Intergovernmental Studies, Kingston: Queen's University Working Paper 17.

Agranoff, Robert and Juan Antonio Ramos Gallarín (1997), "Toward Federal Democracy in Spain: An Examination of Intergovernmental Relations," *Publius: Journal of Federalism*, Vol. 27, No. 4, pp. 1–38.

Beer, Samuel H. (1988), "Introduction," in Timothy Conlan, *New Federalism: Intergovernmental Reform from Nixon to Reagan*, Washington, DC: Brookings Institution.

Bendix, Reinhard and Seymour Martin Lipset (1957), "Political Sociology: An Essay," *Current Sociology*, Vol VI, No. 2, pp. 79–169.

Bowen, John R. and Roger Peterson (1999), "Introduction: Critical Comparisons," in John R. Bowen and Roger Petersen (eds), *Critical Comparisons in Politics and Culture*, Cambridge: Cambridge University Press, pp. 1–20.

Burgess, Michael (1995), "Federalism and the European Union: Political Change and Continuity in the European Community," in C. Lloyd Brown-John (ed.), *Federal Type Solutions and European Integration*, Lanham and London: University Press of America, pp. 57–82.

Castles, Francis G. and John Uhr (2005), "Australia: Federal Constraints and Institutional Innovations," in Herbert Obinger, Stephan Leibfried and Francis G. Castles (eds), *Federalism and the Welfare State: New World and European Experiences*, Cambridge: Cambridge University Press, pp. 51–88

Crouch, Colin (2001), "Breaking Open Black Boxes: The Implications for Sociological Theory of European Integration," in Anand Menon and Vincent Wright (eds), *From the Nation State to Europe? Essays in Honour of Jack Hayward*, Oxford: Oxford University Press, pp. 195–213.

Dubnick, Mel and Alan Gitelson (1981), "Nationalizing State Policies," in Jerome J. Hanus (ed.), *The Nationalization of State Government*, Lexington: D.C. Heath, pp. 39–74.

Eckstein, Harry (1961), *A Theory of Stable Democracy*, originally published as Research Monograph Number 10 by the Center of International Studies, Princeton University, reprinted as Appendix in Harry Eckstein (1966). *Division and Cohesion in Democracy: A Study of Norway.* Princeton: Princeton University Press, pp. 225–288.

Eckstein, Harry (1973), "Authority Patterns: A Structural Basis for Political Inquiry," *American Political Science Review*, Vol. 67, No. 4, pp. 1142–1161.

Erk, Jan (2006), "Does Federalism Really Matter?" *Comparative Politics*, Vol. 39, No. 1, pp. 103–120.

Erk, Jan (2007), "Federalism as a Growth Industry," *Publius: The Journal of Federalism*, Vol. 37.

Erk, Jan (2007), "Real Constitution, Formal Constitution, and Democracy in the European Union," *Journal of Common Market Studies*, Vol. 45.

Erk, Jan and Alain-G. Gagnon (2000), "Constitutional Ambiguity and Federal Trust: The Codification of Federalism in Belgium, Canada and Spain," *Regional and Federal Studies*, Vol. 10, No. 1, pp. 92–111.

Galligan, Brian (1989), "Federal Theory and Australian Federalism: A Political Science Perspective," in Brian Galligan (ed.), *Australian Federalism*, Melbourne: Longman Cheshire.

Galligan, Brian (1995), "Labor and the Australian Constitution," in Galligan, *A Federal Republic: Australia's Constitutional System of Government*, Melbourne: Cambridge University Press, pp. 91–109.

George, Alexander (1979), "Case Studies and Theory Development: The Method of Structured Focused Comparison," in Paul Gordon Lauren (ed.), *Diplomacy: New Approaches in History, Theory and Policy*, New York: Free Press, pp. 43–68.

Golden, Miriam (1999), "Case Studies in Contemporary Job Loss," in John R. Bowen and Roger Peterson (eds), *Critical Comparisons in Politics and Culture*, Cambridge: Cambridge University Press, pp. 110–135.

Grimm, Dieter (1995), "Does Europe Need a Constitution?" *European Law Journal*, Vol. 1, No. 3, pp. 282–302.

Grodzins, Morton and Daniel Elazar (1974), "Centralization and Decentralization in the

American Federal System," in Robert A. Goldwin (ed.), *A Nation of States: Essays on the American Federal System*, Second Edition, Chicago: Rand McNally.

Kiser, Edgar (1996), "The Revival of Narrative in Historical Sociology: What Rational Choice Theory Can Contribute," *Politics and Society*, Vol. 24, No. 3, pp. 249–271.

Knill, Christoph and Andrea Lenschow (2001), "Seek and Ye Shall Find: Linking Different Perspectives on Institutional Change," *Comparative Political Studies*, Vol. 34, No. 2, pp. 187–215.

Koelble, Thomas (1995), "The New Institutionalism in Political Science and Sociology," *Comparative Politics*, Vol. 27, No. 2, pp. 231–243.

Koelble, Thomas (1995), "Towards a Theory of Nationalism," *Nationalism and Ethnic Politics*, Vol. 1, No. 4, pp. 73–89.

Laitin, David D. (1998), "Towards a Political Science Discipline: Authority Patterns Revisited," *Comparative Political Studies*, Vol. 31, No. 4, pp. 423–443.

Laski, Harold (1939), "The Obsolescence of Federalism," *New Republic*, Vol. 3, pp. 367–369.

Levi, Margaret and Michael Hechter (1985), "A Rational Choice Approach to the Rise and Decline of Ethnoregional Political Parties," in Edward A. Tiryakian and Ronald Rogowski (eds), *New Nationalisms of the Developed West: Towards and Explanation*, Boston: Allen and Unwin, pp. 128–146.

Lichbach, Mark I. (1997), "Social Theory and Comparative Politics," in Mark Irving Lichbach and Alan S. Zuckerman (eds), *Comparative Politics: Rationality, Culture, and Structure*, Cambridge: Cambridge University Press, pp. 239–278.

Lipset, Seymour Martin and Stein Rokkan (1967), "Cleavage Structures, Party Systems, and Voter Alignments: An Introduction," in Seymour Martin Lipset and Stein Rokkan (eds), *Party Systems and Voter Alignments: Cross-National Perspectives*, New York: Free Press, pp. 1–64.

Livingston, William S. (1952), "A Note on the Nature of Federalism," *Political Science Quarterly*, Vol. 67, pp. 81–95.

Livingston, William S. (1968), "Canada, Australia and the United States: Variations on a Theme," in Valerie Earle (ed.), *Federalism: Infinite Variety in Theory and Practice*, Itasca: Peacock, pp. 140–152.

Ma Valles, Josep and Montserrat Cuchillo Foix (1988), "Decentralisation in Spain: A Review," *European Journal of Political Research*, Vol. 16, No. 4, pp. 395–407.

Mayer, Lawrence (1970), "Federalism and party behavior in Australia and Canada," *The Western Political Quarterly*, Vol. 23, No. 4, p. 795–807.

McCloskey, Donald N. (1991), "History, Differential Equations, and the Problem of Narration," *History and Theory*, Vol. 30, No. 1, pp. 21–36.

Martin, David (1978), "The Religious Condition in Europe," in Salvador Giner and Margaret Scotford Archer (eds), *Contemporary Europe: Social Structure and Cultural Patterns*, London: Routledge and Kegan Paul, pp. 228–287.

Moreno, Luis (1994), "Ethnoterritorial Concurrence and Imperfect Federalism in Spain," in Bertus de Villiers (ed.), *Evaluating Federal Systems*, Dordrecht, Boston and London: Martinus Nijhoff, pp. 162–193.

Moreno, Luis (1999), "Asymmetry in Spain: Federalism in the Making," in Robert Agranoff (ed.), *Accommodating Diversity: Asymmetry in Federal States*, Baden-Baden: Nomos, pp. 149–168.

North, Douglas (1990), "Institutions and Their Consequences for Economic Performance," in Karen Schweers Cook and Margaret Levi (eds), *The Limits of Rationality*, Chicago and London: University of Chicago Press, pp. 383–401.

Parkin, Andrew and Vernon Marshall (1994), "Federalism and the Australian Labour Party," in Campbell Sharman (ed.), *Parties and Federalism in Australia and Canada*, Canberra: Federalism Research Centre, The Australian National University, pp. 73–98.

Pierson, Paul (1995), "Fragmented Welfare States: Federal Institutions and Development of Social Policy," *Governance*, Vol. 8, No. 4, pp. 449–478.

Pontusson, Jonas (1995), "From Comparative Public Policy to Political Economy: Putting Political Institutions in their Place and Taking Interests Seriously," *Comparative Political Studies*, Vol. 28, No. 1, pp. 117–147.

Resnick, Philip (2003), "Un ou plusieurs Demos? Impératifs fédéreaux ou confédéraux dans les États multinationaux," in Jules Duchastel (ed.), *Fédéralismes et mondialisation: l'avenir de la démocratie et de la citoyenneté*, Montreal: Athéna, pp. 199–214.

Riker, William (1990), "Political Science and Rational Choice," in James E. Alt and Kenneth A. Shepsle (eds), *Perspectives on Positive Political Economy*, Cambridge: Cambridge University Press, pp. 163–181.

Rogowski, Ronald (1998), "Eckstein and the Study of Private Governments: An Appreciation, Critique, and Proposal," *Comparative Political Studies*, Special Issue: A Tribute to Harry Eckstein, Vol. 31, No. 4, pp. 444–463.

Rydon, Joan (1993), "The Australian Tradition of Federalism and Federation," in Michael Burgess and Alain-G. Gagnon (eds), *Comparative Federalism and Federation; Competing Traditions and Future Directions*, Toronto: University of Toronto Press, pp. 227–243.

Sartori, Giovanni (1969), "From the Sociology of Politics to Political Sociology," in Seymour Martin Lipset (ed.), *Politics and the Social Science*, New York: Oxford University Press, pp. 65–100.

Scheiber, Harry N. (2002), "American Federalism as a Working System and as a Constituional Model," in Jürgen Rose and Johannes Ch. Traut (eds), *Federalism and Decentralization: Perspectives for the Transformation Process in Eastern and Central Europe*, Hamburg: Lit Verlag, and New York: Palgrave, pp. 51–70.

Schnapper, Dominique (2004), "Linguistic Pluralism as a Serious Challenge to Democratic Life," in Philippe van Parijs (ed.), *Cultural Diversity versus Economic Solidarity: Proceedings of the Seventh Franqui Colloqium*, Brussels: De Boeck Université, pp. 213–225.

Sil, Rudra (2000), "The Foundations of Eclecticism: The Epistemological Status of Agency, Culture, and Structure in Social Theory," *Journal of Theoretical Politics*, Vol. 12, No. 3, pp. 353–387.

Skocpol, Theda (1984), "Emerging Agendas and Recurrent Strategies in Historical Sociology," in Theda Skocpol (ed.), *Vision and Method in Historical Sociology*, New York: Cambridge University Press.

Swenden, Wilfried (2001), "Comparative Federalism and Higher Education: Some Thoughts for Reflection," *European Journal of Education Law and Policy*, Vol. 5, pp. 153–158.

Tarlton, Charles D. (1965), "Symmetry and Asymmetry as Elements of Federalism: A Theoretical Speculation," *The Journal of Politics*, Vol. 27, pp. 861–874.

Watts, Ronald (1994), "Contemporary Views on Federalism," in Bertus de Villiers (ed.), *Evaluating Federal Systems*, Dordrecht, Boston and London: Martinus Nijhoff, pp. 1–29.

Wibbels, Erik (2006), "Madison in Bagdad? Decentralization and Federalism in Comparative Politics," *Annual Review of Political Science*, Vol. 9, pp. 165–188.

Zimmerman, Joseph F. (1981), "Frustrating National Policy: Partial Federal Preemption," in Jerome J. Hanus (ed.), *The Nationalization of State Government*, Lexington: D.C. Heath, pp. 95–102.

Zuckerman, Alan (1975), "Political Cleavages: A Conceptual and Theoretical Analysis," *British Journal of Political Science*, Vol. 5, No. 2, pp. 231–248.

Austria

Official documents, reports, statistics and parliamentary sessions

Institut für Föderalismus (2002), *26. Bericht über den Föderalismus in Österreich*, Vienna: Wilhelm Braumüller.

20. Sitzung des Nationalrates der Republik Österreich, Freitag, 8. Juli 1966, Stenographische Protokolle über die Sitzungen des Nationalrates, XI. Gesetzgebungsperiode, II. Band, Vienna: Druck der österreichischen Staatsdruckerei.

106. Sitzung des Nationalrates der Republik Österreich, Mittwoch, 18 Juli 1962, Stenographische Protokolle über die Sitzungen des Nationalrates, 1962, IX. Gesetzgebungperiode, V. Band, Vienna: Druck der österreichischen Staatsdruckerei.

111. Sitzung des Nationalrates der Republik Österreich, Mittwoch 10 Juli 1974, Stenographische Protokolle über die Sitzungen des Nationalrates, XIII. Gesetzgebungperiode, 8. Band, Vienna: Druck der österreichischen Staatsdruckerei.

194. Sitzung des Bundesrates der Republik Österreich, Freitag, 20 Juli 1962, Stenographische Protokolle über die Sitzungen des Bundesrates 1959 bis 1962, IX. Gesetzgebungperiode der Republik Österreich, V. Band, Vienna: Druck der österreichischen Staatsdruckerei.

244. Sitzung des Bundesrates der Republik Österreich, Freitag 22 Juli 1966, Stenographische Protokolle über die Sitzungen des Bundesrates der Republik Österreich, 1966 bis 1967, XI Gesetzgebungsperiod, 1967, Vienna: Druck der österreichischen Staatsdruckerei.

334. Sitzung des Bundesrates der Republik Österreich, Dienstag 16. und Mittwoch 17. Juli 1974, Stenographische Protokolle über die Sitzungen des Bundesrates der Republik Österreich, 1974 bis 1975, XIII. Gesetzgebungsperiode, Vienna: Druck der österreichischen Staatsdruckerei.

Stenographische Protokoll, 116. Sitzung des Nationalrates der Republik Österreich, V. Gesetzgebungsperiode, Mittwoch 13 July 1949, Vienna: Druck der österreichische Staatsdruckerei.

Stenographische Protokolle, 46. Sitzung des Bundesrates der Republik Österreich, Freitag 15. Juli 1949, Vienna: Druck der österreichische Staatsdruckerei.

Stenographische Protokolle des Nationalrates der Republik Österreich, VI. Gesetzgebungsperiode, 15 October 1952, Anfragebeantwortung 494/A.B. vom 3. September 1952, 1. und 2. Beiblatt, Vienna: Druck der österreichische Staatsdruckerei.

Verfassungsgerichthof (1996) [1954], "Fernmeldegesetz slg. 2721, 1954," *Die Judicatur des Verfassungsgerichthofes 1919–1964, I. Band*, Vienna: Druck und Verlag der österreichischen Staatsdruckerei.

Books

Adamovich, Ludwig K. and Bernd-Christian Funk (1984), *Österreichisches Verfassungrecht*, Second Edition, New York and Vienna: Springer.

Adamovich, Ludwig K., Bernd-Christian Funk and Gerhart Holzinger (1997), *Österreichisches Staatsrecht, Bands I und II*, New York and Vienna: Springer.

Altenstetter, Christa (1969), *Der Föderalismus in Österreich, unter besonderer Berücksichtigung der politischen Verhältnisse von 1945–1966*, Heidelberg: Quelle and Meyer.

Engelbrecht, Helmut (1988), *Geschichte des österreichischen Bildungswesens; Erziehung und Unterricht auf dem Boden Österreichs, Band V, Von 1918 bis zur Gegenwart*, Vienna: Österreichischer Bundesverlag.

Ermacora, Felix (1967), *Quellen zum österreichischen Verfassungsrecht (1920)*, Vienna: Ferdinand Berger und Söhne.

Ermacora, Felix (1976), *Österreichischer Föderalismus: Vom patrimonialen zum kooperativen Bundesstaat*, Vienna: Wilhelm Braumüller.

Ermacora, Felix (1989), *Materialen zur österreichischen Bundesverfassung: Die Länderkonferenzen 1919/20 und die Verfassungsfrage*, Vienna: Wilhelm Braumüller.

Ermacora, Felix with Gerhard Baumgartner and Gerhard Strejcek (1998), *Österreichische Verfassungslehre*, Vienna: Verlag Österreich.

Esterbauer, Fried (1976), *Kriterien föderativer und konföderativer Systeme unter besonderer Berücksichtigung Österreichs und der Europäischen Gemeinschaften*, Vienna: Wilhelm Braumüller.

Esterbauer, Fried (2000), *Demokratische Leistungsfähigkeit des Föderalismus*, Vienna: Wilhelm Braumüller.

Feldinger, Norbert (1990), *Nachkriegsrundfunk in Österreich: Zwischen Föderalismus und Zentralismus von 1945 bis 1957*, Munich: Saur.

Funk, Bernd-Christian (1980), *Das System der bundestaatlichen Kompetenzverteilung im Lichte der Verfassungsrechtsprechung*, Vienna: Wilhelm Braumüller.

Funk, Bernd-Christian (1996), *Einführung in das österreichische Verfassungsrecht*, Graz: Leykam.

Grießer, Johannes (1989), *Der Österreichische Rundfunk als Thema der Parlamentarische Auseinandersetzung von 1970 bis 1983*, Vienna: Universität Wien.

Gulick, Charles A. (1948), *Austria: From Habsburg to Hitler, Volume I: Labor's Workshop of Democracy*, with a foreword by Walter Federn, Berkeley and Los Angeles: University of California Press.

Juranek, Markus (1999), *Schulverfassung und Schulverwaltung in Österreich und in Europa, Volume I*, Vienna: Verlag Österreich.

Kelsen, Hans (1925), *Allgemeine Staatslehre*, Berlin: Julius Springer.

Kelsen, Hans (1970) [1923], *Österreichisches Staatsrecht: Ein Grundriss Entwicklungsgeschichtlich Dargestellt*, Tübingen: Scientia.

Khol, Andreas and Alfred Stirneman (eds) (1981), *Österreichischen Jahrbuch für Politik 1980*, Munich: R. Oldenbourg, and Vienna: Verlag für Geschichte und Politik.

Koja, Friedrich (1975), *Entwicklungstendenzen des österreichischen Föderalismus*, St Pölten and Vienna: Niederösterreichische Juristische Gesellschaft.

Lebitsch-Buchsteiner, Sigrid (2001), *Die bundesstaatliche Rücksichtnahmepflicht*, Vienna: Wilhelm Braumüller.

Lehmbruch, Gerhard (1967), *Proporzdemokratie: Politisches System und Politische Kultur in der Schweiz und in Österreich*, Tübingen: J.C.B. Mohr.

Magenschab, Hans (1973), *Demokratie und Rundfunk: Hörfunk und Fernsehen im politischen Prozeß Österreichs*, Vienna and Munich: Herold.

Owerdieck, Reinhard (1987), *Parteien und Verfassungsfrage in Österreich: Die Entstehung des Verfassungsprovisoriums der Ersten Republik 1918–1920*, Munich: R. Oldenbourg.

Pelinka, Anton (1998), *Austria: Out of the Shadow of the Past*, Boulder: Westview.

Pelinka, Anton and Sieglinde Rosenberger (2000), *Österreichische Politik: Grundlagen, Strukturen, Trends*, Vienna: WUV.

Pernthaler, Peter (1992), *Der differenzierte Bundesstaat: Theoretische Grundlagen, praktische Konsequenzen und Anwendungsbereiche in der Reform des österreichischen Bundestaats*, Vienna: Wilhelm Baumüller.

Pernthaler, Peter (1996), *Algemeine Staatslehre und Verfassungslehre*, Second Edition, Vienna: Springer.

Pernthaler, Peter (1998), *Der Verfassungskern: Gesamtänderung und Durchbrechung der Verfassung im Lichte der Theorie, Rectsprechung und europäischen Verfassungskultur*, Vienna: Manzsche.

Ringhofer, Kurt (1977), *Die österreichische Bundesverfassung*, Vienna: Verlag des österreichischen Gewerkschaftbundes.

Rosner, Andreas (2000), *Koordinationinstrumente der österreichischen Länder*, Vienna: Wilhelm Braumüller.

Schäffer, Heinz and Harald Stolzlechner (eds) (1993), *Reformbestrebungen im österreichischen Bundesstaatsystem*, Vienna: Wilhelm Braumüller.

Schlesinger, Rudolf (1945), *Federalism in Central and Eastern Europe*, London: Kegan Paul.

Slapnicka, Helmut (1953), *Zwischen Zentralismus und Föderalismus*, Kitzinger-Main: Holzner.

Trabesinger, Arno (1997), *Der Vertretung der Interessen der österreichischen Bundesländer gegenüber dem Bund*, Vienna: Universität Wien.

Twaroch, Paul and Wolfgang Buchner (2000), *Rundfunkrecht in Österreich*, Vienna: Juridica Verlag.

Wadl, Gerald (1998), *Möglichkeiten und Herausforderungen für den Föderalismus in Österreich*, Vienna: Universität Wien.

Walter, Robert (1984), *Die Entstehung des Bundesverfassungsgesetzes 1920 in der Konstituierenden Nationalversammlung*, Vienna: Manzche.

Walter, Robert and Heinz Mayer (2000), *Grundriß des österreichischen Bundesverfassungsrechts*, Ninth Edition, Vienna: Manzche.

Weber, Karl (1980), *Kriterien des Bundesstaates: Eine systematische, historische und rechtsvergleichende Untersuchung des Bundesstaatlichkeit der Schweiz, der Bundesrepublik Duetschland und Österreichs*, Vienna: Wilhelm Braumüller.

Wedl, Kurt (1969), *Der Gedanke des Föderalismus in Programmen Politischer Parteien Deutschland und Österreichs*, Munich and Vienna: Günter Olzag.

Werndl, Josef (1984), *Die Kompetenzverteilung zwischen Bund und Ländern: Ihre Ausgangslage, Entwicklung und Bedeutungsverschiebung auf der Grundlage des Bundesverfassungsgesetzes von 1920*, Vienna: Wilhelm Braumüller.

Zdarzil, Herbert and Nikolaus Severinski (eds) (1998), *Österreichische Bildungspolitik in der Zweiten Republik*, Vienna: Kaiser.

Articles and chapters

Adamovich, Ludwig K. (1973), "Die Zukunft des Föderalismus in Österreich," Heinz Laufer and Frank Pilz (eds), *Föderalismus: Studientexte zur bundesstaatlichen Ordnung*, Munich: Wilhelm Goldman, pp. 360–371.

Bernhard, Reinhold (1988), "Kulturpolitik in den Ländern Österreichs," in Peter Pernthaler (ed.), *Föderalistische Kulturpolitik*, Vienna: Wilhelm Braumüller, pp. 67–78.

Bußjäger, Peter (2000), "Modernisierungsprobleme im österreichischen föderalen System," *Zeitschrift für Politik*, Vol. 49, No. 2, pp. 149–159.

Davy, Ulrike (1986), "Zur Bedeutung des bundesstaatlichen Rücksichtnahmegebotes für Normenkonflickte," *Österreichische Juristen-Zeitung*, Vol. 41, No. 8, pp. 225–234.

Dermutz, Suzanne (1983), "Bildungspartnerschaft. Historische Entwicklung und Merkmale des bildungspolitischen Systems in Österreich," *Österreichische Zeitschrift für Politikwissenschaft*, Vol. 83, No. 1, pp. 19–32.

Erk, Jan (2004), "Austria: A Federation without Federalism," *Publius: Journal of Federalism*, Vol. 34, No. 1, pp. 1–20.

Ermacora, Felix (1970), "Vorstellungen und Wirklichkeit im österreichischen Föderalismus 1848–1970," Felix Ermacora, Heinrich Koller, Hans Klecatsky, Gertrude Welan and Manfried Welan (eds), *Föderalismus in Österreich*, Munich and Salzburg: Anton Puslet, pp. 85–92.

Goldinger, Walter (1969), "Die Stellung der Länder in der Verfassung der Republik Österreich," in Institut für Österreichkunde (ed.), *Der österreichische Föderalismus und seine historischen Grundlagen*, Vienna: Ferdinand Hint, pp. 117–122.

Hormer, Franz (1997), "Das österreichische Bildungssystem," in Herbert Dachs, Peter Gerlich, Herbert Gottweis, Franz Hormer, Helmut Kramer, Volkmar Lauber, Wolfgang C. Müller and Emerich Tálos (eds), *Handbuch des politischen System Österreich*, Third Edition, Vienna: Manzche, pp. 483–490.

Katschthaler, Hans (1984), "Bildungspolitik in Österreich 1979 bis 1983," in *Österreichischen Jahrbuch für Politik 1983*, Andreas Khol and Alfred Stirneman (eds), Munich: R. Oldenbourg, and Vienna: Verlag für Geschichte und Politik, pp. 701–724.

Langer, Josef (1999), "Last in, First out? – Austria's Place in the Transformation of National Identity," in Hanspeter Kriesi, Klaus Armingeon, Hannes Siegrist and Andreas Wimmer (eds), *Nation and National Identity: The European Experience in Perspective*, Zurich and Chur: Ruegger, pp. 153–173.

Lechner, Elmar (1995), "Schule," in Emmerich Tálos, Herbert Dachs, Ernst Hanisch and Anton Staudinger (eds), *Handbuch des politischen Systems Österreichs, Erste Republic 1918–1933*, Vienna: Manzche, pp. 504–515.

Luther, Kurt Richard (1997), "Bund–Länder Beziehungen: Formal- und Realverfassung," in Herbert Dachs, Peter Gerlich, Herbert Gottweis, Franz Hormer, Helmut Kramer, Volkmar Lauber, Wolfgang C. Müller and Emmerich Tálos (eds), *Handbuch des politischen System Österreich*, Third Edition, Vienna: Manzche, pp. 907–919.

Luther, Kurt Richard and Wolfgang C. Müller (1992), "Consociationalism and the Austrian Political System," *West European Politics*, Vol. 15, No. 1, pp. 1–15.

Luther, Richard (1986), "The Revitalization of Federalism and Federation in Austria," in Michael Burgess (ed.), *Federalism and Federation in Western Europe*, London: Croom and Helm, pp. 154–186.

Mayer, Heinz (1986), "Neue Wege der Kompetenz interpretation?" *Österreichische Juristen-Zeitung*, Vol. 41, No. 17, pp. 513–520.

Morscher, Siegbert (1981), "Pro Vorarlberg," in *Österreichischen Jahrbuch für Politik 1980*, Andreas Khol and Alfred Stirneman (eds), Munich: R. Oldenbourg, and Vienna: Verlag für Geschichte und Politik, pp. 31–54.

Morscher, Siegbert (1985), "Weschselseitige Rücksichtnahmepflicht Bund–Länder," *Juristische Blätter*, Vol. 107, No. 15/16, pp. 479–481.

Motz, Michael (1978), "Zur Lage des Föderalismus in Österreich," in *Österreichischen Jahrbuch für Politik 1977*, Andreas Khol and Alfred Stirneman (eds), Munich: R. Oldenbourg, and Vienna: Verlag für Geschichte und Politik, pp. 109–122.

Müller, Wolfgang C. (1992), "Austrian Governmental Institutions: Do They Matter?" *West European Politics*, Vol. 15, No. 1, pp. 123–124.

Müller, Wolfgang C. (1997), "Die Österreichische Volkspartei," in Herbert Dachs, Peter Gerlich, Herbert Gottweis, Franz Hormer, Helmut Kramer, Volkmar Lauber, Wolfgang C. Müller and Emmerich Tálos (eds), *Handbuch des politischen System Österreich*, Third Edition, Vienna: Manzche, pp. 265–285.

Nick, Rainer (1988), "Die Bundesländer und das österreichische Parteiensystem," Anton Pelinka and Fritz Plasser (eds), *Das österreichische Parteiensystem*, Vienna, Cologne and Graz: Böhlau, pp. 410–418.

Obinger, Herbert (2005), "Austria: Strong Parties in a Weak Federal Polity," in Herbert Obinger, Stephan Leibfried and Francis G. Castles (eds), *Federalism and the Welfare State: New World and European Experiences*, Cambridge: Cambridge University Press, pp. 181–221.

Öhlinger Theo (1988), "Centralizing and Decentralizing Trends in the Austrian Constitution," in C. Lloyd Brown-John (ed.), *Centralizing and Decentralizing Trends in Federal States*, Lanham: University Press of America, pp. 225–236.

Pelinka, Anton (1971), "Parteien und Verbände," in Herbert Dachs, Peter Gerlich, Herbert Gottweis, Franz Hormer, Helmut Kramer, Volkmar Lauber, Wolfgang C. Müller and Emmerich Tálos (eds), *Demokratie und Verfassung in Österreich*, Vienna, Frankfurt and Zurich: Europa, pp. 265–327.

Pernthaler, Peter (1988), "Kulturpolitik in Österreich. Verfassungsrechtliche und verfassungspolitische Rahmenbedingungen," in Pernthale (ed.), *Föderalistische Kulturpolitik*, Vienna: Wilhelm Braumüller, pp. 9–28.

Pernthaler, Peter (1992), "Zum Begriff von Föderalismus und Bundesstaat in Österrreich," in Herbert Schambeck (ed.), *Föderalismus und Parlamentarismus in Österreich*, Vienna: Österreichische Staatsdruckerei, pp. 35–52.

Pernthaler, Peter (1999), "Das föderalistische system österreichs," in Reinhard Meier-Walser and Gerhard Hirscher (eds), *Krise und Reform des Föderalismus, Analysen zu Theorie und Praxis bundstaatlicher Ordnungen*, Munich: Olzog, pp. 210–225.

Plaser, Fritz (1997), "Massenmedien und Politikvermittlung," in Herbert Dachs, Peter Gerlich, Herbert Gottweis, Franz Hormer, Helmut Kramer, Volkmar Lauber, Wolfgang C. Müller and Emerich Tálos (eds), *Handbuch des politischen System Österreich*, Third Edition, Vienna: Manzche, pp. 463–482.

Pulzer, Peter (1974), "Austria: The Legitimizing Role of Political Parties," in Kenneth McRae (ed.), *Consociational Democracy: Political Accomodation in Segmented Societies*, Toronto: McClelland and Stewart, pp. 157–178.

Rack, Reinhard (1995), "Federalism: Making the Community More Attractive to Europeans: The Austrian Point of View," in C. Lloyd Brown-John (ed.), *Federal-Type Solutions and European Integration*, Lanham and London: University Press of America, pp. 395–407.

Schambeck, Herbert (1984), "Entwicklungstendenzen und Perspectiven des Föderalismus in Österreich," in Stephan Koren, Karl Pisa and Kurt Waldheim (eds), *Politik für die Zukunft*, Vienna and Cologne: Herman Böhlaus, pp. 139–154.

Schambeck, Herbert (1992), "Zum Werden und zu den Aufgaben des österreichischen Föderalismus," in Herbert Schambeck (ed.), *Föderalismus und Parlamentarismus in Österreich*, Vienna: Österreichische Staatsdruckerei, pp. 17–20.

Schausberger, Franz (1992), "Föderalismus und Länderrechte – Ein Problem im Zuge eines österreichieschen EG-Beitritts?" in Andreas Khol and Alfred Stirneman (eds),

Österreichischen Jahrbuch für Politik 1991, Munich: R. Oldenbourg, and Vienna: Verlag für Geschichte und Politik, pp. 357–377.

Stampfer, Bernd (1981), "Zur Situation des Föderalismus in Österreich," in Andreas Khol and Alfred Stirneman (eds), *Österreichischen Jahrbuch für Politik 1980*, Munich: R. Oldenbourg, and Vienna: Verlag für Geschichte und Politik, pp. 5–30.

Ucakar, Karl (1997), "Verfassung: Geschichte und Prinzipien," in Herbert Dachs, Peter Gerlich, Herbert Gottweis, Franz Horner, Helmut Kramer, Volkmar Laubner, Wolfgang C. Müller and Emerich Tálos (eds), *Handbuch des Politischen Systems Österreichs*, Third Edition, Vienna: Manzche, pp. 84–98.

Wandruszka, Adam (1977) [1954], "Östrreichs Politische Struktur. Die Entwicklung der Parteien und politischen Bewgungen," in Heinrich Benedikt (ed.), *Geschichte der Republik Österreich*, Vienna: Verlag für Geschichte und Politik, pp. 289–348.

Weber, Karl (1995), "Föderalismus," in Emmerich Tálos, Herbert Dachs, Ernst Hanisch and Anton Staudinger (eds), *Handbuch des politischen Systems Österreichs, Erste Republic 1918–1933*, Vienna: Manzche, pp. 123–134.

Wollansky, Gertraud (1983), "Schulpolitik in Österreich: Ein Überblick," *Österreichische Zeitschrift für Politikwissenschaft*, Vol. 83, No. 1, pp. 5–18.

Belgium

Official documents, reports, statistics and parliamentary sessions

Annales Parlementaire de Belgique, Chambre des Réprésentants, Session Ordinaire 1979–80/Parlementaire Handelingen van België, Kamer der Volksvertegenwoordigers, Gewone Zitting 1979–80, Dewarichtet: Brussels.

Conseil de la Communauté Française, Session 1980–81, Séance du mardi 4 novembre 1980, *Compte Rendu Intégral*.

Déclaration de l'Exécutif, Conseil de la Communauté Française, Session 1980–81, Séance du mardi 4 novembre 1980, *Compte Rendu Intégral*.

Ministrie van de Vlaamse Gemeenschap (1995), *Een regering voor de Vlamingen*.

OESE (Doorlichting van het Educatief Overheidsbeleid) (1991), Ministerie van de Vlaamse Gemeenschap, Department Onderwijs, Ministère de l'Education, de la Recherche et de la Formation; Verwaltung de Deutschsprachigen Gemeinschaft, Abteilung Unterricht, *Het Educatief Bestel in België: Van Convergentie naar Divergentie*, Brussels.

Overeenkomst van 8 februari 1984 betreffende de onderwijsaangelegenheden die krachtens de Grondwet niet tot de bevoegheid van de Gemeenschappen behoren, reproduced in Jan De Groof (ed.) (1990), *De Scholpactwet: Coördinatie en annotatie*, Brussels: Story Scienta and Centrum voor Politieke, Economische en Sociale Studies CEPESS: p. 103.

Séance du jeudi 27 juni 1963/Vergadering van donderdag 27 juni 1963, *Chambre des Réprésentants, Annales Parlementaires/ Kamer der Volksvertegenwoordigers, Parlementaire Handelingen*, Dewarichtet: Brussels.

Séance du mercredi 18 février 1970/Vergadering van woensdag 18 februari 1970, *Annales Parlementaire de Belgique, Chambre des Réprésentants, Session Ordinaire 1969–1970/Parlementaire Handelingen van België, Kamer der Volksvertegenwoordigers, Gewone Zitting 1969–1970*, Dewarichtet: Brussels.

Séance Plenieres jeudi 7 juillet 1988/Plenaire Vergadering van donderdag 7 juli 1988 (1989), *Annales Parlementaires et Rapports nominatifs des Commissions, Chambre des Réprésentants de Belgique, Session Extraordinaire 1988*, Dewarichtet: Brussels.

Le Soir (1999), *L'avenir des Belges, le fédéralisme à l'épreuve*.

Vlaamse Executieve (1983), Standpuntbepaling van de Vlaamse Executieve i.v.m.'de communautarisering van het onderwijs', 27 April 1983, reproduced in Jan de Groof (ed.) (1990), *De Schoolpactwet: Coördinatie en annotatie*, Brussels: Story Scienta Scienta and Centrum voor Politieke, Economische en Sociale Studies CEPESS.

Books

Alen, André (1990), *Belgium: Bipolar and Centrifugal Federalism*, Brussels: Ministry of Foreign Affairs.

Alen, André and Rusen Ergec (1994), *Federal Belgium After the Fourth State Reform of 1993*, Brussels: Ministry of Foreign Affairs.

Bouckaert, Gert and Tom Auwers (1999), *De Modernisering van de Vlaamse Overheid*, Brugge: Die Keure.

Brasinne, Jacques (1994), *La Belgique fédérale*, Crisp: Brussels.

Bruwier, Marinette, Nicole Caulier-Mathy, Claude Desame and Paul Gerin (1990), *1886 La Wallonie nèe de la grève?'* Bruxelles: Éditions Labor.

Carette, Christian, Jan de Groof, Patrick Peeters, Jan Vermeire (1993), *La Legislation des Media, Le cadre normatif général, Les normes administratives et techniques relatives aux radio- et télécommunications*, Cepess: Brussels.

Coppieters, Franz (1974), *The Community Problem in Belgium*, Brussel: Institut Belge d'Information et de Documentation.

Delwit, Pascal, Jean-Michel De Waele and Paul Magnette (1999) (eds), *Gouverner la Belgique, Clivages et compromis dans une société complexe*, Presses Universitaires de France: Paris.

Derenne, Christophe and Colette De Troy (eds) (1997), *Belgique: Disparition d'une nation européennes*, Brussels: Éditions Luc Pire.

Dewachter, Wilfried (1992), *De duelistische identiteit van de Belgische maatschappij*, Koninklijke Nederlandse Akademie van Wetenschappen, Amsterdam: Noord-Hollandsche.

Dieckhoff, Alain (ed.) (1996), *Belgique, La Force de la désunion*, Paris: Éditions Complexe.

Fitzmaurice, John (1983), *The Politics of Belgium: Crisis and Compromise in a Plural Society*, New York: St Martin's Press.

Hooghe, Liesbeth (1991), *A Leap in the Dark: Nationalist Conflict and Federal Reform in Belgium*, Ithaca: Cornell Studies in International Affairs Western Societies Papers.

Huyse, Lucien (1970), *Passiviteit, Pacificatie en Verzuiling in de Belgische Politiek*, Antwerp and Utrecht: Standaard Wetenschappelijke Uitgeverij.

Jaumain, Serge (ed.), *La réforme de l'Etat ... et après? L'impact des débats institutionnels en Belgique et au Canada*, Brussels: ULB.

Mabille, Xavier (1997), *Histoire politique de la Belgique: Facteurs et acteurs de changement*, reviewed and updated new edition, Brussels: Crisp.

Maes, Rudolf (1985), *La Decentralisation Territoriale; Situation et Perspectives*, Brussels: Rapport au Ministre de l'Intérieur et de la Fonction publique.

McRae, Kenneth (1986), *Conflict and Compromise in Multilingual Societies: Belgium*, Waterloo: Wilfrid Laurier University Press.

Neels, Leo, Dirk Voorhoof, Hans Maertens (eds) (1996), *Medialex: Selectie van bronnen van de media- en informatie wetgeving*, Fourth Edition, Antwerp: Kluwer.

Senelle, Robert (1971), *La Revision de la Constitution 1967–1970*, Brussels: Ministere des Affaires Etrangers et du Commerce Exterieur.

Senelle, Robert (1978), *La Reforme de l''Etat Belge*, Brussels: Ministere des Affaires Etrangers, du Commerce Exterieur et de la Cooperation au Developpement.

Senelle, Robert with Edgard Van de Velde and Emiel Clement (1999)*Kronieken van de Vlaamse Staatswording, Over de Identiteit van het Vlaming-Zijn*, Lannoo, Tielt.

Van Cauwenberghe, Jean Claude (ed.) (1998), *Oser être Wallon!* Gerpinnes: Éditions Quorum.

Wigny, Pierre (1972), *La Troisième Revision de la Constitution*, Brussels: Bruylant.

Witte, Els and Harry Van Velthoven (1998), *Taal en Politiek, De Belgische casus in een historisch perspectief*, Brussels: VUB.

Witte, Els, Jan De Groof and Jeffrey Tyssens (eds) (1999), *Het Schoolpact van 1958: Onstaan, graondlijnen en toepassing van een Belgisch compromis/Le pacte scolaire de 1958: Origines, principes et application d'un compromis belge*, Brussels: Vrije Universiteit Brussels.

Articles and chapters

Alen, André (1994), "Le Fédéralisme Belge," in André Alen, Jean Beaufays, Gonzales d'Alcantara, Frank Delmartino, Kris Deschouwer, Rusen Ergec and Henry Tulkens, *Le Fédéralisme: Approches politique, économique et juridique*, De Boeck: Brussels, pp. 135–185.

Alen, André and Patrick Peeters (1999), "The Competences of the Communities in the Belgian Federal State: The Principle of Exclusivity Revisited," *European Public Law*, Vol. 3, No. 2, pp. 165–173.

Aunger, Edmund A. (1993), "Regional, National, and Official Languages in Belgium," *International Journal of the Sociology of Language*, Special Issue: *Sociology of Language in Belgium Revisited*, Vol. 104, pp. 31–48.

Beaufays, Jean (1998), "Petite Histoire d'un jeune État binational," in Marco Martiniello and Marc Swyngedouw (eds), *Où va la Belgique? Les soubresauts d'une petite démocratie européenne*, Paris: L'Harmattan, pp. 123–136.

Berckx, Cathy and Karel Rimanque (1996), "L'Influence des Sociaux-Chrétiens sur l'évolution des institutions 1945–1995," in Wilfried Dewachter, Georges-Henri Dumont, Micehl Dumoulin, Manu Gérard, Emiel Lamberts, Xavier Mabille and Mark Van den Wijngaert (eds), *Un Parti Dans l'Histoire 1945–1995, 50 Ans d'Action du Parti Social Chrétien*, Louvain-la-Neuve: Ducolot.

Breuning, Marijke (1997), "Nationalism and Nationalist Parties: A Comparison of the Flemish Volksunie and Vlaams Blok," *Nationalism and Ethnic Politics*, Vol. 3, No. 1, pp. 1–27.

Covell, Maureen (1985), "Possibly Necessary But Not Necessarily Possible: Revision of the Constitution in Belgium," in Keith G. Banting and Richard Simeon (eds), *Redesigning the State; The Politics of Constitutional Change*, Toronto and Buffalo: University of Toronto Press, pp. 71–95.

De Groof, Jan (1994) "The Belgian Model for Constitutional Rights on Education," in Jan De Groof (ed.), *Subsidiarity and Education, Aspects of Comparative Educational Law, First Report of the International Educational Law Association*, Leuven and Amersfort: Acco, pp. 305–312.

De Groof, Jan (1996), "Les Sociaux-Chrétiens et l'enseignement," in Wilfried Dewachter, Georges-Henri Dumont, Michel Dumoulin, Manu Gérard, Emiel Lamberts,

Xavier Mabille and Mark Van den Wijngaert (eds), *Un Parti Dans l'Histoire 1945–1995, 50 Ans d'Action du Parti Social Chrétien*, Louvain-la-Neuve: Ducolot, pp. 567–584.

Delmartino, Frank (1986), "Belgium: A Regional State or a Federal State in the Making," in Michael Burgess (ed.), *Federalism and Federation in Western Europe*, London, Sydney, Dover and New Hampshire: Croom Helm, pp. 35–58.

Delpérée, Francis (1991), "Le fédéralisme en Belgique," in *Le fédéralisme en Europe*, Barcelona: ICPI, pp. 89–99.

Delpérée, Francis (1999), "Le fédéralisme de confrontation," in Pascal Delwit, Jean-Michel De Waele and Paul Magnette (eds), *Gouverner la Belgique, Clivages et compromis dans une société complexe*, Paris: Presses Universitaires de France, pp. 53–70.

Deprez, Kas (1992), "The Dutch Language in Flanders," in Theo Hermans, Louis Vos and Lode Wils (eds), *The Flemish Movement, A Documentary History 1780–1990*, London and Atlantic Highlands: Athlone, pp. 416–429.

Deschouwer, Kris (2002), "Causes and Effects of Constitutional Changes in Multilingual Belgium," in Stephen Brooks (ed.), *The Challenge of Cultural Pluralism*, Westport: Praeger, pp. 121–140.

Destatte, Philippe (1998), "La Wallonie dans l'enseignement de l'histoire," in Jean Claude Van Cauwenberghe (ed.), *Oser être Wallon!*, Gerpinnes: Éditions Quorum, pp. 45–54.

Dewachter, Wilfried (1998), "Belgique: La Déchirure," *Politique internationale*, Vol. 78, pp. 177–190.

De Winter, Lieven, André-Paul Frognier and Jaak Billiet (1998), "Y a-t-il encore des Belges? Vingt ans d'enquêtes sur les identités politiques territoriales," in Marco Martiniello and Marc Swyngedouw (eds), *Où va la Belgique? Les soubresauts d'une petite démocratie européenne*, Paris: L'Harmattan, pp. 123–136.

Dierickx, Guido (1984), "The Management of Subcultural Conflict: The Issue of Education in Belgium 1950–1975," *Acta Politica*, Vol. 19, No. 1, pp. 85–95.

Dumont, Hugues and Georges-Henri Dumont (1996), "La Politique Culturelle Sociale-Chrétienne sous le Signe de l'autonomie et du pluralisme," in Wilfried Dewachter, Georges-Henri Dumont, Michel Dumoulin, Manu Gérard, Emiel Lamberts, Xavier Mabille and Mark Van den Wijngaert (eds), *Un Parti Dans l'Histoire 1945–1995, 50 Ans d'Action du Parti Social Chrétien*, Louvain-la-Neuve: Ducolot, pp. 555–564.

Erk, Jan (2003), "'Wat We Zelf Doen, Doen We Beter': Belgian Substate Nationalisms, Congruence and Public Policy," *Journal of Public Policy*, Vol. 23, No. 2, pp. 201–224.

Erk, Jan (2005), "From Vlaams Blok to Vlaams Belang: The Belgian Far-Right Renames Itself," *West European Politics*, Vol. 28, No. 3, pp. 493–502.

Erk, Jan (2005), "Substate Nationalism and the Left–Right Divide: Critical Junctures in the Formation of Nationalist Labour Movements in Belgium," *Nations and Nationalism*, Vol. 11, No. 4, pp. 551–70.

Frognier, Andre P., Michel Quevit and Marie Stenbock (1982), "Regional Imbalances and Centre–Periphery Relationships in Belgium," in Stein Rokkan and Derek Urwin (eds), *The Politics of Territorial Identity: Studies in European Regionalism*, London: Sage Publications, pp. 251–278.

Heisler, Martin O. (1990), "Hyphenating Belgium: Changing State and Regime to Cope with Cultural Division," in Joseph V. Montville (ed.), *Conflict and Peacemaking in Multiethnic Societies*, Lexington: Lexington Books, pp. 177–195.

Hill, Keith (1974), "Belgium: Political Change in a Segmented Society," in Richard Rose (ed.), *Electoral Behaviour: A Comparative Handbook*, New York and London: Macmillan, pp. 29–107.

Hondeghem, Annie (1998), "La Politisation de l'Administration en Belgique: Vers une nouvelle culture?" *Revue française d'Administration publique*, Special Issue: *Les fonctionnaires et la politique dans les pays de l'union européene*, Vol. 86, pp. 255–266.

Hooghe, Liesbeth (1995), "Belgian Federalism and the European Community," in Barry Jones and Michael Keating (eds), *The European Union and the Regions*, Clarendon Press: Oxford, pp. 135–165.

Huyse, Luc (1981), "Political Conflict in Bicultural Belgium," in A. Lijphardt (ed.), *Conflict and Coexistence in Belgium, The Dynamics of a Culturally Divided Society*, Berkeley: Institute of International Studies, University of California, pp. 107–126.

Jongen, François (1998), "Radiodiffusion et Culture en Droit Belge," in Hugues Dumont and Alain Strowel (eds), *Politique culturelle et droit de la radio-télévision*, Brussels: Publications des Facultés universitaire Saint-Louis.

Lentzen, Évelyne (1998), "La processus de fédéralisation," in Marco Martiniello and Marc Swyngedouw (eds), *Où va la Belgique? Les soubresauts d'une petite démocratie européenne*, Paris: L'Harmattan, pp. 31–43.

Lijphardt, Arend (1981), "The Belgian Example of Cultural Coexistence in Comparative Perspective," in A. Lijphardt (ed.), *Conflict and Coexistence in Belgium, The Dynamics of a Culturally Divided Society*, Berkeley: Institute of International Studies, University of California, pp. 1–12.

Lorwin, Val (1974), "Belgium: Conflict and Compromise," in Kenneth McCrae (ed.), *Consociational Democracy, Political Accommodation in Segmented Societies*, Ottawa: The Carleton Library, McClelland and Stewart Limited, pp. 179–206.

Magnette, Paul (1999), "Le régime parlementaire. De l'orléanisme au fédéralisme," in Pascal Delwit, Jean-Michel De Waele and Paul Magnette (eds), *Gouverner la Belgique, Clivages et compromis dans une société complexe*, Paris: Presses Universitaires de France, pp. 71–112.

Mughan, A. (1985), "Belgium: All Periphery and No Centre?" in Yves Meny and Vincent Wright (eds), *Centre–Periphery Relations in Western Europe*, London: George Allen and Unwin, pp. 273–299.

Murphy, Alexander B. (1993), "Linguistic Regionalism and the Social Construction of Space in Belgium," *International Journal of the Sociology of Language*, Special Issue: *Sociology of Language in Belgium Revisited*, Vol. 104, pp. 49–64.

Murphy, Alexander B. (1995), "Belgium's Regional Divergence: Along the Road to Federation," in Graham Smith (ed.), *Federalism: The Multiethnic Challenge*, London and New York: Longman, pp. 73–100.

O'Neill, Michael (1998), "Re-Imagining Belgium: New Federalism and the Political Management of Cultural Diversity," *Parliamentary Affairs: A Journal of Comparative Politics*, Vol. 51, Vol. 2, pp. 241–258.

Peeters, Patrick (1994), "Federalism: A Comparative Perspective – Belgium Transforms from a Unitary to a Federal State," in Bertus de Villiers (ed.), *Evaluating Federal Systems*, Dordrecht, Boston and London: Martinus Nijhoff, pp. 194–207.

Scholsem, Jean-Claude (1998), "La nouvelle Belgique fédérale," in Marco Martiniello and Marc Swyngedouw (eds), *Où va la Belgique? Les soubresauts d'une petite démocratie européenne*, Paris: L'Harmattan.

Seiler, Daniel (1977), "Clivages, régions et science politique: application d'un schéma d'analyse aux cas de la Suisse et de la Belgique," *Canadian Journal of Political Science*, Vol. X, No. 3, pp. 447–472.

Seiler, Daniel-Louis (1998), "Non-lieu," in Marco Martiniello and Marc Swyngedouw (eds), *Où va la Belgique? Les soubresauts d'une petite démocratie européenne*, Paris: L'Harmattan.

Seiler, Daniel-Louis (1999), "Un État entre importation et implosion: consociativité, partitocratie et lotissement dans la sphère publique en Belgique," in Pascal Delwit, Jean-Michel De Waele and Paul Magnette (eds), *Gouverner la Belgique, Clivages et compromis dans une société complexe*, Paris: Presses Universitaires de France, pp. 15–52.

Senelle, Robert (1989), "Constitutional Reform in Belgium: From Unitarism Towards Federalism," in Murray Forsyth (ed.), *Federalism and Nationalism*, Leicester and London: Leicester University Press, pp. 51–95.

Senelle, Robert (1990), "The Current Constitutional System," in René Bryssinck, Marina Boudart and Michel Boudart (eds), *Modern Belgium*, Belgium: Modern Belgium Association, pp. 169–220.

Servaes, Jan (1998), "Médias et politique," in Marco Martiniello and Marc Swyngedouw (eds), *Où va la Belgique? Les soubresauts d'une petite démocratie européenne*, Paris: L'Harmattan, pp. 161–172.

Sonntag, Selma K. (1993), "The Politics of Compromise: The Enactment of Regional Unilingualism," *International Journal of the Sociology of Language*, Special Issue: *Sociology of Language in Belgium Revisited*, Vol. 104, pp. 9–30.

Stengers, Jean (1981), "Belgian National Sentiments," in A. Lijphardt (ed.), *Conflict and Coexistence in Belgium, The Dynamics of a Culturally Divided Society*, Berkeley: Institute of International Studies, University of California, pp. 46–59.

Uyttendaele, Marc (1997), "La Belgique: un modèle de fédéralisme panaché," in Serge Jaumain (ed.), *La réforme de l'Etat ... et après ? L'impact des débats institutionnels en Belgique et au Canada*, Brussels: Université Libre de Bruxelles, pp. 37–46.

Van Dam, Denise (1997), "Les mouvements sociaux d'hier, germes du nationalisme ou du régionalisme d'aujourd'hui," in Serge Jaumain (ed.), *La réforme de l'Etat ... et après ? L'impact des débats institutionnels en Belgique et au Canada*, Brussels: ULB.

Vandeweyer, Luc (1989), "Gesprekken tussen federalisten in de jaren zestig. De Vlaamse Volksbeweging op zoek naar bondgenoten in Wallonië," *Res Publica*, Vol. 31, No. 1, pp. 35–48.

Van Dyck, Ruth (1996), "'Divided We Stand.' Regionalism, Federalism and Minority Rights in Belgium," *Res Publica*, Vol. 38, No. 2, pp. 429–446.

Witte, Els (1992), "Belgian Federalism: Towards Complexity and Asymmetry," *West European Politics*, Vol. 15, No. 4, pp. 95–117.

Zolberg, Aristide R. (1974), "The Makings of Flemings and Walloons: Belgium 1830–1914," *Journal of Interdisciplinary History*, Vol. 5, No. 2, pp. 179–235.

Zolberg, Aristide R. (1977), "Splitting the Difference: Federalization without Federalism in Belgium," in Milton Esman (ed.), *Ethnic Conflict in the Western World*, Ithaca and London: Cornell University Press, pp. 103–142.

Canada

Official documents, reports, statistics and parliamentary sessions

Caplan, Gerald and Florian Sauvageau (1986), *Rapport du Groupe de travail sur la politique de la radiodiffusion*, Ottawa: Ministère des Approvisionnement et Services.

Citizens' Forum on Canada's Future (1991), *Report to the People and Government of Canada*, Ottawa: Ministry of Supply and Services.

The Constitutional Committee of the Québec Liberal Party (1980), *A New Canadian Federation*, Montreal.

Le Devoir (1976), "Jean-Paul L'Allier expose sa politique: la culture ou rien," May 29, 1976, pp. 1, 20.

Le Droit (1977), "Radio, television et unité nationale," 25 July 1977, p. 7.

The Globe and Mail, "For a Federal Role in Education," April 14, 1993, p. A-16.

Maclean's, "Special Report: What's Wrong at School," January 11, 1993, p. 4.

Organisation for Economic Cooperation and Development (1976), *Reviews of National Policies for Education – Canada*, Paris: OECD.

La Presse (1985), "L'avenir de la television francophone au Canada," *La Presse*, 22 May 1985, p. C-1.

Report of the Task Force on Canadian Unity (Pepin-Robarts Report) (1979), *A Future Together*, Ottawa: Queen's Printer.

Le Soleil, "O'Neill craint l'intervention d'Ottawa dans le contôle de la radiodiffusion," April 7, 1977, p. F-1.

Tremblay, Arthur (1955), *Contribution à l'étude des problèmes et des besoins de l'enseignement dans la province de Québec, Commission Royale d'Enquête su le Problèmes Constitutionnels*, Québec.

Books

Banting, Keith (1987), *The Welfare State and Canadian Federalism*, Second Edition, Montreal and Kingston: McGill-Queen's University Press.

Cameron, David M. (1991), *More Than an Academic Question: Universities, Government and Public Policy in Canada*, Halifax: Institute for Research on Public Policy.

Cook, Ramsay (1967), *Canada and the French Canadian Question*, Toronto: Macmillan.

Foley, Michael (1989). *The Silence of Constitutions: Gaps, "Abeyances" and Political Temperament in the Maintenance of Government*, London: Routledge.

Gagnon, Alain-G. and Mary-Beth Montcalm (1990), *Québec: Beyond the Quiet Revolution*, Scarborough: Nelson.

Kymlicka, Will (1998), *Finding Our Way: Rethinking Ethnocultural Relations in Canada*, Toronto: Oxford University Press.

Laramée, Alain (ed.) (1993); *Les communications au Québec*, Montreal: Saint-Martin.

McRoberts, Kenneth (1997), *Misconceiving Canada*, Toronto: Oxford University Press.

Nielsen, Greg Marc (1994), *Le Canada de Radio-Canada: Sociologie critique et diagolisme culturel*, Toronto: Éditions du Gref.

Proulx, Gilles (1976), *L'Aventure de la Radio*, Montreal: Édition La Presse.

Proulx, Gilles (1986), *La Radio: d'hier à aujourd'hui*, Québec: Libre expression.

Raboy, Marc (1990), *Missed Opportunities: The Story of Canada's Broadcasting Policy*, Montreal and Kingston: McGill-Queen's University Press.

Rocher, François and Miriam Smith (eds) (1995), *New Trends in Canadian Federalism*, Peterborough: Broadview.

Saywell, John (1969) (eds), *Canadian Annual Review for 1968*. Toronto: University of Toronto Press.

Scott, Frank and Michael Oliver (eds) (1964), *Quebec States Her Case: Speeches and Articles from Quebec in the Years of Unrest*, Toronto: Macmillan

Siegel, Arthur (1983), *Politics and the Media in Canada*, Toronto: McGraw-Hill.

Simeon, Richard (1972), *Federal–Provincial Diplomacy: The Making of Recent Policy in Canada*, Toronto: University of Toronto Press.

Simeon, Richard and Ian Robinson (1990), *State, Society and the Development of Canadian Federalism*, Toronto: University of Toronto Press.

Smiley, Donald V. (1983), *Canada in Question: Federalism in the Eighties*, Third Edition, Toronto: McGraw-Hill Ryerson,

Smiley, Donald and Ronald Watts (eds) (1985), *Intrastate Federalism in Canada*, Toronto: University of Toronto Press.

Stevenson, Garth (1982), *Unfulfilled Union: Canadian Federalism and National Unity*, Toronto: Gage.

Thomas, David M. (1997), *Whistling Past the Graveyard: Constitutional Abeyances, Quebec, and the Future of Canada*, Toronto: Oxford University Press.

Webber, Jeremy (1994), *Reimagining Canada: Language, Culture, Community anthe Canadian Constitution*, Montreal and Kingston: McGill-Queen's University Press.

Weir, Austin (1965), *The Struggle for National Broadcasting in Canada*, Toronto: McClelland and Stewart.

Westmacott, Martin and Hugh Mellon (eds) (1998), *Challenges to Canadian Federalism*, Scarborough: Prentice Hall.

Articles and chapters

Bakvis, Herman (1981), *Federalism and the Organisation of Political Life: Canada in Comparative Perspective*, Kingston: Institute of Intergovernmental Relations, Queen's University.

Bakvis, Herman and Grace Skogstad (2002), "Canadian Federalism: Performance, Effectiveness, and Legitimacy," in Herman Bakvis and Grace Skogstad (eds), *Canadian Federalism: Performance, Effectiveness, and Legitimacy*, Don Mills: Oxford University Press.

Banting, Keith (2005), "Canada: Nation-Building in a Federal Welfare State," in Herbert Obinger, Stephan Leibfried and Francis G. Castles (eds), *Federalism and the Welfare State: New World and European Experiences*, Cambridge: Cambridge University Press, pp. 89–137.

Beauchemin, Jean-Marie (1976), "Perception francophone du rapport ou Alice au pays merveilles," in *Reactions to the OECD Review – Canada, 1976 Conference of the Canadian Education Association*, Toronto: The Canadian Education Association, pp. 19–27.

Beckton, Clare and A. Wayne Mackay (1986), "Institutional and Constitutional Arrangements: An Overview," in Clare Beckton and A. Wayne Mackay (eds), *Recurring Issues in Canadian Federalism*, Toronto: University of Toronto Press, pp. 1–76.

Behiels, Michael (1985), "Quebec Confronts the New Federalism," in Michael Behiels, *Prelude to Québec's Quiet Revolution: Liberalism versus Neo-nationalism 1945–1960*, Montreal and Kingston: McGill-Queen's University Press, pp. 185–219.

Brossard, Jacques (1974), "Fédéralisme et status particulier," in Adrian Popovici (ed.), *Problèmes de droit contemporain: Mélanges Louis Baudoin*, Montreal: Les Presses de l'Université de Montréal, pp. 425–444.

Burgess, Michael (2001), "Competing National Visions: Canada–Québec Relations in a Comparative Perspective," in Alain-G. Gagnon and James Tully (eds), *Multinational Democracies*, Cambridge: Cambridge University Press, pp. 257–274.

Cairns, Alan (1977), "The Governments and Societies of Canadian Federalism," *Canadian Journal of Political Science*, Vol. X, No. 4, pp. 695–725.

Coulombe, Pierre (1998), "Québec in the Federation," in Martin Westmacott and Hugh

Mellon (eds), *Challenges to Canadian Federalism*, Scarborough: Prentice Hall, pp. 187–197.

Covell, Maureen (1987), "Federalization and Federalism: Belgium and Canada," in Herman Bakvis and William M. Chandler (1987), *Federalism and the Role of State*, Toronto, Buffalo and London: University of Toronto Press, pp. 57–81.

Cutler, Fred and Matthew Mendelsohn (2001), "What Kind of Federalism do Canadians (outside Québec) want?" *Policy Options*, Vol. 22, No. 8, pp. 23–29.

Cutler, Fred and Matthew Mendelsohn (2001), "Canadians Can't Make Sense of Inter-governmental Disputes: Institutions of Federalism are Outdated," *Globe and Mail*, 31 July, p. A-11.

Demers, François (1993), "La presse écrite: fin de cycle, fin de siècle," in Alain Laramée (ed.), *Les communications au Québec*, Montreal: Saint-Martin, pp. 35–54.

Elton, David K. (1977). "Public Opinion and Federal–Provincial Relations: A Case Study of Alberta," in J. Peter Meekison (ed.), *Canadian Federalism: Myth or Reality?* Third Edition, Toronto: Methuen.

Erk, Jan (2002), "Le Québec entre la Flandre et la Wallonie: Une comparaison des nationalismes sous-étatiques belges et du nationalisme québécois," *Recherches sociographiques*, Vol. 48, No. 3, pp. 499–516.

Erk, Jan (2006), "'Uncodified Workings and Unworkable Codes': Canadian Federalism and Public Policy," *Comparative Political Studies*, Vol. 39, No. 4, pp. 441–462.

Fletcher, Frederick J. and Martha Fletcher (1989), "Federalism and Communication Policy: Communications and Confederation Revisited," in David P. Shugarman and Reg Whitaker (eds), *Federalism and Political Community: Essays in Honour of Donald Smiley*, Peterborough: Broadview Press, pp. 385–405.

Fox, Francis M. (1981), "The Federal Interest," in J.W. George Ivany and Michael E. Manley-Casimir (eds), *Federal–Provincial Relations: Education Canada*. Toronto: Ontario Institute for Studies in Education, pp. 54–57.

Gagnon, Alain-G. (1991), "Everything Old is New Again: Canada, Québec and Constitutional Impasse," in Frances Abele (ed.), *How Ottawa Spends: The Politics of Fragmentation 1991–92*, Ottawa: Carleton University Press, pp. 63–105.

Gagnon, Alain-G. and Jan Erk (2001), "Legitimacy, Effectiveness and Canadian Federalism; On the Benefits of Ambiguity," in Herman Bakvis and Grace Skogstad (eds), *Canadian Federalism: Performance, Effectiveness and Legitimacy*, Toronto: Oxford University Press, pp. 317–330.

Gagnon, Alain-G. and Joseph Garcea (1988), "Quebec and the Pursuit of Special Status," in Martin Westmacott and R.D. Olling (eds), *Perspectives on Canadian Federalism*, Scarborough: Prentice Hall, pp. 304–325.

Gibbins, Roger (1987), "Federal Societies, Institutions, and Politics," in Herman Bakvis and William Chandler (eds), *Federalism and the Role of the State*, Toronto, Buffalo and London: University of Toronto Press, pp. 15–31.

Gibbins, Roger (1998), "Federalism and Regional Alienation," in Martin Westmacott and Hugh Mellon (eds), *Challenges to Canadian Federalism*, Scarborough: Prentice Hall, pp. 40–52.

Hargraves, Susan (1981), "Federal Intervention in Canadian Education," in J.W. George Ivany and Michael E. Manley-Casimir (eds), *Federal–Provincial Relations: Education Canada*, Toronto: Ontario Institute for Studies in Education, pp. 23–33.

Henry, Shawn (2002), "Re-visiting Western Alienation," in Lisa Young and Keith Archer (eds), *Regionalism and Party Politics in Canada*, Toronto: Oxford University Press, pp. 77–91.

Hurley, James Ross (2002), "Canadian Federalism: Idiosyncratic Characteristics, Evolution and Lessons Learned," in Jürgen Rose and Johannes Traut (eds), *Federalism and Decentralisation: Perspectives for the Transformation Process in Eastern and Central Europe*, Hamburg: Lit, and New York: Palgrave, pp. 141–154.

Kymlicka, Will (1998), "Multinational Federalism in Canada: Rethinking the Partnership," in Roger Gibbins and Guy Laforest (eds), *Beyond the Impasse, Toward Reconciliation*, Montreal: Institute for Research on Public Policy, pp. 15–50.

Kymlicka, Will (2001), "Minority Nationalism and Multination Federalism," in Kymlicka, *Politics in the Vernacular: Nationalism, Multiculturalism and Citizenship*, Oxford and New York: Oxford University Press, pp. 91–119.

Lorimer, Rowland (1995), "The Future of English-Language Publishing," in Kenneth McRoberts (ed.), *Beyond Quebec: Taking Stock of Canada*, Montreal and Kingston: McGill-Queen's University Press, pp. 202–217.

McRoberts, Kenneth (1997), "Trudeau and the New Federal Orthodoxy: Denying the Quebec Question," in Kenneth McRoberts, *Misconceiving Canada: The Struggle for National Unity*, Toronto: Oxford University Press, pp. 55–76.

Meadwell, Hudson (2002), "Is a 'True' Multination Federation a Cure for Our Ills?" in Patrick James, Donald Abelson and Michael Lusztig (eds), *The Myth of the Sacred: The Charter, the Courts, and the Politics of the Constitution in Canada*, Montreal and Kingston: McGill-Queen's University Press, pp. 219–238.

Miller, Mary Jane (1995), "Will English-Language Television Remain Distinctive," in Kenneth McRoberts (ed.), *Beyond Quebec: Taking Stock of Canada*, Montreal and Kingston: McGill-Queen's University Press, pp. 182–201.

Noël, Alain (2000), "General Study of the Framework Agreement," in Alain-G. Gagnon and Hugh Segal (eds), *The Canadian Social Union Without Quebec*, Montreal: Institute for Research on Public Policy, pp. 9–36.

Petter, Andrew (1989), "Federalism and the Myth of the Federal Spending Power," *The Canadian Bar Review*, Vol. 68, No. 3, pp. 449–455.

Raboy, Marc (1997), "Media, Nationalism and Identity in Canada and Quebec," *Res Publica*, Vol. 2, No. 2, pp. 315–323.

Resnick, Philip (1994), "Toward a Multinational Federalism: Asymmetrical and Confederal Alternatives," in F. Leslie Seidle (ed.), *Seeking a New Canadian Partnership: Asymmetrical and Confederal Options*, Montreal: Institute for Research on Public Policy, pp. 71–89.

Robinson, Ian and Richard Simeon (1999), "The Dynamics of Canadian Federalism," in James Bickerton and Alain-G. Gagnon (eds), *Canadian Politics*, Third Edition, Peterborough: Broadview Press, pp. 239–261.

Rose, Jonathan (1998), "Federalism, Broadcasting, and the Search for Community," in Martin Westmacott and Hugh Mellon (eds), *Challenges to Canadian Federalism*, Scarborough: Prentice Hall, pp. 129–143.

Ryan, Claude (1977), "Les deux solitudes à Radio Canada," *Le Devoir*, 30 July 1977, p. 4.

Simeon, Richard (1977), "Regionalism and Canadian Political Institutions," in J. Peter Meekison (ed.), *Canadian Federalism: Myth or Reality?* Third Edition, Toronto: Methuen, pp. 292–304.

Simeon, Richard (1989), "We are all Smiley's People: Some Observations on Donald Smiley and the Study of Federalism," in David P. Shugarman and Reg Whitaker (eds), *Federalism and Political Community: Essays in Honor of Donald Smiley*. Peterborough: Broadview Press.

Simeon, Richard (2004), "Canada: Federalism, Language, and Regional Conflict," in Ugo M. Amoretti and Nancy Bermeo (eds), *Federalism and Territorial Cleavages*, Baltimore and London: The Johns Hopkins University Press, pp. 93–122.

Smiley, Donald (1968), "Rowell-Sirois Report, Provincial Autonomy and Post War Canadian Federalism," in J. Peter Meekison (ed.), *Canadian Federalism: Myth or Reality?* First Edition, Toronto: Methuen, pp. 65–81.

Smiley, Donald (1977), "Territorialism and Canadian Political Institutions," *Canadian Public Policy*, Vol. III, No. 4, pp. 449–457.

Smith, Brian R.D. (1981), "The Need for Intergovernmental Cooperation," in J.W. George Ivany and Michael E. Manley-Casimir (eds), *Federal–Provincial Relations: Education Canada*, Toronto: Ontario Institute for Studies in Education, pp. 58–62.

Smith, David.E. (1989), "Broadcasting in the Federation: National Power, Divided Purpose," in David P. Shugarman and Reg Whitaker (eds), *Federalism and Political Community: Essays in Honour of Donald Smiley*, Peterborough: Broadview Press, pp. 361–383.

Smith, Jennifer (2003), "The Constitutional Debate and Beyond," in François Rocher and Miriam Smith (eds), *New Trends in Canadian Federalism*, Second Edition, Peterborough: Broadview Press, pp. 45–66.

Stein, Michael (1971), "Federal Political Systems and Federal Societies," in J. Peter Meekison (ed.), *Canadian Federalism: Myth or Reality?* Second Edition, Toronto: Methuen, pp. 34–48.

Vipond, Robert (1989), "1787 and 1867: The Federal Principle and Canadian Confederation Reconsidered," *Canadian Journal of Political Science*, Vol. 22, No. 1, pp. 3–25.

Williams, Colin H. (1995), "A Requiem for Canada?" in Graham Smith (ed.), *Federalism: The Multiethnic Challenge*, Longman: London and New York, pp. 31–72.

Germany

Official documents, reports, statistics and parliamentary sessions

Der Bundesminister für Bildung und Wissenschaft (1970), *Bildungsbericht '70, Report of the Federal Government on Education, The Federal Governments Concept for Educational Policy*, English version.

Der Bundesminister für Bildung und Wissenschaft (1978), *Bericht der Bundesregierung über die strukturellen Probleme des föderativen Bildungssystem*, Bonn.

Bundesverfassungsgericht (1952), "Urteil vom 20. Februar 1952 'Finanzausgleich'," *Entscheidungen des Bundesverfassungsgerichts*, Tübingen: J.C.B. Mohr.

Bundesverfassungshof (1952), "Urteil vom 21 Mai 1952 (2 BvH 2/52). Verteilung von Bundeswohnungsbaumitteln an die Länder. Formen der Einflußnahme der Länder auf die Bildung des Bundeswillens. Rechtspflicht zu bundesfreundlichen Verhalten," *Entscheidungen des Bundesverfassungsgerichts 1952*, Tübingen: J.C.B. Mohr.

Bundesverfassungsgericht (1956), "Urteil vom 1. December 1954, Schranken der Befugnis des Bundes zur Rahmengesetzgebung gemäß Art.75 GG, Besoldunggesetz für das Land Nordrhein-Westphalen 9. Juni 1954," *Entscheidungen des Bundesverfassungsgerichts*, Tübingen: J.C.B. Mohr.

Bundesverfassungsgericht (1957), "Urteil vom 26. März 1957. Reichskonkordat vom 20. Juli 1933. Niedersächsisches Gesetz über das öffentliche Schulwesen von 14. September 1954," *Entscheidungen des Bundesverfassungsgerichts*, Tübingen: J.C.B. Mohr.

Bundesverfassungsgericht (1959), "Urteil vom 30. Juli 1958," *Entscheidungen des Bundesverfassungsgerichts*, Tübingen: J.C.B. Mohr.

Bundesverfassungsgericht (1972), "Absoluter Numerus Clausus für Medizinstudium," *Entscheidungen des Bundesverfassungsgericht*, Band 33, Tübingen: J.C.B. Mohr.

Bundesverwaltungsgericht (1966), "Gültigkeit des Staatsvertrag über die Errichtung des Zweiten Deutsches Fernsehens," *Entscheidungen des Bundesverwaltungsgerichts*, Band 22, Berlin: Carl Heymanns.

Christlich-Demokratische Union (CDU) (1993), *Erziehung, Ausbildung und Bildung in unserer freiheitlichen Demokratie: Für die humane Leistungsschule und ein leistungfähiges Hochschulsystem.*

Deutscher Ausschuss für das Erziehungs- und Bildungwesen (1959), *Empfehlungen und Gutachten des Deutschen Ausschuss für das Erziehungs- und Bildungwesen; Rahmenplan zur Umgestaltung und Vereinheitlichung des allgemeinbildendenden öffentlichen Schulwesens*, Stuttgart: Ernst Klett Verlag.

Frei Demokratische Partei (FDP) (1991), *Soziale Chancen durch liberale Marktwirtschaft.*

Geschäftsordnung der Ständigen Konferenz der Kultusminister der Länder in der Bundesrepublik Deutschland, according to the resolution dated 19.11.1955.

Gesetz über die Errichtung von Rundfunkanstalten des Bundesrechts vom 29.11.1960.

Max-Planck-Institute für Bildungforschung (1979), *Das Bildungwesen in der Bundesrepublik Deutschland*, Reinbeck bei Hamburg: Rowohlt Tachenbuch Verlag.

Ministerpräsidenten des Landes Nordrhein-Westfalen/Bildungskommission Nordrhein-Westfalen (1995), *Zukunft der Bildung-Schule der Zukunft: Denkschrift der Kommission "Zukunft der Bildung-Schule der Zukunft,"* Neuwied: Luchterhand.

Noelle, Elisabeth and Erich Peter Neumann (eds) (1956), "Die Regierungen," *Jahrbuch der öffentlichen Meinung 1947–1955*, Allensbach: Institut für Demoskopie.

Noelle, Elisabeth and Erich Peter Neumann (eds) (1967), "Wissenschaftsrat," *Jahrbuch der öffentlichen Meinung 1965–67*, Allensbach and Bonn: Institut für Demoskopie.

Noelle, Elisabeth and Erich Peter Neumann (eds) (1974), "Entscheidungsbefugnis," *Jahrbuch der öffentlichen Meinung 1968–1973*, Allensbach and Bonn: Institut für Demoskopie.

Organisation for Economic Co-operation and Development (1972), *Reviews of National Policies for Education: Germany*, Paris: OECD.

Satzung der Arbeitgemeinschaft der öffentlich-rechtlichen Rundfunkanstalten der Bundesrepublik Deutschland (9/10.6.1950).

Staatsvertrag über Mediendienste (Mediendienste-Staatsvertrag) vom 20. Januar–12. Februar 1997.

Sozialdemokratische Partei Deutschlands (SPD) (1989), *Grundsatzprogramm der SPD.*

Ständige Konferenz der Kultusminister der Länder in der Bundesrepublik Deutschland (1955), "Die Kultusministerkonferenz und ihre Arbeit von 1952 bis 1955," from *Niederscriften über die Sitzungen des Plenums vom 28–29.4.1955/18.19.1955, 46–49 Sitz.*, Bonn: KMK.

Ständige Konferenz der Kultusminister der Länder in der Bundesrepublik Deutschland (1995), "Hohenheimer Memorandum zur Bildungs-, Wissenschafts- und Kulturpolitik im geeinten Deutschland," in *Handbuch für die Kultusminister-Konferenz*, Bonn: KMK.

Books

Abromeit, Heidrun (1992), *Die verkappte Einheitsstaat*, Opladen: Leske und Budrich.

Blair, Philip (1981), *Federalism and Judicial Review in West Germany*, Oxford: Clarendon.

Brill, Hermann Louis, Erwin Scheu and Hermann C.W. Aubin (eds) (1950), *Die Bundesländer: Beiträge zur Neugliederung der Bundesrepublik*, Frankfurt am Main: Institut zur Förderung öffentlicher Angelegenheiten.

Denninger, Erhard with Peter Becker, Ulrich Hammer, Andreas Kehler, Jürgen Lüthje, Peter Hauck, Hans-Albert Lennartz, Henning Schrimpf and Bernard Nagel MCL (1984), *Hochschulrahmengesetz: Kommentar*, Munich: C.H. Beck.

Deuerlein, Ernst (1972), *Föderalismus: Die historischen und philosophischen Grundlagen des föderativen Princips*, Munich: Paul List.

Frey, Kurt (1976), *Konstruktiver Föderalismus: Gesammelte kulturpolitische Beiträge 1948–1975*, Deutsches Institute für Internationale Pädagogische Forschung: Studien und Dokumentationen zur deutschen Bildungsgeschichte, Weinheim und Basel: Beltz Verlag.

Führ, Christoph (1996), *Deutsches Bildungswesen seit 1945; Grundzüge und Probleme*, Bonn: Inter Nationes.

Furchner, Klaus (1960), *Von der Notwendigkeit der Rundfunkneuordnung in der Bundesrepublik Deutschland*, Würzburg: Johan Wilhelm Nauman.

Hahn, H.-J. (1998), *Education and Society in Germany*, Oxford and New York: Berg.

Hearnden, Arthur (1974), *Education in the Two Germanies*, Boulder: Westview Press.

Hearnden, Arthur (1976), *Education, Culture, and Politics in West Germany*, London: Pergamon Press.

Heckel, Heckel, Herman Avenarius and Helmut Fetzer (1986), *Schulrechtskunde: Ein Handbuch für Praxis, Rechtsprechung und Wissenschaft*, Sixth Edition, Neuwied and Dramstadt: Luchterhand.

Hermann, Günther (ed.) (1977), *Rundfunkgesetze: Fernsehen und Hörfunk Textsammlung*, Second Edition, Köln, Berlin, Bonn and Munich: Carl Heymanns

Hermann, Günther (1994), *Rundfunkrecht; Fernsehen und Hörfunk mit neuen Medien*, Munich: C.H. Beck.

Hochstetter, Herbert (1972), *Gesetz zur Vereintlichung und Ordnung des Schulwesens in Baden-Württemberg (Schulverwaltunggesetz)*, Fourth Edition, Stuttgart: Kohlhammer.

Hesse, Konrad (1962) *Der unitarische Bundesstaat*, Karlsruhe: C.F. Müller.

Jarausch, Konrad H. and Volker Gransow (eds) (1994), *Uniting Germany, Documents and Debates, 1944–1993*, Providence and Oxford: Berghahn Books.

Jeffery, Charlie and Peter Savigear (eds) (1991), *German Federalism Today*, Leicester and London: Leicester University Press.

Katzenstein, Peter (1987), *Policy and Politics in Western Germany: The Growth of a Semi-Sovereign State*, Philadelphia: Temple University Press.

Kühn, Heinz (1971), *Rundfunkneuordnung und bundesstaatliche Struktur*, Düsseldorf: Landesregierung Nordrhein-Westphalia.

Kühn, Heinz, Karl Holzamer and Peter Lerche (1972), *Rundfunkneuordnung und bundesstaatliche Struktur*, Munich: C.H. Beck.

Laufer, Heinz and Ursula Münch (1998), *Das Föderative System der Bundesrepublik Deutschland*, Opladen: Leske und Budrich.

Lüders, Carl-Heinz (1953), *Die Zuständigkeit zur Rundfunkgesetzgebung*, Bonn: Köllen Verlag.

Merkl, Peter (ed.) (1999), *The Federal Republic of Germany at Fifty*, New York and London: New York University Press.

Michael, Berthold and Heinz-Herman Schepp (eds) (1993), *Die Schule in Staat und Gesellschaft; Dokumente zur deutschen Schulgeschichte im 19. und 20. Jahrhundert*, Göttingen and Zürich: Muster-Schmidt Verlag.

Peters, Hans (1954), *Zuständigkeit des Bundes im Rundfunkwesen*, Berlin, Göttingen and Heidelberg: Springer.

Picht, Georg (1964), *Die deutsche Bildungskatastrophe, Analyse und Dokumentation*, Olten and Freiburg im Breisgrau: Walter Verlag.

Poeppelt, Karin S. (1978), *Zum Bildungsgesamtplan der Bund–Länder-Kommission: Die Einfügung des Artikels 91b in das Grundgesetz und der Prozeß der Bildungsplanung für den Elemantar-, Primar- und Sekundarbereich in der Bund-Länder-Kommission für Bildungsplanung*, Weinheim and Basel: Beltz Verlag.

Rebmann, Kurt, Martin Ott and Werner Storz (1964), *Das baden-württembergische Gesetz über die Presse (Landespressegesetz) vom 14. Januar 1964 nebst dem Modellenentwurf eines Landespressegesetzes*, Stuttgart: Kohlhammer.

Rudzio, Wolfgang Rudzio (1991), *Das politische System der Bundesrepublik Deutschland*, Third Edition, Opladen: Leske und Budrich.

Sanford, John (1976), *The Mass-Media of the German-Speaking Countries*, London: Oswald Wolff.

Scharpf, Fritz W., Bernd Reissert and Fritz Schnabel (1976), *Politikverflechtung: Theorie und Empirie des kooperativen Föderalismus in der Bundesrepublik*, Kronberg: Scriptor Verlag.

von Friedeburg, Ludwig (1989), *Bildungsreform in Deutschland: Geschichte und gesellschaftlicher Widerspruch*, Frankfurt am Main: Suhrkamp Verlag.

Walper, Karl Heinz (1966), *Föderalismus*, Berlin: Colloqium Verlag.

Articles and chapters

Baumert, Jürgen and Dietricht Goldschmidt (1980), "Centralization and Decentralization as Determinants of Educational Policy in the Federal Republic of Germany," *Social Science Information*, Vol. 19, pp. 1029–1098.

Blair, Philip (1991), "Federalism, Legalism and Political Reality: The Record of the Federal Constitutional Court," in Charlie Jeffery and Peter Savigear (eds), *German Federalism Today*, Leicester and London: Leicester University Press, pp. 1–7.

Erk, Jan (2003), "Federalism and Mass Media Policy in Germany," *Regional and Federal Studies*, Vol. 13, No. 2, pp. 107–127.

Erk, Jan (2003), "Federal Germany and its Non-Federal Society: Emergence of an all-German Educational Policy in a System of Exclusive Provincial Jurisdiction," *Canadian Journal of Political Science*, Vol. 36, No. 2, pp. 295–317.

Exler, Ulrich (1992), "Financing German Federalism: Problems of Financial Equalization in the German Unification Process," *German Politics*, Vol. 1, No. 3, pp. 22–37.

Färber, Gisela (1992), "Länderfinanzausgleich und Gemeindefinanzen – Anmerkungen zu einigen häufig übersehenen Tatsachen," in Kurt Bohr (ed.), *Föderalismus, Demokratische Struktur für Deutschland und Europa*, Munich: C.H. Beck, pp. 85–122.

Gellner, Winand (1989), "Federalism and Controversy Over the New Media in West Germany," *Publius: Journal of Federalism*, Special Issue: *German Federalism*, Vol. 19, No. 4, pp. 133–145.

Glaeßner, Joachim Gert and Werner Reutter (2001), "Verfassung, Politik und Politikwissenschaft," in Gert-Joachim Glaeßner and Werner Reutter (eds), *Verfassungspolitik und Verfassungswandel: Deutschland und Großbritannien im Vergleich*, Wiesbaden: Westdeutscher Verlag, pp. 9–28.

Gunlicks, Arthur (1989), "Introduction," *Publius: Journal of Federalism*, Special Issue: *Federalism and Intergovernmental Relations in West Germany: A Fortieth Year Appraisal*, Vol. 19, No. 4, pp. 1–15.

Gunlicks, Arthur (1993), "The Future of Federalism in the Unified Germany," in Christopher Anderson, Karl Kaltenthaler and Wolfgang Luthardt (eds), *The Domestic Politics of German Unification*, Boulder and London: Lynn Reiner, pp. 155–174.

Helms, Ludger (2002), "Das föderative System der Bundesrepublik Deutschland im internationalen Vergleich," *Zeitschrift für Politik*, Vol. 49, No. 2, pp. 125–148.

Hesse, Joachim Jens (1987), "The Federal Republic of Germany: From Cooperative Federalism to Joint Policy-Making," *West European Politics*, Vol. 10, No. 4.

Hesse, Joachim Jens (1995), "Effects and Outputs in Federal Type Solutions and Their Implications for European Integration – The Case of Germany," in C.Lloyd Brown-John (ed.), *Federal-Type Solutions and European Integration*, Lanham, New York and London: University Press of America.

Holzamer, Karl (1972), "Rundfunkneuordnung und bundesstaatliche Struktur," in Heinz Kühn, Karl Holzamer and Peter Lerche, *Rundfunkneuordnung und bundesstaatliche Struktur*, Munich: C.H. Beck.

Hrbek, Rudolph (1973), "Das Problem der Neugliederung des Bundesgebietes," in Heinz Laufer and Frank Pilz (eds), *Föderalismus, Studientexet zur bundesstaatlichen Ordnung*, Munich: Wilhelm Golsmann Verlag.

Karpen, Ulrich (1976), "Plannung des Hochschulwesens und Grundgesetz," in Ulrich Karpen and Franz-Ludwig Knemeyer, *Verfassungsprobleme des Hochschulwesens*, Paderborn: Ferdinand Schöningh, pp. 9–43.

Kloepfer, Michael (1979), "Bildungsföderalismus, Mängelbericht und Grundgesetz: Verfassungrechtliche Anmerkungen zur Zentralisierung im Bildungwesen," in Peter Döring (ed.), *Nachlese zum 16. Bildungspolitischen Gespräch: Bildungspolitik im föderativen Bundesstaat*, Frankfurt am Main: DIPF.

Kommers, Donald (1989), "The Basic Law of the Federal Republic of Germany: An Assessment After Forty Years," in Peter Merkl (ed.), *The Federal Republic of Germany at Forty*, New York and London: New York University Press, pp. 133–159.

Kommers, Donald P. (1994), "The Federal Constitutional Court in the German Political System," *Comparative Political Studies*, Vol. 26, Vol. 4, pp. 299–326.

Lehmbruch, Gerhard (1996), "German Federalism and the Challenge of Unification," in Joachim Jens Hesse and Vincent Wright (eds), *Federalizing Europe? The Costs, Benefits and Preconditions of Federal Political Systems*, Oxford: Oxford University Press, pp. 169–203.

Mackenstein, Hans and Charlie Jeffery (1999), "Financial Equalization in the 1990s: On the Road Back to Karslruhe?" in Charlie Jeffery (ed.), *Recasting German Federalism: The Legacies of Unification*, London: Pinter, pp. 155–176.

Maier, Hans (1998), "Die Kultusministerkonferenz im Föderalen System," in Sekretariat der Ständige Konferenz der Kultusminister der Länder in der Bundesrepublik Deutschland (ed.), *Einheit in der Vielfalt: 50 Jahre Kultusministerkonferenz 1948–1998*, Neuwied, Kniffel and Berlin: Luchterhand, pp. 21–33.

Pridham, Geoffrey (1973), "A 'Nationalization' Process? Federal Politics and State Elections in West Germany," *Government and Opposition*, Vol. 8, No. 4, pp. 455–473.

Raschert, Jürgen (1980), "Bildungspolitik im kooperativen Föderalismus. Die Entwicklung der länderübergriefenden Plannung und Koordination des Bildungswesens der Bundesrepublik Deutschland," in Max-Planck-Institute für Bildungforschung, Projektgruppe Bildungsbericht (Jürgen Baumert, Achim Lescinsky, Jens Naumann, Jürgen Raschert and Peter Siewert as editors, in cooperation with Diether Hopf, Helmut Köhler, Lothar Krappman, Gottfried Pfeffer and Luitgard Trommer-Krug), *Bildung in der Bundesrepublik Deutschland: Daten und Analysen, Vol. 1*, Stuttgart: Klett-Cotta, pp. 103–215.

Renzsch, Wolfgang (1989), "German Federalism in Historical Perspective: Federalism as a Substitute for a National State," *Publius: Journal of Federalism*, Special Issue: *German Federalism*, Vol. 19, No. 4, pp. 17–33.

Schneider, Steffen (2004), "Labour Market Policy and the Unemployment Crisis in the Federal Republic of Germany: Institutional Sclerosis or Corporatist Renewal?" in Alain Noël (ed.) (2004), *Federalism and Labour Market Policy: Comparing Different Governance and Employment Strategies*, Montreal and Kingston: McGill-Queen's University Press.

Smith, Gordon (1976), "Politics of Centrality," *Government and Opposition*, Vol. 11, No. 4, pp. 398–407.

Stern, Klaus (1969), "Föderative und unitarische Aspekte im deutschen Rundfunkwesens," in Hans R. Klecatsky, Klaus Stein, Ulrich Weber and Svente Bergström, *Rundfunkrecht und Rundfunkpolitik: Referate und Reden aus wissenschaftlichen Veranstalungen des Instututs Rundfunkrecht an der Universität zu Köln*, Munich: C.H. Beck.

Sturm, Roland (1992), "The Changing Territorial Balance," in Gordon Smith, William E. Paterson, Peter H. Merkl and Stephen Padgett (eds), *Developments in German Politics*, Durham: Duke University Press, pp. 119–134.

Sturm, Roland (1999), "The Constitution Under Pressure: Emerging Asymmetrical Federalism in Germany?" in Robert Agranoff (ed.), *Accommodating Diversity: Asymmetry in Federal States*, Baden-Baden: Nomos, pp. 118–136.

Tiburtius, Joachim (1959), "Kulturpolitik: Sache der Länder oder des Bunds," in Ossip K. Flechtheim (ed.), *Bund und Länder*, Berlin: Colloqium Verlag.

Vogel, Bernard (1998), "Auf dem Weg zur Inneren Einheit: KMK Reflex und Impuls kultureller Identität," in Sekretariat der Ständige Konferenz der Kultusminister der Länder in der Bundesrepublik Deutschland (ed.), *Einheit in der Vielfalt: 50 Jahre Kultusministerkonferenz 1948–1998*, Neuwied, Kniffel and Berlin: Luchterhand.

Voigt, Rüdiger (1989), "Financing the German Federal System in the 1980s," *Publius: Journal of Federalism*, Special Issue: *German Federalism*, Vol. 19, No. 4, pp. 99–103.

von der Heydte, Friedrich (1960), "Föderalismus und Rundfunkordnung," from Deutsche Tagespost, 27 January 1969, reproduced in Klaus Furchner (1960), *Von der Notwendigkeit der Rundfunkneuordnung in der Bundesrepublik Deutschland*, Würzburg: Johan Wilhelm Nauman.

Switzerland

Official documents, reports, statistics and parliamentary sessions

Amtliches Bulletin der Bundesversammlung/Bulletin officiel de l'Assemblée fédérale, 21 March 1984.

Conférence des gournements cantonaux (ed.) (1997), *Réforme de la Constitution comme réforme du fédéralisme: Le projet de Constitution 1995 du point de vue des cantons*, Zurich: Schultess.

Conférence intercantonale de l'instruction publique de la Suisse romande et du Tessin, CIIP (1999), *Politiques de l'Éducation et Chemin de traverse: 125 ans de collaboration intercantonale en Suisse romand*, Neuchâtel: CIIP.

Föderalismusheurings/Le Fédéralisme reexamine: Protokolle von zehn öffentlichen Befragungen in Solothurn zum Zustand des schweizerischen Föderalismus/Les procès-verbaux des dix consultations publiques à Soleure sur l'état du fédéralisme suisse,

15.9.1972–28.4.1973, three volumes, (1973), Zurich: Benziger Verlag and Solothurn: Stiftung für eidgenössische Zusammenarbeit/Fondation pour la collaboration confédérale.

Institut romand de recherche et de documentation pédagogiques, IRDP (1990), *Le Concordat: forme vivante de la démocratie suisse. Journée d'étude de l'Institut romand de recherche et de documentation pédagogiques à l'occasion du 20ᵉ anniversaire de sa création juridique*, Neuchâtel, 16 June 1989, Cousset (Fribourg): Delval and IRDP.

Konferenz der Kantonsregierungen (1997), *Verfassungsreform als Föderalismusreform: Der Verfassungsentwurf 1995 aus der Sicht der Kantone*, Zurich: Schultess.

OECD (1990), *Bildungspolitik in der Schweiz*, Bern: EDK.

Sitzung vom 17. December 1968/Séance du 17 décembre 1968, Ständerat-Conseil des États (1968), *Amtliches Bulletin der Bundesversammlung/Bulletin officiel de l'Assemblée fédérale*, Bern: Verbandsdruckerei AG.

l'Union romande des éditeurs de journaux et périodiques (URJ) (ed.) (1996), *Presse Romande du Miracle à la réalité*, Renens: URJ.

Books

Abderhalden, Ursula (1999), *Möglichkeiten und Grenzen der interkantonalen Zusammenarbeit*, Fribourg: Universitätsverlag Freiburg.

Amstutz, Hans (1996), *Das Verhältnis zwischen deutscher und französischer Scwhweiz in den Jahren 1930–1945*, Aargau, Frankfurt am Main and Salzburg: Sauerländer.

Aubert, Jean-François (1978), *Exposé des institutions politiques de la Suisse à partir de quelques affaires controversées*, Lausanne: Payot.

Bassand, Michel and François Hainard (1985), *Dynamique, socio-culturelle réginale*, Laussane: Presses Polytechniques Romandes.

Basta, Lidja R. and Thomas Fleiner (eds) (1996), *Federalism and Multiethnic States: The Case of Switzerland*, Fribourg: Institut du fédéralisme.

Bildungspolitik im schweizerischen Föderalismus: Festschrift für Prof. Dr. Eugen Egger (1985), Bern and Stuttgart: Paul Haupt.

Boegli, Laurance (1998), *Les concordats intercantonaux: Quels enjeux pour la démocratie*, Chavannes-près-Renens: Idheap.

Büchi, Christoph (2000), *"Röstigraben": Das Verhältnis zwischen deutscher und französischer Schweiz, Geschichte und Perspectiven*, Zurich: Neue Zürcher Zeitung.

Busino, Giovanni (ed.) (1985), "Les politiques scolaire des Cantons Romands et du Tessin," Special Issue: *Revue Européene des sciences sociales*, Vol. XXIII, No. 70.

Charpilloz, Alain and Geneviève Grimm-Gobat (1982), *La Romandie Dominée*, Lausanne: Pierre-Marcel Favre.

Chenaux, Jean-Philippe (1986), "La Presse d'opinion en Suisse romande ou la bataille des idées," Éditions du *Journale de Genève* et de *la Gazette de Lausanne*.

Codding, George Arthur, Jr. (1961), *The Federal Goverment of Switzerland*, Boston: Houghton Mifflin.

De Mestral, Aymon (1971), *Suisse romande/Suisse alémanique. Qu'est-ce qui ne va pas?* Lausanne: Éditions Nouvelle Revue de Lausanne.

de Reynold, Gonzague (1938), *Conscience de la Suisse*, Neuchâtel.

Du Bois, Pierre (ed.) (1983), *Union et division des Suisses: Les relations entre Alémaniques, Romands et Tessinois aux XIXe et XXe siècles*, Lausanne: Éditions l'air.

Du Bois, Pierre (1999), *Alémaniques et Romands entre unité et discorde. Histoire et actualité*, Lausanne: Favre.

Dunand, Fabien (1991), *Le modèle suisse*, Paris: Éditions Payot.

Faganini, Hans Peter (1991), *Föderalistischer Aufgabenverbund in der Schweiz*, Bern and Stuttgart: Paul Haupt.

Fleiner, Thomas, Peter Forster, Alexander Misic and Urs Thalmann (eds) (2000), *BV-CF 2000. Die neue schweizerische Bundesverfassung: Föderalimus, Grundrechte, Wirtschaftsrecht und Staatsstruktur/La nouvelle Constitution suisse: Fédéralisme, droits fundamentaux, droit économique et structure de l'État*, Basel, Geneva and Munich: Helbing and Lichtenham.

Frenkel, Max (1984), *Föderalismus und Bundesstaat, Band I Föderalismus; System, Recht und Probleme des Bundesstaates im Spannungfeld von Demokratie und Föderalismus*, Bern and Frankfurt am Main: Peter Lang.

Germann, Raimund E. and Jean-Marie Muller (eds) (1989), *La dynamique fédéraliste en Suisse*, Bern: Société Suisse des Sciences Administrative.

Germann, Raimund E. and Ernst Weibel with Hans Peter Graf (eds) (1986), *Handbuch Politisches System der Schweiz, Band 3 Föderalismus/Manuel Système politique de la suisse, Volume3 Fédéralisme*, Bern and Stuttgart: Paul Haupt.

Giger, Hans (ed.) (1991), *Bildungspolitk im Umbruch: Staatsmonopol in der Weiterbildung*. Zurich: Verlag Neue Zürcher Zeitung.

Golaz, Eric, Moritz Gubler, François Logez, Olivier Meuwly, Jean Paschoud, Olivier Weniger (eds) (1990), *Perspectives Media: Fédéralisme et concentration des médias/ Media Perspectiven: Föderalismus und Medienkonzentration*, Lausanne: Société d'étudiants Helvetica.

Government and Opposition (1988), Special Issue: "Can the Confederation Helvetica be imitated?" Vol. 23: No. 1.

Grin, François (1999), "Language Policy in Multilingual Switzerland: Overview and Recent Developments," *ECMI Brief No. 2*, Flensburg: European Centre for Minority Issues.

Hafelin, Ulrich (1969), *Der cooperative Föderalismus in der Schweiz*, Basel: Helbing and Lichterhahn.

Hänni, Peter (2000), *Schweizerische Föderalismus und Europäische Integration: Die Rolle der Kantone in einem sich wandelnden internationalen Kontext*, Zurich: Schultess.

Jarnen, Ottfried, Patrick Donges, Matthias Künzler, Wolfgang Schulz, Thorsten Held and Uwe Jürgen (2001), *Der Schweizerische öffentliche Rundfunk im Netzwerk: Möglichkeiten der Absicherung und Bindung der SRG an dei Gesellschaft*, Zurich: Institut für Publizistikwissenschaft und Medienforschung der Universität Zürich.

Kägi-Diener, Regula (2000), *Brevier des Föderalismus: Eine Einführung in den Föderalismus aufgrung der Erfahrungen im schweizerischen Bundesstaat*, Bern: Schweizerischen Helsinki-Vereinigung and Zurich: Neue Zürcher Zeitung.

Knüsel, René (1994), *Les minorités ethnolinguistique autochtones à territoire: L'exemple du cas helvétique*, Lausanne: Payot.

Kölz, Alfred (1998), *Der Weg der Schweiz zum Bundesstaat: 1789–1798–1848–1998: Historische Abhandlungen*, Zürich and Chur: Rüegge.

Kreis, Georg (1993), *Die Schweiz unterwegs: Schlussbericht des Nationales Forschungsprogramm 21 'Kulturelle Vielvalt und Nationale Identität'*, Basel: Helbing and Lichtenhahn.

Kriesi, Hanspeter (1998), *Le Système Politique Suisse*, Paris: Economica.

Kriesi, Hanspeter, Boris Wernli, Pascal Sciarini and Matteo Gianni (1996), *Le clivage linguistique: Problèmes de compréhension entre les communautés linguistiques en Suisse*, Berne: Office fédéral de la statistique.

Knüsel, René and Julian Hottinger (1994), *Regionalist Movements and Parties in Switzerland: A Study Case on the 'Lega dei Ticinesi'*, Laussane: Institut de hautes études en administration publique.

Knüsel, René and Daniel-L. Seiler (eds) (1984), *Vous avez dit "Suisse romande"?* Lausanne: Institut de Science Politique.

Laserre, David (1967), *Etapes du fédéralisme. L'expérience suisse*, Second Edition, Lausanne: Éditions Recontre.

Lezzi, Maria (2000), *Porträts von Schweizer Euroregionen: Grenzüberschreitende Ansätze zu einem europäischen Föderalismus*, Basel and Frankfurt am Main: Helbing and Lichtenhahn.

Linder, Wolf (1998), *Swiss Democracy: Possible Solutions to Conflict in Multicultural Societies*, Second Edition, London: Macmillan and New York: St Martin's Press.

Lüthy, Herbert (1966), "Politische Probleme der Mehrsprachigkeit in der Schweiz," *Civitas*, Vol. 22, pp. 38–45.

Martin, William (1971), *Switzerland: From Roman Times to the Present*, New York: Praeger.

McRae, Kenneth D. (1983), *Conflict and Compromise in Multilingual Societies*, Waterloo: Sir Wilfrid Laurier University Press.

Meier, Werner A. and Michael Schanne (1995), *La paysage médiatique Suisse*, Zurich: Pro Helvetia.

Meier, Werner A., Heinz Bonfadelli and Michael Schanne (1993), *Medienlandschaft Schweiz im Umbruch: Vom öffentlichen Kulturgut Rundfunk zur elektronischen Kioskware*, Basel and Frankfurt am Main: Helbing and Lichtenhahn.

Melich, Anna (1990), *Identité Nationale et Media Comptemporains: Les Suisses, la pluri-culture et les plurimedia*, Laussane: LEP.

Miéville, Daniel-S. (ed.) (1996), *"La Suisse est-elle soluble dans l'Europe?" Journal de Genève et Gazette de Lausanne*.

Neidhart, Leonard (1975), *Föderalismus in der Schweiz*, Zurich: Benziger.

Neuberger, Gregory (ed.) (2000), *Föderalismus in Bewegung – Wohin steuert Helvetia?*, Zurich: Franz Ebner.

Neuen Helvetischen Gesellschaft/Nouvelle Société Helvétique (1965), *Der Föderalismus vor der Zukunft/Le fédéralisme face à l'avenir*, Special Issue of *Jahrbuch Neuen Helvetischen Gesellschaft/Annuaire de la Nouvelle Société Helvétique*, Vol. 36.

Neuen Helvetischen Gesellschaft/Nouvelle Société Helvétique (1968), *Nebeneinander- und miteinander? Beiträge für ein bessere Zusammenarbeit auf kulturellem Gebiet/Les uns à coté des autres? Essais pour une meilleure coopération sur le plan culturel*, Special Issue of *Jahrbuch Neuen Helvetischen Gesellschaft/Annuaire de la Nouvelle Société Helvétique*, Vol. 39.

Nüssli, Kurt (1985), *Föderalismus in der Schweiz: Konzepte, Indikatoren, Daten*, Grüsch: Verlag Ruegger.

Rohr, Jean (1987), *La Démocratie en Suisse*, Paris: Economica.

Schmid, Carol (1981), *Conflict and Consensus in Switzerland*, Berkeley: University of California Press.

Schmitt, Nicolas (1996), *Federalism: The Swiss Experience*, Pretoria: HSRC.

Starck, Dorothee (1999), *Föderalismus in der Schweiz: Darstellung der Strukturen und der praktischen Erfahrungen*, Speyer: Hochschule für Verwaltungswissenschaften.

Steinberg, Jonathan (1996), *Why Switzerland?* Second Edition, Cambridge: Cambridge University Press.

Steinemann, Matthias, Sabine Zaugg, Roman Gattlen (2000), *Medien und Identität: Eine*

Studie zum Beitrag von Radio- und Fernsheprogrammen zur gesellschaftlichen und kulturellen Integration in der Schweiz, Bern: SRG/SSR.

Trechsel, Alexandre H. (1995), *Clivages en Suisse: Analyse des impact relatifs des clivages sur l'électorat suisse lors des élections fédérales*, Geneva: Université de Genève.

Tschoumy, Jacques-André (1989), *Souveraineté et Interdépendances*, Neuchâtel: IRDP.

Von Blumenthal, Viktor (1991), *Bildungspolitik in der Schweiz: Vergleichende Datum und Analysen zur Entwicklung in den 80er Jahren*, Munich: Minerva.

Von der Weid, Nicolas, Roberto Bernhard and François Jeanneret (2002), *Bausteine zum Brückenschlag zwischen Deutsch- und Welschschweiz/Élements pour trait d'union entre la Suisse alémanique et la Suisse romande*, Biel: Éditions Libertas Suisse.

Weibel, Ernst (1990), *Institutions politiques romandes: Les mécanismes institutionnels et politiques des cantons romands et du jura bernois*, Fribourg: Éditions Universitaires Fribourg.

Weibel, Ernest with Cordelia Monnier and Marie-Laure Béguin (1997), *La Cohésion nationale menacée?/Ist der nationale Zusammenhalt in Frage gestellt?* Neuchâtel: Université de Neuchâtel.

Windisch, Uli (1992), *Les relations quoditiennes entre Romands et Suisse allemande: Les cantons bilingues de Fribourg et du Valais*, Volume 1, Lausanne: Payot.

Windisch, Uli (1992), *Les relations quoditiennes entre Romands et Suisse allemande: Les cantons bilingues de Fribourg et du Valais*, Volume 2, Lausanne: Payot.

Wuerth, Andreas (1999), *Die SRG und ihr Integrationsauftrag: Wandel-Gründe-Konsequenzen*, Bern, Stuttgart and Vienna: Paul Haupt.

Articles and chapters

Andrey, Georges (1976), "La Conscience politique romande. Petite contribution à l'étude du fédéralisme Suisse (1848–1975)," *Annuaire Suisse de Science Politique/Schweizerisches Jahrbuch für Politische Wissenschaft*, Vol. 16, pp. 151–161.

Armingeon, Klaus (2000), "Swiss Federalism in Comparative Perspective," in Ute Wachendorfer-Schmidt (ed.), *Federalism and Political Performance*, New York and London: Routledge. pp. 112–129.

Bächtiger, Andre and Jürg Steiner (2004), "Switzerland: Territorial Cleavage Management as paragon and Paradox," in Ugo M. Amoretti and Nancy Bermeo (eds), *Federalism and Territorial Cleavages*, Baltimore and London: The Johns Hopkins University Press, pp. 27–54.

Beaufays, Jean (1995), "Observations on Switzerland: A Model for Belgium," in C. Lloyd Brown-John (ed.), *Federal-Type Solutions and European Integration*, Lanham, New York and London: University Press of America.

Bogdanor, Vernon (1988), "Federalism in Switzerland," *Government and Opposition*, Vol. 23, No. 1, pp. 69–90.

Boillat, Jean-Marie (1999), "De la conference intercantonale des chefs des departments de l'instruction publique de la Suisse romande et du Tessinn (CDIP/SR+I) à la Conférence intercantonale de l'instruction publique (CIIP)," in Conférence intercantonale de l'instruction publique de la Suisse romande et du Tessin, CIIP, *Politiques de l'Éducation et Chemin de traverse: 125 ans de collaboration intercantonale en Suisse romand*, Neuchâtel: CIIP, pp. 9–13.

Braun, Dietmar (1999), "Bildungs-, Wissenschafts- und Kulturpolitik," in Ulrich Klöti, Peter Knoepfel, Hanspeter Kriesi, Wolf Linder and Yannis Papadopoulos (eds), *Handbuch der Schweizer Politik/Manuel de la politique suisse*, Zurich: Verlag Neue Zürcher Zeitung, pp. 841–879.

Camartin, Iso (1985), "Les relations entre les quatre régions linguistiques," in Robert Schlöpfer (ed.), *La Suisse aux quatre langues*, Geneva: Éditions Zoe, pp. 253–284.

Cavadini, Jean (1985), "La Suisse multilingue et le fédéralisme en matière d'éducation," *Bildungspolitik im schweizerischen Föderalismus: Festschrift für Prof. Dr. Eugen Egger*, Bern and Stuttgart: Paul Haupt.

Corboud Fumagalli, Adrienne (1996), "Une Suisse ou trios regions?" *Medienwissenschaft Schweiz*, Vol. 1, pp. 11–17.

Dörig, Hans Rudolf (1988), "Kulturpflege im Schweizerischen Bundesstaat," in Peter Pernthaler (ed.), *Föderalistische Kulturpolitik*, Vienna: Wilhelm Braumüller, pp. 29–41.

Erk, Jan (2003), "Swiss Federalism and Congruence," *Nationalism and Ethnic Politics*, Vol. 9, No. 2, pp. 50–74.

Fleiner, Thomas and Alexandre Misic (1999), "Der Föderalismus in der Schweiz," in Reinhard Meier-Walser and Gerhard Hirscher (eds), *Krise und Reform des Föderalismus, Analysen zu Theorie und Praxis bundstaatlicher Ordnungen*, Munich: Olzog, pp. 246–264.

Hega, Gunther (2000), "Federalism, Subsidiarity and Educational Policy in Switzerland," *Regional and Federal Studies*, Vol. 10, No. 1, pp. 1–35.

Heller, Geneviève (1987), "L'école vaudoise: entre l'identité Suisse et l'identité cantonale," in François de Capitani and Georg Germann (eds), *Auf dem Weg zu einer schweizerischen Identität 1848–1914*, Fribourg: Universitätsverlag Freiburg Schweiz, pp. 245–271.

Hesse, Konrad (1989), "Die neue Ordnung des Rundfunks in der Schweiz und der Bundesrepublik Deutschland," in Walter Haller, Georg Müller, Alfred Kölz and Daniel Thürer (eds), *Festschrift für Ulrich Häfelin zum 65. Geburtstag*, Zurich: Schultness, pp. 149–165.

Hottinger, Julian T. (1997), "La Suisse, une démocratie consociative ou de concordance?" *Revue Internationale de Politique Comparée*, Vol. 4, No. 3, pp. 625–638.

Hottinger, Julian T. (2000), "La diversité culturelle," in Thomas Fleiner, Peter Forster, Alexander Misic and Urs Thalmann (eds), *BV-CF 2000. Bundesverfassung: Föderalismus, Grundrechte, Wirtschaftsrecht und Staatsstruktur/La nouvelle Constitution suisse: Fédéralisme, droits fondamentaux, droit économique et structure de l'État*, Basel, Geneva and Munich: Helbling and Lichtenhahn.

Hughes, Christopher (1993), "Cantonalism: Federation and Confederacy in the Golden Epoch of Switzerland," in Michael Burgess and Alain-G. Gagnon (eds), *Comparative Federalism and Federation; Competing Traditions and Future Directions*, Toronto: University of Toronto Press, pp. 154–167.

Hürlimann, Hans (1985), "Bildungspolitische Spannungsfelder im Föderativstaat," in *Bildungspolitik im schweizerischen Föderalismus: Festschrift für Prof. Dr. Eugen Egger*, Bern and Stuttgart: Paul Haupt.

Klöti, Ulrich (1997), "Malaise Romand – Oder Helvetische Krise?" in Ernest Weibel with Cordelia Monnier and Marie-Laure Béguin (eds), *La Cohésion nationale menacée?/Ist der nationale Zusammenhalt in Frage gestellt?*, Neuchâtel: Université de Neuchâtel.

Klöti, Ulrich and Kurt Nüssli (1986), "Constitutional Reform in Switzerland: Task-Distribution, Political Ideas and Financial Interests," in Michael Burgess (ed.), *Federalism and Federation in Western Europe*, London, Sydney and Dover: Croom and Helm, pp. 187–203.

Kreis, Georg (1994), "Die Schweizerische Föderalismusdebatte seit 1960," in Thomas

Fröschl (ed.), *Föderationsmodelle und Unionstrukturen: Über Staateverbindungen in der frühen Neuzeit vom 15. zum 18. Jahrhundert*, Vienna: Verlag für Geschichte und Politik and Munich: R. Oldenbourg, pp. 177–192.

Kriesi, Hanspeter (1999), "State Formation and Nation Building in the Swiss Case," in Hanspeter Kriesi, Klaus Armingeon, Hannes Siegrist and Andreas Wimmer (eds) (1999), *Nation and National Identity: The European Experience in Perspective*, Zurich and Chur: Ruegger, pp. 13–28.

Linder, Wolf (1999), "Politische Kultur," in Ulrich Klöti, Peter Knoepfel, Hanspeter Kriesi, Wolf Linder and Yannis Papadopoulos (eds), *Handbuch der Schweizer Politik/Manuel de la politique suisse*, Zurich: Verlag Neue Zürcher Zeitung, pp. 13–33.

Rohrer, Ursula (1985), "Geschichte der Schweizerischen Konferenz der Kantonalen Erziehungsdirektoren," *Bildungspolitik im schweizerischen Föderalismus: Festschrift für Prof. Dr. Eugen Egger*, Bern and Stuttgart: Paul Haupt.

Schaltegger, Christoph A. (2001) "Ist der Schweizer Föderalismus zu kleinräumig?" *Schweizerische Zeitschrift für Politikwissenschaft* Vol. 7, No. 1, pp. 1–18.

Schindler, Dietrich (1989), "Differenzierter Föderalismus," in Walter Haller, Georg Müller, Alfred Kölz and Daniel Thürer (eds), in *Festschrift für Ulrich Häfelin zum 65. Geburtstag*, Zurich: Schultness.

Schmid, Gerhard (1993), "Bildungspolitik, Forschungspolitik, Kulturpolitik, Medienpolitik," in Gerhard Schmid (ed.), *Handbuch Politisches System der Schweiz, Band 4, Politikbereiche*, Bern, Stuttgart and Vienna: Paul Haupt.

Schmitt, Nicolas (1994), "Switzerland," in Jutta Kramer and Hans-Peter Schneider (eds), *Federalism and Civil Societies*, Baden-Baden: Nomos.

Schmitt, Nicolas (1995), "Swiss Cantons and Europe," in C. Lloyd Brown-John (ed.), *Federal-Type Solutions and European Integration*, Lanham, New York and London: University Press of America.

Schmitt, Nicolas (1999), "Fédéralisme et fusion de cantons: l'importance du territoire," in Jean-Philippe Chenaux, Olivier Delacrétaz, Nicolas Schmitt and Marco Taddei (eds), *La Suisse éclatée: Quand las "fusiologues" jouent avec le feu*, Lausanne: Centre Patronal.

Taddei, Marco (1999), "Les fusions cantonales à la mode alémanique," in Jean-Philippe Chenaux, Olivier Delacrétaz, Nicolas Schmitt and Marco Taddei (eds), *La Suisse éclatée: Quand las "fusiologues" jouent avec le feu*, Lausanne: Centre Patronal.

Tschoumy, Jacques-André (1985), "L'innovation scolaire en suisse romande," in Giovanni Busino (ed.), *Les politiques scolaire des Cantons Romands et du Tessin*, Special Issue of *Revue Européene des sciences sociales*, Vol. XXIII, No. 70, 161–176.

Touret, Paul (1999), "Affirmations Régionales et Thématiques Fédéralistes en Romandie et en Wallonie," in Philippe Destatte (ed.), *L'idée fédéraliste dans les États-nations*, Maastricht: Presses InterUniversitaires Européennes, pp. 405–418.

Vatter, Adrian (1999) "Föderalismus," in Ulrich Klöti, Peter Knoepfel, Hanspeter Kriesi, Wolf Linder and Yannis Papadopoulos (eds), *Handbuch der Schweizer Politik/Manuel de la politique suisse*, Zurich: Verlag Neue Zürcher Zeitung, pp. 77–108.

Wälti, Sonja (1996), "Institutional Reform of Federalism: Changing the Players rather than the Rules of the Game," *Swiss Political Science Review*, Vol. 2, No. 2, pp. 113–141.

Weibel, Ernst (1986), "Les rapports entre les groups linguistiques," in Raimund E. Germann and Ernst Weibel with Hans Peter Graf (eds) (1986), *Handbuch Politisches System der Schweiz, Band 3 Föderalismus*, Bern and Stuttgart: Paul Haupt.

Widmer, Thomas and Christof Buri (1992), "Brüssel oder Bern: schlägt das Herz der

'Romands' eher für Europa?" *Annuaire Suisse de science politique*, Vol. 32, pp. 363–88.

Windisch, Uli (1998), "Médias et communication politique en démocratie directe: quinze theses," in Uli Windisch, *La Suisse: clichés, délire, réalité*, Lausanne: L'Age d'homme, pp. 79–94.

Wuerth, André (1999), "Mediensystem und politische Kommunikation," in Ulrich Klöti, Peter Knoepfel, Hanspeter Kriesi, Wolf Linder and Yannis Papadopoulos (eds), *Handbuch der Schweizer Politik/Manuel de la politique suisse*, Zurich: Verlag Neue Zürcher Zeitung, pp. 337–386.

Index